Ames
Gibson
Sharaff

3-4   139
13-14   142-4
22   145
30   147 paey eua
                   -9
32 Cinotaukeer
dchitect 57-60 -62
                 quai scene
59 paris   Ames   Eel°a
             80   158
             82   154 101
             98-9
             101   167-8
             105-6 198
             111-12
             114-15
          color 125
          color 132-ucdor
          " "134-5
                136
          color 89.40

151
Sharaff
colo

The Magic Factory

How MGM Made An American in Paris

DONALD KNOX

Foreword by Andrew Sarris

PRAEGER PUBLISHERS
New York · Washington · London

PRAEGER PUBLISHERS
111 Fourth Avenue, New York, N.Y. 10003, U.S.A.
5, Cromwell Place, London SW7 2JL, England

Published in the United States of America in 1973
by Praeger Publishers, Inc.

Library of Congress Cataloging in Publication Data

Knox, Donald, 1936—
  The magic factory.

  1. An American in Paris. [Motion picture]
2. Metro-Goldwyn-Mayer, inc.   I. Title.
PN1997.A343K5   791.43'7   72-89638

Printed in the United States of America

For my mom and dad

CONTENTS

vii

Foreword

by Andrew Sarris

I am fully aware that it has become culturally fashionable to bemoan the recent flood of film books. But not for me. Actually, we haven't even begun to catch up with decades and decades of lost time in accumulating information on the art, sociology, history, and iconography of motion pictures. As a result there are huge gaps everywhere, and even the dullest pedantry must be welcomed as a temporary filler. Even so, there are times when I feel that oral histories are beginning to come out of our ears. Talk, talk, and more talk, all into the omnipresent tape recorder, the survivors of the time machine ransacking their memories for the benefit of posterity, but too often also squirting out the bile of bloated egos. I mention my feelings on the subject simply to emphasize my conviction that Donald Knox has avoided the usual pitfalls of the oral-history approach to the subject of film by managing to have his witnesses talk shop rather than settle old scores. Hence, I strongly recommend *The Magic Factory* to all serious scholars of film. I must add, however, that this enterprise, like all others of a similar nature, can be useful more as a supplement to critical judgment than as a substitute for it. By gathering and orchestrating his precious testimony as he has, Knox has enabled us to understand the workings of a particularly intricate process of collective creation: the Metro musical in its Golden Age (1944–55).

Of course, I find it a bit frightening that film critics and historians seeking to apportion proper credit for each and every one of the thousands of interesting movies ever made would have to immerse themselves in thousands of books. I tend to prefer some middle way between functional presumption by the critic about creative roles and endless recollections poured into a tape recorder. Hence, my well-known predilection for a very tentative form of auteurism, in which the director is considered the hypothetically dominant figure in the film-making process until a pattern of contributions has been established. The director-*auteur* is not even a real person as such, but a field of magnetic force around which all agents and elements of the film-making process tend to cluster. If his magnetic force is strong enough and selective enough, he can come to be regarded after a time as an authentic *auteur*. If his magnetic force is weak and erratic, he will be denigrated in time as a mere *metteur en scène*. Where then does all this leave us with Vincente Minnelli and *An American in Paris?* At first glance, Minnelli seems to have been reduced to the same level as the office boy (Rick Ingersoll) and the script timer (Nora Janney), and certainly no higher than Arthur Freed, Alan Jay Lerner, Gene Kelly, John Green, Preston Ames, and Leslie Caron. But, as we proceed through the maze of monologues, we begin to perceive the temporal pattern of movie-making, beginning with inspiration and ending with execution. It is not simply a group grope of complementary craftsmen, but also a relay race with the writer and the producer, say, starting off the first leg of the race with an idea, and the director and performers crossing the finish line with an image.

Nonetheless, if *An American in Paris* were the only evidence of Minnelli's existence, there would be no problem in treating him as a key member of a smoothly functioning team. Indeed, Minnelli was not even on the set the whole time the picture was being shot, but sneaked off to do another assignment, *Father's Little Dividend*, while the final ballet of *An American in Paris* was being rehearsed and set up. And besides, of all genres, the musical is probably the least amenable to directorial-auteurist analysis, especially musicals with creative choreographer-performers like Gene Kelly and Fred Astaire. Hence, it would be idiotic to analyze *An American in Paris* exclusively as an episode in Vincente Minnelli's directorial career. If there were indeed one ultimate *auteur* haunting the whole project, it would have to be the ghost of George Gershwin, from whose melodious compositions so much of the *mise en scène* took its cues.

And yet, something that always baffled me about *American in Paris* has finally been clarified by the assorted testimonies in *The Dream Factory*. It always struck me that there was a fatal emotional rupture in the plot between the black-and-white Beaux Arts Ball and the climactically rainbowish *American in Paris* ballet. Despite the conventionally happy ending of romantic reconciliation between Kelly and Caron, the film ends in a somber, downbeat mood that I have never been able to explain or evaluate or even attribute. But suddenly, in the midst of *The Magic Factory*, the ill-starred (in career terms) Nina Foch mentions that her best scene ended on the cutting room floor. It was a scene at the Beaux Arts Ball in which she inquires drunkenly why no one likes her. All concerned felt that this scene established too much sympathy for the discarded patroness character at the expense of the two dancing lovers, and this, after all, was a musical, and not a grim slice of life. And so the Foch scene was neatly excised, but somehow the problem was never solved. Why? I am still not completely sure, but I think I can postulate two related hypotheses, one involving Minnelli's morbidly beautiful *mise en scène*, and the other involving Alan Jay Lerner's misogynous tendencies as a dramatist (tendencies given much fuller play in *My Fair Lady* and *On a Clear Day You Can See Forever*, the latter film an underrated masterpiece exquisitely expressing both Minnelli's morbidity and Lerner's misogyny). In a very curious way, the collaboration of Minnelli and Lerner tends to achieve the jangling disharmony of a forced union of Edgar Allan Poe and George Bernard Shaw.

However, this mini-insight is merely what one reader managed to extract from Donald Knox's invaluable contribution to film scholarship. Other readers may be stimulated more by the book's evocation of the last days of the studio system in Hollywood; or the hilarious contretemps between Alan A. Antik, the technical expert on Paris, and Minnelli, the delirious dreamer of Paris, on what constituted reality and what constituted inaccuracy; or Leslie Caron's iconoclastic description of Hedda Hopper on one of her safaris to the set; or the genuine respect and affection expressed by so many of the participants toward their colleagues, despite the back-biting reflexes of the movie business.

It strikes me suddenly that I am unfair to Mr. Knox's editorial enterprise when I describe the recollections he has gathered as "monologues." "Interviews" is closer to the mark. Unlike the self-styled superstars in the interview field, Mr. Knox does not flaunt his own plumage in the face of his subject. Quite the contrary. He listens in the darkness, all the better to illuminate the utterances issuing from the past. And it would be a poor reward indeed for his commendable modesty to have his interviewees be credited with much of the pithiness and pertinence for which the interviewer himself is undoubtedly responsible. All in all, he has done the job with an admirably selfless craftsmanship befitting his glorious subject.

Acknowledgments

From the earliest beginnings, back in the days of the Movie Buff and the Philadelphia Pie and Wine Film Festival, it was David Mallery and his love for the movies that made this project possible. George Stevens, Jr. found the way to make it happen. This Research Associate project was funded by the Louis B. Mayer Foundation and was administered by the American Film Institute's Center for Advanced Film Study.

Danny Selznick first mentioned *An American in Paris* to me as perhaps the way to investigate the MGM system. Howard Strickling gave valuable assistance in helping me to contact the people who speak in this book. To the people who comprise all the pages of this book, let me say that, for me, they represent all that was wonderful about *Metro-Goldwyn-Mayer*.

Helen Seitz and Pat London spent many hours arranging my screenings. Ron Haver, Jim Silke, and Ann Schlosser took turns pointing me in the right direction. A place to think and to write was supplied by Ken and Susan Smith and Donald and Ellura McPherson. The pieced-together drafts were made into legible manuscript by Ann Powers and Harriet Diamond. Preston Ames was not only patient with my tape recorder on more than one occasion; he also gave valuable time in helping me track down many of the "lost" illustrations that appear in this book. The libraries of the Theater Arts Department at UCLA, at the University of Southern California, of the American Academy of Motion

xiii

Picture Arts and Sciences, and of the American Film Institute provided me supportive material.

I would also like to mention the staff at The American Film Institute's Center for Advanced Film Studies, whose warmth and enthusiasm enhanced a memorable year. My wife Betsy and our sons Neil and Alexander took the dour days in stride and gave in return the love that made up all the good days.

A 16-mm print of *An American in Paris* may be rented for nontheatrical exhibition from Films Incorporated, 1144 Wilmette Avenue, Wilmette, Illinois 60091.

PREFACE

As the Hollywood movie companies divest themselves of their stages and lots, and auction off such props as the red shoes Judy Garland wore down the yellow brick road, the unique system they created for manufacturing motion pictures recedes into memory. The Magic Factory traces the decision-making circuitry that went into the act of producing a single studio film. Both the studio I chose to study, Metro-Goldwyn-Mayer (MGM), and one of the products they produced, *An American in Paris,* present a fine opportunity to illuminate the system and the way of life the studios engendered.

I chose *An American in Paris* because the picture reveals several key factors that went into the making of a major studio film. Preceded by *The Pirate* and *On the Town,* and followed by *Singin' in the Rain* and *The Band Wagon, An American in Paris* fits snugly into a genre in which MGM excelled—the Technicolor musical. Because it was a musical, its production involved nearly every department at Metro's Culver City studio. The film featured a star of the first magnitude, Gene Kelly, and developed a new star, Leslie Caron. (Discovering and promoting new talent were MGM specialties.) Also, *An American in Paris* won six Academy Awards, including Best Picture of 1951. Although Academy Awards do not necessarily indicate excellence, the six Oscars won by *An American in Paris* do make it representative of the type of picture that the "old Hollywood" stood for, in the best sense of that phrase.

I also chose *An American in Paris* because, either in theaters or on television, hundreds of millions of people have seen it. Lastly, I chose this film for study because most of the people who made it are still alive and were willing to be interviewed for a book in the form of an oral memoir.

However, several key people who contributed to the film died before this project began: Oscar Levant; Carol Haney, Gene Kelly's dance assistant; Al Raboch, Minnelli's first assistant director; Conrad Salinger, who did much of the orchestrating; and, finally, the head of MGM's peerless sound department, Douglas Shearer. Their expertise and warmth, alas, are missing from the following pages. Alfred Gilks, the cinematographer, has also passed away. However, in February, 1952, he wrote a magazine piece explaining his role in the making of *An American in Paris*. His words in this book are from this article, and are printed with the permission of the magazine, *The American Cinematographer*.

The people who speak in this book were selected mainly on the basis of their importance in making the decisions that affected the creative conception of the movie. It is for this reason that I did not seek out camera crews, grips, gaffers, script clerks, lab technicians, or any of the hundreds of other personnel who made this picture an archetype of excellence in studio craftsmanship.

Interestingly, what emerged from the hundred or so hours of interviewing is the importance of the system itself in producing the work. By "system," I mean the forty-odd department units that made up the studio structure. The MGM departments represented the armature on which the studio's artistry was displayed. In this study, these departments emerge from obscurity to share in the production glow normally reserved for producer, director, and star. The system provided excellence and style at every level, from the Art Department, which re-created Paris with exacting verisimilitude on a back lot in Culver City, to the Camera Department, which could provide a cameraman as talented as Ray June in order to light a single difficult set. The heroes of this system, not unlike the anonymous town artisans who created the great Gothic cathedrals, are the men in the departments. Without them, it would have been impossible for the lion's roar to have been the loudest in the land. In that sense, this study of the making of *An American in Paris* reveals the strong possibility, at least in musicals, that the studio was in fact the *auteur*. No single person made *An American in Paris*; it was a studio creation.

In many instances, creative functions overlapped; for instance, the remarkable relationship of John Green, Saul Chaplin, and Conrad Salinger in the area of music. In other cases, like Nora Janney's solitary role in timing the script, one person was totally responsible for one facet of the completed work. Answering the question of how the picture was made is much like assembling a jigsaw puzzle. No one participant knows the whole pattern. Together, however, they answer the riddle of how a group of distinguished artists could work for an organization that was half a time-clocked factory and half a wonderland and create a unified body of work.

It must be remembered that *An American in Paris* was not produced within a vacuum. The system was not geared to producing a single motion picture. In 1950, MGM made 16 cartoons, 12 "Traveltalks," 9 "Pete Smith Specialties," 8 "People on Parades," 104 "News of the Days" and 41 features, one of which happened to be *An American in Paris*. The studios in those days were still a flourishing and fruitful way of life, successfully combining the complex business and industrial worlds of the twentieth century with the artistry and nostalgia of nineteenth-century romanticism. It was a curious mixture—of an industry anchored in the present, yet yearning for the past. The present, in 1950, was reflected in 19,048 American movie houses, containing 11,977,081 seats for which an audience paid an average of 52.86¢ per admission. The past was seen in such titles as *Home Town Story, Showboat, Angels in the Outfield, Across the Wide Missouri,* and *An American in Paris*— all produced by Metro in 1950.

During the hours of interviewing, a feeling of nostalgia would seep into each narrative, so the following pages are permeated with a certain feeling of melancholy. But, in fact, I learned it was more than just nostalgia. It was, rather, a yearning for something these craftsmen and artists felt was good, which they had helped to create, and which no longer exists. Whether it all added up to art has yet to be determined. Toscanini perhaps summed up the process best by saying, when explaining Beethoven's Eroica Symphony, "Some people hear in the music Napoleon while others hear Alexander the Great. I hear *allegro con brio*."

This book is conceived as an "oral history" narrative. Most of the people interviewed told me their stories in their homes. The others talked to me at Greystone, the American Film Institute's home in Beverly Hills. Between 1950–51, when the film was made, and the time when we were talking about it, 1970, some memories quite naturally became fogged. Whenever I encountered conflicting stories, I would ask several participants about the event in question. In this way, a consensus was almost always reached as to what actually did happen at a particular time. Wherever possible, dates and places have been cross-checked with memos, press releases, or news stories of the time and then, where necessary, corrected in the text. (When Arthur Freed told me he met George and Ira Gershwin at Chappells, his memory was in error. Mr. Freed first met the Gershwins at T. B. Harms, and it is this kind of factual correction that I have taken upon myself to make.) In a few instances, I have retained two versions of a story. A case in point is the telling of how the money to produce the ballet sequence was acquired. In this instance, two differing accounts were told to me by Dore Schary and Alan Jay Lerner. I have chosen to tell both versions because, as far as I can determine, both happened, with neither party knowing what the other had done.

The name "oral history" may be an unfortunate choice for the book's genre. It doesn't begin to describe that genre's beautiful strength, and it is misleading (for most of the same reasons, in fact, that the name *"cinema-verité"* is misleading). It assumes a *de facto* truth but disregards honesty. What is forgotten is that, by definition, oral history is as much concerned with people as with events. It is the people involved, and not the event itself, that is fascinating. The primary demand put upon an editor compiling oral history is that he not misrepresent his people. An editor is always asked to assess if he has recorded history or memoir, as if one is different from, or more important than, the other. I, for one, do not think it is all that important in this book to know whether the narrators as individuals, or as a group, are telling *the* truth. More significantly, they are telling *a* truth—about themselves and about an event they shared at a time when they all were the best in the world at what they did. It is *this* truth they are all talking about. Listen.

DONALD KNOX

January, 1973

THE PEOPLE (*in alphabetical order*)

Preston Ames (Art Director)
Alan A. Antik (Technical Advisor)
Leslie Caron (Actress)
Saul Chaplin (Music Codirector)
Joe Cohn (MGM Vice-President)
Adrienne Fazan (Editor)
Nina Foch (Actress)
Arthur Freed (Producer)
George Gibson (Head of the Scenic Art Department)
Alfred Gilks (Cinematographer)
Keogh Gleason (Set Decorator)
John Green (Executive in Charge of Music and Music Codirector)
Rick Ingersoll (Office Boy)
Honore (Nora) Janney (Script Timer)
Gene Kelly (Actor and Choreographer)
Alan Jay Lerner (Author and Screenwriter)
Lilly Messinger (Literary Consultant)
Vincente Minnelli (Director)
Mary Ann Nyberg (Freed Unit Dress Designer)
Dore Schary (Executive Vice-President in Charge of Production)
Irene Sharaff (Costume Designer)
Howard Strickling (Head of the Publicity Department)
Walter Strohm (Head of the Production Department)
Emily Torchia (Leslie Caron's Publicist)
Ed Woehler (Unit Production Manager)

PART I

1

The People

Preston Ames (Art Director):

Coming to MGM was basically an economic thing. I had just finished schooling in Paris in 1932 and had my degree in architecture. I then worked with Arthur Brown, Jr., in San Francisco for four fruitful years. Then that episode was terminated, and in the height of the Depression I was left not knowing what to do. A good friend suggested I go to Hollywood and see what I could do in the motion picture business. I was introduced to Cedric Gibbons, the supervising art director at MGM, through a cousin of mine who happened to know him. Three months later, I went to work with him. You never worked *for* this man; you always worked *with* him. The year was 1936. I started out as a draftsman. That's the way everybody started in those days.

From draftsman you were eventually promoted to the position of art director; it's that simple, and it's not that simple. It was really a question of supply and demand and talent and also of recognizing your ability from a point of view of personality. Could you get along with people, and did you have a mind for taking responsibility? This, after all, is what an art director has—great, great responsibility. He's responsible for the visual quality of the picture. If he's given a certain amount of money, he has to spend it wisely. He has to be able to get along with his director; he has to get along with the people he works with, his supervisors, his

3

producer. He also has to have a knowledge of photography, cinematography, and of lighting. All of these things come by just going out, watching, learning, and doing the various aspects of this thing called "art
direction." I became an art director after ten years or so on the boards as
a draftsman. There were a lot of pictures being done, and everybody was
busy, and I was kind of next in line. Mr. Gibbons called me in one day
(everybody was "Mr." in that era, and it was beautiful in that respect
because there was a certain dignity about it all). He said, "Mr. Ames,
here is a script." Just that simple. I never did the picture, but I worked
like hell on it. I broke it down and made every kind of effort to show
that I knew what I was doing. It was sort of a test. Then I was given
something else, and that's just the way it happened.

I had a pretty good hunch that Cedric Gibbons was responsible for
my getting the job on *An American in Paris*, because the director didn't
know me. Mr. Gibbons remembered that I had lived five years in France
as an architectural student, and he felt, rightly so, that I would be very
much at home with this picture. I had no fears about doing those things
which I had known in Paris—the streets and the *quais* and the cafés.
It was a kind of built-in thing. I was psyched and ready for it. I had no
fear. I was ready to go.

Alan A. Antik (Technical Advisor):

I was born and raised in Paris. I became an officer in the French Army
and was assigned to the Maginot Line. In 1940, during an air raid on my
outpost, I was wounded, received the *Croix de guerre*, and sent back to
Paris. After recovering I was reassigned to French Army Counterintelli-
gence, the Troisième Bureau. With the surrender of France, I was noti-
fied by friends that I had been put on a list of the most wanted men by
Nazi Intelligence. So naturally I went underground. Later on in 1940, I
was smuggled to Spain and caught one of the last freighters to America.

After the war, I was stuck in New York and, because I spoke Spanish
fluently, I was made a Spanish-language dubbing director for MGM.
Eventually, to save money, Arthur Loew, who was the head of the Inter-
national Productions Department, moved my operation to Mexico City.
All of a sudden, real trouble started with the Mexican producers when
our dubbed product began to threaten their national product. So Mr.
Loew called me up from New York and said, "Look Alan, I'm afraid we

have too much pressure and there is no way of compromising but liquidating the whole thing. You better come back here."

So, with my wife and two sons, I drove back to New York. When I arrived in New York, they really did me a dirty trick. Mr. Loew didn't speak to me, but another vice president said, "I have a message for you from Mr. Loew. He's very sorry, but we have to terminate our relationship. We'll give you six months' salary." I said, "I'm not interested in six months' salary. I don't understand it, because I received so many compliments and I was so very useful to you." So he said, "Mr. Loew is going to write about you to the studio." Loew's contact was L. K. Sidney, who was one of the MGM big shots. So he wrote two very nice letters about me, recommending me very highly.

We drove out here, and I rented a little house in Beverly Glen. I was a little bit downhearted because all of a sudden, out of something, nothing. So. L. K. Sidney said, "We'll get you fixed up," but nothing happened. At this time I met Arthur Freed. Freed was absolutely charming, he said, "I may have something wonderful for you because I'm planning to make *An American in Paris*. We're going to do 40 per cent of this picture in Paris, Minnelli is going to direct it, and, because of your background and knowledge, I want you to be in charge of all the second-unit operation in France and later on advise us in the studio." I said, "Fine," and signed a contract.

Leslie Caron (Actress):

I was very anemic as a child. I had spent the war in Paris, mostly. Food was very scarce even after the war. When I came here in 1950, we were still rationed, so it was nine years of food deprivation during the most important years of my growth. Consequently, I wasn't very strong.

My mother had been a dancer and she obviously regretted having stopped, and I suppose those long mornings when she would tell me about her dancing days paid off. My father is French, and my mother was American of French descent. She was the one that really groomed me into being a ballet dancer. She said she didn't want me to be one, but she all the same filled my head with the desire to be one. You know, being a ballet dancer is a bit like being a race horse: You have to be groomed carefully.

When I was fifteen, I joined the Ballets des Champs-Elysées. I joined this company as a member of the corps de ballet, with little solo parts which I did right away, and within a year I became a premiere dancer. That's the rank just below prima ballerina. For the big opening night in Paris, there was a ballet where I played the sphinx in *Oedipus and the Sphinx*. The choreographer was David Lichine. It was an extraordinary opening night which was a great success in the press and at the box office, and Gene Kelly happened to be there.

Gene Kelly (Actor and Choreographer):

In 1947 or '48, I went to see a ballet in Paris called *The Sphinx*. It was a ballet by David Lichine, and sitting on top of a huge pedestal was a girl, I later learned, in a black wig with long claws and heavy makeup on. She was the sphinx, and she moved very well. It so happened that Eddie Constantine's wife, Hélène, who had worked for me at MGM, was one of the leading dancers with this group. Eddie saw me in the audience and said, "Let's go back and say hello to Hélène," so I went back and said, "I'd like to meet the charming girl who played the sphinx." We went to her dressing room, but she had already gone home. She was only fifteen, but she looked about twenty-one with all that makeup on. They told me her name and that her mother was an American and that she could speak a little English.

Arthur Freed (Producer):

Two years later, we began to cast *An American in Paris* and Gene went on vacation to New York. He had showed me some pictures of a girl he called the Cat Girl, with long fingernails, who he had seen in Paris a year or two before and whose name was Leslie Caron. I called him on the phone and said, "Gene, I don't want to bust up your holiday, but would you fly to Paris and make a couple of tests because we haven't got a girl." I said there was an actress named Versois who was kind of a star, and I said, "Make a test of her." Then I said, "While you do it, make a test of the little Cat Girl, Leslie Caron."

Gene Kelly:

When we were doing *An American in Paris,* Leslie was seventeen, but I knew that she wouldn't look that young. So I asked Freed to get permission to go and make a test of this girl named Leslie Caron. I just felt that we just couldn't make the picture without a real French girl— it just wouldn't be right—anymore than we could have made it without Guetary or Chevalier, a Frenchman playing a Frenchman, against Levant and myself.

Leslie Caron:

MGM was supposed to do *An American in Paris,* and Gene Kelly remembered me and came to France to look me up. The go-between was the husband of one of my colleagues in the company. He later became quite a famous movie star, but in those days he didn't have a penny, and he was just laying about—Eddie Constantine. Eddie was the husband of Hélène Constantine, who shared a dressing room with me. One day I got a call from Eddie, who said, "Gene Kelly is in Paris, and he'd like to see you about a musical." And I said, "Oh, come off it Eddie! Me, in movies?" I was a very classical ballet dancer, and I liked classical music and serious books and serious films. I was very blue-stocking in those days, but I told my mother, and she said, "Well, I think you should meet him and see." So a meeting was arranged, and Eddie took me to meet Gene Kelly at the George V Hotel. Gene said he meant to do a test with me. I wasn't very interested in making films, frankly. I much preferred dancing on the stage. It was terrific fun traveling with the company—you know, going to Greece or Lebanon, Egypt, Switzerland, Scotland—it was just a beautiful life. But my health wasn't what it ought to be. So my mother said, "Well, perhaps filming would be easier for you. Why don't you try it?" There was no talk of money at this point. I was totally uninterested anyway, but I condescended to shoot the test. I was very nervous all the same.

Arthur Freed:

The two tests came over, and Vincente and Benny Thau and I went down and ran them, and I asked Gene which one he liked, but he wouldn't say. He wanted to see which one we liked. So we ran the Versois test and it was pretty good. Then we ran Leslie Caron's test. Vincente, Benny, and I requested that they be run over, and they were. Then we each wrote down on a piece of paper which one we liked. We all liked Leslie.

Vincente Minnelli (Director):

Well, she was so marvelous. She was so much better then the other girl. She had that wonderful gamine quality.

Arthur Freed:

She had such reality. She was a wonderful dancer, and there was a kind of real quality about her. It's awfully hard to explain the quality of a person; it hits you.

Leslie Caron:

I made the test and promptly forgot about it; I was doing other things, and I wasn't very interested. Two weeks later, an agent, the brother of Jules Stein (I can't remember his first name), calls me up and says that MGM has picked up my option and that they want me in Hollywood in three days and that it's a seven-year contract, et cetera, et cetera. That very night I was to go to the opening of *Gone with the Wind*, which was at last arriving in Paris after the war. It was an awful lot to swallow in one day.

I had no clothes at all at that time because my father's business had deteriorated—he had made some bad transactions—and so, as I always do in the case of complete panic, I started making clothes myself. That was the best thing I could think of doing. I didn't read the papers, so

I didn't know much of MGM, but all the same, America and a film; so I was quite excited. I made myself a dress, a blue dress.

Saul Chaplin (Music Codirector):

I started as a songwriter in the late 1930's, when I wrote, with Sammy Cahn, at least ten standards, things like "Please Be Kind." I came out to California in 1940 as a member of Columbia's Music Department. I did everything imaginable in that department for eight years. Then, in 1949, Metro started doing a picture called *On the Town*. They needed a vocal arranger, because Hugh Martin and Kay Thompson, who were the staff vocal arrangers, were on another project. The combination of Metro's need, and my close association with Leonard Bernstein and Betty Comden and Adolph Green, whose *On the Town* was now about to be filmed, clinched the deal for me. I might also add that, while I was at Columbia, I did *Cover Girl* with Gene Kelly, and, as he was co-directing *On the Town*, he also became instrumental in my being hired at Metro. After *On the Town*, I signed a term deal with them, and stayed for nine years.

Adrienne Fazan (Editor):

I started working for the picture business in the late 1920's for First National. I was an assistant editor for Alexander Hall in the Colleen Moore Unit. Her husband was the producer, and everyone worked for them. Then Warner Brothers bought First National and, naturally, things changed. Also, sound pictures came out at that time. Not every theater had sound equipment, so they made silent films out of sound films, and this gave me the chance to cut the silent pictures from the sound pictures, adding titles and so forth. That was a wonderful chance for me; it really started me.

I started working at MGM in 1930, cutting films in the shorts department. Carey Wilson was the producer, and "What Do You Think?" was the name of the series. He made excellent shorts, and it was wonderful training. Then I changed jobs. At that time, MGM made foreign-language films—German, Italian, French, what have you. I could still speak German, so I got a job as a German-film editor. They brought real German or French or Italian actors to MGM and made pictures. They remade some of the big pictures like *The Big House,* which was remade in four or five different languages. They also hired foreign directors. I would cut the German-language version. Then I started cutting regular features. In 1950, at the time of *An American in Paris,* I had worked for MGM twenty years. My God!

Nina Foch (Actress):

I was seven years with Columbia, in which I did an awful lot of pictures. I made a picture opposite Glenn Ford called *Undercover Man.* I was in *Song to Remember,* and I made a picture opposite George Raft which I wouldn't call one of the higher moments in my aesthetic career. They used to have the twelve-week layoff, you know, at the end of each year. Before I went on to sign a new contract, I took my twelve-week layoff and went to New York and did *The Respectful Prostitute,* the Sartre play, and got marvelous notices.

After I had the experience of *The Respectful Prostitute,* I decided I could become a *really* good actress. Actually, I was a half-ass B-plus movie star at that time, and I realized I didn't have to be. So I went into Harry Cohn, with forty weeks to go now, mind you, before even option time on my new contract, and without asking my agent about it, and I said, "Look, I can stay here and be a half-ass B-plus actress for you and get nowhere, or I can go to New York and really get to be good, I think. I think I can be really . . . I mean a great actress." That man . . . I liked that man; he'd scare people to death, but he was very smart, canny; he kept his word. There were all kinds of crazy things about Harry Cohn that were great. When you were tough with him, of course, your knees were shaking, but, when your position was a cool, valid one which made sense to him, he always understood that. Temperament, bad behavior—he loved to give people a hard time if they tried things on him. But he got my pitch, and he said, "All right, kid, go ahead." Well, my agent was furious. Here I am now, making a real potful every week; I mean I worked my way up to a fairly decent salary. Seven years is a long time.

I then did *Twelfth Night* on Broadway and had an enormous success, and it was from there that I was tested for *An American in Paris.* I tested for it and got it. The other contender, I believe, was Celeste Holm. She did not get it, as you know.

Arthur Freed:

I first met George and Ira Gershwin up at the publishers on 45th Street in New York, T. B. Harms. I was writing songs then, and all the other songwriters, Vincent Youmans and Herb Brown and myself, used to go up there and play each other's songs. It was like a clubroom for us.

We weren't starving though, because Max Dreyfus—he owned T. B. Harms—would give us a little drawing account. He always gave us enough drawing account to live on. That would encourage us to keep writing and offer them the songs.

I can't tell you how many songwriters have become producers. I go back to George M. Cohan, to Rodgers and Hammerstein, to Buddy DeSilva—they all started as songwriters and became important producers. Louis B. Mayer was very interested in musicals, and I started with *Broadway Melody*. I wrote the songs, and they were rather big hit songs. After that, Mayer and I became very friendly. He eventually said, "I want you to get into the production of musical pictures." We talked about it for a period of about a year. Actually, I started *The Wizard of Oz*. I bought it from Sam Goldwyn before I was a producer. Then I actually started in 1940 with a full credit on *Babes in Arms*, with Mickey [Rooney] and Judy [Garland].

The main thing I was looking for as a producer was new talent, real talent, and most of the pictures I made were with talented people that I had brought in—people like Stanley Donen, Gene Kelly, and Minnelli.

Mary Ann Nyberg (Freed Unit Dress Designer):

The Freed Unit was on the second floor of the Thalberg Building. It was a corner suite located immediately over the mortuary next door, and we could watch the bodies come and go. We always thought it was very appropriate—great musicals coming out next door to a mortuary. Freed took me in once to show me his particular suite, his suite within the suite, because he had a very large office with orchids and marvelous paintings—beautiful Rufino Tamayos and Rouaults and some others. But he had this huge main office room and then a side room which was sort of a library, a rest room where he could get away, I suppose, if he wanted to. Then that immediately led to his own private bath, which he pridefully showed me because it was a point of status at that time to have your own bath with shower. I opened the shower and it was full of bourbon.

Walter Strohm (Head of the Production Department):

I think that everyone who worked with Freed respected him and was very happy to be with him. He was a contributing producer as far as I was concerned. He was available if you needed him. He didn't interfere with your activities. If he thought you were doing your work, that was fine. He didn't want to be bothered. He wanted the results the best he could get. A lot of producers sort of envied his exalted position. I'd just say that Freed had a glamour around him that he carried about. Freed was kind of the top musical producer in America. He wore the Legion of Honor, and a lot of things like that gave him a little stature.

Preston Ames:

Minnelli and Freed were a very, very close corporation. They thought together and worked together. Mr. Freed was a producer in the sense that he was a real producer in letting Minnelli, the director, have, to a point, his own reign. Obviously, when things got sticky Freed would step in and help, but he never pushed Minnelli to do it one way or the other. If that's the way Minnelli wanted it, that's the way it was going to be done. That's why he hired the man to do the picture.

Alan Jay Lerner (Author and Screenwriter):

It's true that Arthur has the tendency to start a sentence on Wednesday and finish it on Friday, but somehow it reached a point where you understood what he was trying to say. I feel that those times when he was inarticulate were seldom due to the fact that he didn't know what he wanted. It was more likely that he didn't want to upset you or hurt you. Eventually he got around to saying what he wanted, and most of the time he was right. In fact, I have a hard time remembering a time when he wasn't.

George Gibson (Head of the Scenic Art Department):

I was essentially a theatrical scenic artist. I had worked in the 1920's as an assistant scenic artist in London, Edinburgh, Glasgow and for a while in Wolverhampton. You know, I worked pretty well all over Great Britain at one time or another at various theaters, and I worked with the Harker brothers in London for a while. It was *the* scenic studio. They did all those big operettas, *No, No, Nanette, Desert Song,* and *New Moon.* It was a long jump to Hollywood, but it was a phase of my education, you know.

Scenic art originated in the theater many years ago. The scenic artist functioned as a designer and painter of large pictorial backgrounds and stage settings intended to depict the locale, interior or exterior, of the play being enacted on the stage. In the motion picture industry, the scenic artist is responsible for the projection of the functional part of the set in which the action takes place onto a two-dimensional surface, which is called the backing, in order to convey the illusion of continuing reality.

Anyway, about coming to America, it's the old urge, greener pastures and all that. I had heard so much about the United States. My thoughts were always of the theater, and, when I came to the United States in 1930, my first thought was theater. I worked first in the theater in Los Angeles. I would help paint backings for their stage presentations. My initiation to the motion picture business was through *Cavalcade,* with Clive Brook and Diana Wynyard. Gradually, as the theater began to fail here, because the Depression was a little longer in hitting the West Coast, the picture business gradually became a whole-time thing for me. I want to stress at this time no self-respecting scenic artist would work in the motion picture industry. He was essentially a man concerned with the theater, and the motion picture business was something that he turned his nose up at. However, the arrival of hard times changed my thinking along those lines. I began to realize that the picture business was the only business left for any of us. I worked at Fox and MGM and one or two others off and on until 1934. Jim Basevi at Metro, who was head of special effects, miniatures, process, all this kind of thing, was tremendously impressed with me and with what I had done for him. He spoke to Cedric Gibbons about me, and Gibbons said, "Fine, if we need a man like this, let's have a man like this." So I went to work in the Art Department with the idea of doing scenic work as scenic work arose. Of course, scenic work arose more frequently with each little success we had with it. We did more and more and more until one day in 1937 Cedric Gibbons said to me, "Mr. Gibson we've got to have some place where you can work." Up to this point I'd been working on the stages. I would have a team of artists all working on different levels. Now many odd things used to occur because when you get on a big backing the essential thing is teamwork. When you start off on a scaffold, you have an artist working on one level, another on another level, and another on still another level, and it was very, very difficult to maintain control. We'd start a big pine tree, and it would be one kind of a pine tree at the bottom level and another at the middle level and another kind of pine tree at the third level. You know, it was fraught with problems. A year or so later, with the full support of Gibbons, we got MGM to build a new paint frame for us. That building was the finest and most functional paint frame you could find anywhere.

Well, during World War II things just mushroomed. MGM had to stay on the stages, and thank God this department was here! It answered all the problems. We shot, for example, *30 Seconds over Tokyo* on a sound stage, using backings and a miniature out on Lot 3.

After the war, we got back into the swing again, and we went on from there. Then we came to the one that tested all of us and that put us in the crucible, *An American in Paris*. We had become reconciled to the fact that, given the go ahead and the will to try to do it, anything was possible, even *An American in Paris*.

Keogh Gleason (Set Decorator):

I came to MGM at about the same time that Preston Ames was getting off the boards and becoming an art director. I did a whole bunch of little pictures for MGM. You wouldn't dare call them "B's," which they were. They were economical "A's"; that's what Joe Cohn called them. That meant you didn't spend a cent. If you couldn't dress a set from stock or couldn't cheat it in a corner or use a standing set, you didn't have it. Maybe they would have to rewrite the thing.

The first thing I did with Minnelli, and the reason I got on *An American in Paris*, was a simple little picture. There used to be a thing at Metro between the decorators and Minnelli because he was so difficult about throwing out sets. There were two or three of my colleagues who wouldn't work with Minnelli any more, because he would throw out whole sets. Well, one day, I was called in and told it was my turn for the kiss of fire. It was a "simple" little picture called *Father of the Bride*. It was tricky because it had a big cast: Spencer Tracy, Joan Bennett, Elizabeth Taylor, and Billie Burke. It was a little tale of a man who really gets shot down by the expense of giving his daughter away in marriage. He's supposed to be a $25,000-a-year man. Well, Minnelli says to me, "Of course, at the reception all will be silver." I said, "You mean the gifts." He says, "Oh no, at the reception, before the gifts." I said, "Where does he get silver on $25,000 a year?" He says, "They borrowed it from the neighbors." Well, I decorated the house set, and Minnelli walks in with his entourage, and nobody says a word. They just walk through. No one said a word for ten minutes. Don't you know, it's that old thing that drives you up the wall, when the boss comes and the aides will not say anything until the boss gives them the cue of what to say. Finally, he said, "Keogh, it's perfect," and the others said, "Isn't it marvelous," blah, blah, blah, the whole bit. After that, Ed Willis, who was head of the Set Decorating Department, said, "Keogh you're it!"

John Green (Executive in Charge of Music and Music Codirector):

I wore two hats at Metro: I was the General Music Director of the studio, as well as Executive in Charge of Music. In other words, "If you don't like the music, fellows, holler at Green."

I had been at Metro from 1942 to 1946 as a staff composer-conductor, and I left in December of 1946 to freelance. I freelanced for three years. During that period, I returned to Metro to do *Easter Parade*; so the inner workings of Metro's music business and the Metro Music Department were no secret to me.

One of the first things that I did when I returned in August of 1949 as the Executive in Charge of Music and General Music Director was go through the MGM Orchestra with a rake. This was very unpleasant, and there are still some unpleasant memories of that lurking and lingering around. In one fell swoop, I dismissed twenty-eight of those fifty players in the first week I was there on the job. You see, in reconstructing that whole department, I had the kind of carte blanche that one can only dream of. When they were negotiating with me to come back there as the head, L. B. Mayer said, "I want the finest music department there's ever been in the world of entertainment." I asked him, "Mr. Mayer, is the studio willing to pay for that?" He said, "What do you think we're bringing you here for? Go do it." And indeed I did.

Rick Ingersoll (Office Boy):

In August of 1950, I started working at MGM as an office boy in the publicity department. It was my job, in addition to taking messages and getting the trades, to take guided tours. An American in Paris was the first film I ever saw filmed. It wasn't a closed set, so I used to take small tours through their stage every day.

Honore (Nora) Janney (Script Timer):

When I went to work at the studio, I went as a stenographer in the Script Department. That was about 1936. I went into the stenographic pool, and then from there they assigned the girls to the producers or the directors. I was eventually sent to be secretary to the director George Seitz, who turned out to be a wonderful man. I was supposed to be his secretary, but I ran interference for him a lot and kept people from bothering him. It was after I left Mr. Seitz that I got into timing scripts. That's a job which projects from a shooting script the eventual length or running time of the completed picture. There was an opening, but they had never had a woman do it before. Joe Finn, who was head of estimating, and my boss, said it wasn't right, it wasn't morally right, to lock up a man and a woman in a little office like that together. Of course, I didn't hear about this until some time later. I kept wondering why all the fellows around the production office were snickering. One boy used to come in and spend hours with me while I was timing with my male partner. Years later, he said, "Well, I was just keeping you decent." He was the chaperon.

Gene Kelly:

I always wanted to dance to American music and popular songs and popular American composers, but, when I studied ballet in the 1930's, it didn't fit—it didn't work. There was in the air a great unrest in dancers, but it was all centered in the modern dancers, and by modern dancers I mean specifically Martha Graham and Humphrey Wideman. Martha Graham was the great dean of the whole school then. What Mary Wigman was doing in Germany she was doing over here, to explore and break away from the old classic ballet traditions and do things that emanated from what they liked to call names such as "Earth Source." The difficulty was that this type of dancing didn't fulfill whatever need it was in me that I had. I wanted to dance to Cole Porter and Jerry Kern and Rodgers and Hart and Gershwin. So I began to make up my own kind of dancing.

I auditioned for the Monte Carlo Ballet Russe at one time, and they offered me a job, but I decided not to go with them. I couldn't quite envision myself at forty still doing *Swan Lake* and *Giselle*. Also, at that time the ballet companies were quite conservative. They weren't trying out many things I really wanted to do. So I practically started to try to find a kind of dance of my own. I didn't find it so farfetched to use athletics as a base, you know, and, if I wanted to express elation, I'd do it just as easily by taking a big jump over my leg. It didn't matter whether my hands were in fifth position or not. As a matter of fact, it seemed to me better that they weren't, and quite simplistically it worked well on the New York stage.

Arthur Freed:

When I first signed Gene Kelly, nobody in the studio liked him. They said, "You're not going to put him opposite Judy Garland in *For Me and My Gal*?" I said, "He's perfect for it; he's an Irishman." Eddie Mannix said, "But he's the wrong kind of an Irishman." I had lunch one day with Mayer, and I said, "I want to tell you something: I'm starting the picture next week, and everybody thinks that I'm doing the wrong thing by putting Gene Kelly in this picture opposite Judy." He says, "How do you feel?" I says, "I love him." He says, "Well then, don't listen to all those schmucks."

Gene Kelly:

I came to Hollywood under contract to David Selznick, who loaned me out to MGM to do *For Me and My Gal*. Shortly thereafter, Metro bought out my contract from Selznick. My new MGM contract stated that I was a singer, actor, dancer, director, and choreographer, but I didn't get paid any more for directing and acting and choreographing in the same picture.

I was paid forty weeks out of fifty-two a year, and they could put those weeks anywhere they wanted, which is the old seven-year-contract system. The other twelve weeks I could do what I wanted, unless they wanted to use me. They had a call on my services, but there again, if I said, "Gee, I'm too tired to dance; I need the rest," they'd let me go; they wouldn't pay me. That also worked out well for me because I did a couple of straight pictures where I began to learn to act a little bit. Clark Gable or Robert Taylor rejects, things like that. I had the rare advantage of having become a movie star and also learning a little more. So, as I say, it worked out well for me. I saw myself in rushes, and I was aghast at some of the bad things I did, but I learned, and, although I never turned out to be what I'd call the consummate actor, I did learn from some of those quasi-B pictures. Some weren't bad; *The Black Hand* or *Cross of Lorraine*, they weren't bad, or *The Three Musketeers*.

Alan Jay Lerner:

It was through Lilly Messinger, who was then a script buyer for MGM, that I met Louis B. Mayer.

Lilly Messinger (Literary Consultant):

Alan came into my office in New York to tell me about a play he had written with Frederick Loewe called *The Day Before Spring*. I loved it and told Mr. Mayer about it. On my recommendation, Mr. Mayer requested that Lerner and Loewe come out to MGM and audition the play for them. This they did. Metro liked it so well that they signed a preproduction deal for the play. Unfortunately, the play was not a success and the movie was never made. However, what is fortunate is that Mr. Mayer met Mr. Lerner.

Alan Jay Lerner:

MGM had bought the first play that Frederick Loewe and I wrote, *The Day Before Spring*. At that time, Mayer wanted Loewe and me to come to California. But Miss Messinger said that we should stay in the theater, because that was where we wanted to be. Then Loewe went to Europe for a year, and it was then that I decided it would be a good time for me to do a film. In California I met Mr. Mayer, and through him I went to see Arthur Freed.

Arthur Freed did the sensible thing, as he usually did. He said, "Why don't you come out here for ten weeks. Look around, and, if you find something that you would like to do, then fine. If you don't find something, then there will be no harm done and that will be that." I thought: What a wonderful way to begin!

After about three or four weeks I got involved in a project called *Royal Wedding*. It wasn't very good, but we did it anyway. Right near the end of it, Arthur Freed asked me to do *An American in Paris*.

Vincente Minnelli:

I started out by being under contract to Paramount. That was a miserable thing. I had three shows running on Broadway, but the thing was you had to go to Hollywood. Well, I didn't want to, but they brought me out as a producer. Paramount wasn't doing much, all the shows I'd done in New York were revues with Beatrice Lillie and people like that, and Paramount wasn't doing anything except *Big Broadcast* and things like that which didn't interest me at all. So I spent most of my time out here trying to get out of my contract. I had the feeling that people were looking at me through those shutters. Finally I got out and went back to Broadway. Then Arthur Freed came to see me at my studio and convinced me to come to MGM to do the kind of thing that I liked, you know?

Arthur Freed:

In my trips to New York City, I'd seen some of the things that Vincente directed—sketches and songs with Bea Lillie and things like that. Yip Harburg was a good friend of mine who'd written songs for me (Harburg and [Harold] Arlen did the extra songs for *Cabin in the Sky*). Well, I was in New York one trip around 1942 and was having dinner with Yip, and I said, "I know you're a good friend of this fellow Vincente Minnelli, and I'd like to meet him." He said, "I'll make a date." He called him, and we went up to his apartment, and we talked a little while, and I said, "Minnelli, how about coming out to California?" He said, "I've been there." I said, "What do you mean?" He said, "I was at Paramount and couldn't get to first base, and they paid me off and fired me." I said, "That shouldn't stop you." He said, "Well, I like the pictures you make." I said, "Look, I'll tell you what to do. The thing you did with Paramount was wrong; you went there for $2,000 a week, and they didn't know what you could do." Vincente wasn't the kind of person that pushed it. So I said, "Let me give you a thought: Come out to California, and come into my unit, and sit and don't do a damn thing. You won't be under any obligation; the studio's not going to say, 'Look, we're paying this guy $2,000 a week; what the hell is he doing?' Take your hotel bill and spend six months. I say, if you don't like it, leave after two weeks; there's no contract either way." So he says, "Let me think it over." About a week later, I was back in California and he called me on the telephone: "Do you still want me to come out there?" I said, "Yes. What'll you need for your hotel bill?" He said, "$300 a week." Well, he came out and sat with me, and he went down and watched [Busby] Berkeley work and other things, and then I put him on to direct a little number with Lena Horne.

Vincente Minnelli:

In other words, I was to come out for a year without any title or anything and work with everybody. A lot of the people that I knew in New York were here—Lillian Hellman, Dottie Parker, and Dick Perlman. Any producer could call me in and have me read his script and give ideas. I staged some numbers and shot them. Lena Horne came into the studio at that time, and I did all of her numbers in other pictures. It was a great year.

Arthur Freed:

One of the biggest criticisms of the business was that they wouldn't give young people a chance. Everything had to be Robert Z. Leonard, and so forth and so on. There was a patent on who was a director. I had a hell of a time at the start; that's why I had to make a colored picture with Vincente to start him. Mannix and the front office would all squawk and say, "Hey, you're not going to put him on with Norma Shearer to start with?" I even tried to start him with Harry Rapf and Dore Schary in the B Department, but they wouldn't give him a picture either. Finally I said to Mayer, "I want to make this fellow a director." Mayer was all for it. The only way to start him was to buy a property. I wanted to buy *Porgy and Bess*, but I couldn't get it, so I bought *Cabin in the Sky*. I put Vincente on it, and that started it. We made a deal with him after that.

Vincente Minnelli:

I always liked pictures. I knew from the time that I did *Cabin in the Sky* that this was the thing that I liked. In the theater, you know, you have a wonderful opening night and everything is slick and wonderful and then you go back a couple of weeks later and the light cues are all wrong and they've replaced key figures in the orchestra with scale men and people are kidding the show. But in pictures once you do it you've done it, and I like that.

Alan Jay Lerner:

Vincente doesn't try to do your creating for you. As Kenneth Hyman once said, "A critic is a man who knows direction, but doesn't know how to drive." Well, Vincente knows the direction, but he will let you drive. He knows what the picture should look like. When Vincente is at his best, his pictures have a look, a patina, that nobody else has ever achieved in motion pictures. He is as unique as Lubitsch was in his way.

Arthur Freed:

Minnelli's not shy when he's directing; no sir, he may not be boister-ous, he may not yell, but boy he's made out of iron.

Keogh Gleason (Set Decorator):

When communicating with Minnelli, it's like he tells you the second paragraph before he's told you the first.

George Gibson (Head of the Scenic Art Department):

On *Brigadoon*, it seemed there wasn't a clarification of his ideas. Cedric Gibbons had an idea of doing it one way, but it didn't sit too well with Minnelli, who wanted it another way. So Cedric Gibbons said, "We'll get a hold of Gibson and Ames, and let's talk it over." So, with myself and Preston Ames and Cedric Gibbons in his office, Minnelli outlined all of what he was thinking about. This was grasping at straws; you had to be something of a mind reader to know what Minnelli wanted. After Minnelli left, Cedric Gibbons looked at Ames, and he looked at me, and he said, "Mr. Ames and Mr. Gibson, you may know what has been discussed here, but I don't!" And we didn't either, if you want to know the truth; we didn't either.

Irene Sharaff (Costume Designer):

Well, I've known Vincente for years. I knew him in New York when he was a designer. The first picture I designed with Vincente was *Meet Me in St. Louis*. I can't calculate the number of years I've known him, but it's been quite a long time. I was not under contract at MGM at the time I did *An American in Paris*, but I had worked there quite a few years before. The book of *An American in Paris* had been filmed when I got on the picture. There was just one other section I did, where Leslie does kind of a series of short dances. Vincente had asked me to do the costumes for this too; otherwise I was only connected with the *An American in Paris* ballet sequence.

Walter Strohm:

I was an Assistant Director with the old Metro company before they merged with Goldwyn and with Mayer. The symbol of Metro, when I started out, was a parrot and he threw the letters M-E-T-R-O onto the screen.

At the time of the Metro, Goldwyn, and Mayer merger, I was working and going to school at the same time. My father was also there, and he worked for Joe Cohn. He was head of the Location Department, and I used to work in that. You see, there weren't any unions to speak of. So, when I say I worked in the production office, I mean I worked in the production office in a sort of many-faceted way. Things then sort of grew.

I went to Europe with Rex Ingram for the first picture MGM made there. I was Ingram's Assistant Cameraman. So, you see, I have a long, continuous, faithful torch with MGM. Well actually it was Loew's, Inc., that was the company. *Metro-Goldwyn-Mayer* was not a corporate name. It was only a trade name until the divorcement forced on them by the government. So *Metro-Goldwyn-Mayer* was to Loew's what spearmint chewing gum was to Wrigley.

Emily Torchia (Leslie Caron's Publicist):

I went from school to the switchboard at MGM and never left until two years ago. I eventually began working in publicity, handling the younger players—among them, Leslie Caron when she first arrived from Paris. When they were starting out, I also worked with Lana Turner, Ann Rutherford, Judy Garland, and Elizabeth Taylor. For the most part, I'd arrange interviews and photographic layouts for them.

Ed Woehler (Unit Production Manager):

I went to MGM in 1933. So I was there from 1933 to 1959. In 1933, I worked at Universal in the Production Department when a man by the name of Ed Sedgwick came over to do a picture. I was an assistant on this picture, and, since he liked the way I worked, the way I organized things, he recommended me to Charlie Chick at MGM. Joe

Cohn was the Production Manager at Metro, and Charlie Chick was his assistant. Charlie wanted me to come over to MGM, and, since they had such a great reputation, I came over.

The first picture I did at MGM was a baseball picture called *Death on the Diamond*, with Bob Young, and Ed Sedgwick directed it. The next picture I did was with W. S. Van Dyke, as his First Assistant. Then I did *Naughty Marietta* with him. After that, I did *Mutiny on the Bounty* with Frank Lloyd and then worked again with Van Dyke and Norma Shearer on *Marie Antoinette*. Then I worked as an assistant with George Cukor on quite a few pictures—*The Women, Philadelphia Story, Gone with the Wind, Gaslight*. Once I went with him, he kept me.

MGM had been after me for years to become a unit manager, but I wanted to pursue the directing end. I kept saying, "No, no." Finally, they said, I think it was in '42, "Look Eddie, Cukor's gone now; will you please do us a favor and become a unit manager?" MGM said they'd give me another $100 a week if I would, so I said, "All right." As a unit manager I was on all the George Sidney pictures—*Three Musketeers, Annie Get Your Gun, Showboat*—and then Minnelli got me on *An American in Paris*.

2

THE Studio

Dore Schary (Executive Vice-President in Charge of Production):

After [Irving] Thalberg's death, MGM had been organized by Mayer under a system that was jokingly referred to as a "college of cardinals." Louis B. Mayer was head of the studio, and big-scale decisions came to him. Under him there were a variety of executives—among them, Al Lichtman, Sam Katz, Bernard Hyman, Lawrence Weingarten, and Jim McGuinness. They, in turn, had staffs of producers under them and were split up into units. That system worked during the war years, particularly when there were very few pictures made. Also, where the demands were not nearly as severe and where the strictures of time were not as urgent, it could work. But, after the war, as big motion picture attendance dwindled, the system began to crack because the studio didn't produce as many pictures as they had before; there were so many complicating circumstances, including how to reach a decision on getting something done. That circumstance led to Mr. [Nick] Schenck insisting that there be a production head and Mayer recognizing that one had to be created, or found. That led to my appointment in 1948. I took over authorities which were in my contract and which I insisted on having because I knew the history of MGM (having been there before). I insisted on those prerogatives because without them a production head would be shackled. I insisted that if I were a production

25

head that I have final decisions on most matters. I would, for example, have to clear certain things, i.e., any piece of material that would cost over $75,000. In the main, I would make my decisions on cast, director, writer, cutting, and so on. The need was so great that everybody kept their word and I just turned out product which was badly needed. So, in that first year, I was able to switch an 8 million dollar loss into about a million dollar profit. We began to move.

At that point, the whole business of the so-called college of cardinals disappeared; it simply didn't exist anymore. I never believed such a set-up was practical. If I was going to be in charge of production, I was going to be in charge of production and my contact would be with the individual producers. They would report directly to me. Eddie Mannix was General Manager. Bennie Thau was in charge of actors—essentially their contracts and complaints. Louis Sidney was sort of an aid to Mannix. He was Assistant General Manager and took over duties of general managership assigned to him. Joe Cohn was in charge of physical production—cost of production, and work scheduling, et cetera. Those were the four chief people on the staff. They worked below me. The ultimate production decisions were mine. However, that authority was a little complicated occasionally by their going to Mayer. It so happened, however, that Schenck was very pleased with what was going on at the studio, so he did not permit that ever to become a problem. In the conversations, the "in camera" conversations, that Mayer had with Schenck, he was always told, "Well, what are you talking to me for? He's doing a fine job."

Nick Schenck and New York had no role in terms of the product unless it was something very unusual or very tricky or controversial. In such events, they'd begin to raise questions and then you'd have to argue. If your credit cards were good at the moment, you won the argument. If they were not, you backed away for a while and came up with it again later on.

Keogh Gleason (Set Decorator):

There were so many stars that you couldn't believe it, and all of the stages were filled. There was an excitement going on. Metro was the glamour place. Every star will tell you, during that period, boy, if their agent just got a nibble at Metro, or, "I'm going to be in a Metro picture," you know . . . wow! Sometimes you didn't see your colleagues for days on end or only when we'd get together for a drink at night at that bar that's gone now—The Ready Room. There used to be some interesting characters there at night, anybody from stars on down. Everybody would be exhausted.

Adrienne Fazen (Editor):

Well at MGM there were many people unnecessarily involved. They had more what I called "running around boys and girls." They had so many people, so many assistants . . . it didn't make sense.

Honore (Nora) Janney (Script Timer):

One of the first things I was told there was to be very careful about what I said, because you didn't know who you'd be talking to. It could be a son-in-law or a father-in-law, could be a cousin who went to dinner every Saturday night and told what he had been able to learn.

Mary Ann Nyberg (Freed Unit Dress Designer):

People stood across the street from the Thalberg Building. This wasn't one day a year or when a star was going to come in or something; they stood across the street on the grass, all kinds of people, and just watched. It was really unbelievable.

Gene Kelly (Actor and Choreographer):

I often got calls from people working on other musical pictures at MGM, and they'd say, "Gee, we're sorta stuck on an idea here; what do you think?" I'd go and watch the rehearsals, delighted to be able to help. Then there were times when there were some extreme cases where, for example, I rehearsed six weeks and we were all ready to shoot a picture called *Easter Parade* when I broke my leg. Fred Astaire, luckily for us, had retired. He had decided to quit the business, but we got him to come back in. He got back in shape and did the picture with Judy Garland. Where the stuff that we laid out didn't suit him, we switched it around a bit. It was that continuity of work around there that just happened. At any other studio, the picture would have been canceled for a year and they would have had to pay Judy a salary while she's doing nothing.

John Green (Executive in Charge of Music and Music Codirector):

You have to remember one thing about the musical films of that studio, at least in my time: They had three giants in the field of musical-film production—Arthur Freed, Jack Cummings, and Joe Pasternak. There was such expertise, each in his own way, in these three people. I mean those fellows just wrote the book about what they were doing.

Ed Woehler (Unit Production Manager):

As a unit manager, what we would do is shoot a picture and prepare one at the same time. You'd always be working on a couple of pictures. It didn't give me too much time for myself, but we were dedicated, I mean we just gave our own good life to the studio and didn't resent it. In fact, we accomplished something and were pleased with what we did.

Adrienne Fazan:

There was overtime but the studio made a rule that we could not work overtime without special permission. So I said, "Oh, the hell with you." I worked the overtime, but I didn't put in for it, because I hate that business: "You can't do this." "You can't do that." What the hell! I'm working on a picture for the picture, trying to make it as good as possible. Then they tell me I can't work, I have to go home when I have work to do. I didn't go for that.

Dore Schary:

The studios were like little kingdoms, and, like little kingdoms, there was always somebody wandering around saying, "The King has no clothes on." And, "The King is on his last legs." And, "I don't know why he's doing this." And, "that's a terrible mistake he made." You see, there's a whole underground of gossip about whoever is running the job. It goes all the way from which actress he's trying to get to sleep with him to "How much does he gamble?"

Leslie Caron (Actress):

The seating arrangement in the commissary was a matter of such importance. The most important producers and the most important stars could sit against the back wall so that, as you looked through the commissary, the stars would just line the wall. There was the same girl who was there for years and years—she may still be there, as far as I know—who knew who could sit against the wall and who couldn't. Being invited to the commissary for lunch by a producer was so important that you couldn't refuse the invitation. Then there were places that you shouldn't sit. I remember Ava Gardner breaking all the rules and going in the cafeteria with the truck drivers and grips. That was considered just abominable. So we had all that protocol.

Walter Strohm (Head of the Production Department):

People thought that the money to make the pictures just came out of some mine somewhere and that that was secondary to picturemaking, not realizing the pictures were the mine and, unless we made enough of them and made them good enough to be successful in the sense of paying off the loan, we would all be out of work. We had to make thirty or forty pictures a year to make it pay, but every week the salary was there, and that's more than it is now. People could pick up their good old checks, and it was a wonderful thing. These men who were capable enough to form a company and to be able to borrow the money almost on their own reputations had to show results. They had to have pictures that paid off. They allowed a lot of artistic pictures to be made too, believe me. They knew down in their hearts they were just gambling— gambling right from the beginning. They made artistic pictures, the Thalbergs, the Selznicks, the Mayers. Do you think Gene Kelly's *Invitation to the Dance* wasn't taken with a little bit of concern by our company. The ballet may be the greatest, but is it good box office? But they went ahead and made it. So these things are important. Now they're selling the studio, there are no jobs to speak of in Hollywood. It's truly a disaster area, and you stop and think: When they had it so good, nobody appreciated it.

Preston Ames (Art Director):

The beauty of Cedric Gibbons was that we learned several things that we've never forgotten. One was he allocated responsibility and then allowed you to proceed with that responsibility. If you wanted help, you went for help. If you were in trouble, you explained your case and he judged you accordingly. If you were right, he would back you up to the hilt; if you were wrong, he would forgive you. Secondly, he didn't want you to be just a pretty-picture maker. That he loathed. He felt that was being a little unfair to yourself and that it was being unfair to the director. If you couldn't take that sketch and make it into reality, you were just an artist. And that he wouldn't tolerate.

George Gibson (Head of the Scenic Art Department):

We trained the best in our place. The means were there, because information and knowledge are growing things. Everybody contributed. You'd contribute through discussion. At a coffee break, we didn't sit down and talk about football; we sat down and talked about art. We discussed paint or a show we had seen. Everything built to the assimilation of knowledge. Quite different from what you might say the norm was, because you know how it is when guys sit down for a coffee break: They'll talk about anything but work. But we were always concerned about work.

Nina Foch (Actress):

I went to lunch and dropped some lipstick right down my white linen dress. Well, I looked terrible, and I had an appointment after lunch at the studio. I came sobbing into MGM's wardrobe, saying, "Mary,

Mary, for God's sake, look at me!" She said, "Give me the dress, sweetheart," took the dress, and, like magic, because they had just raided Europe and had every great craftsman that you could lay your fingers on, she brought that white linen dress back to me in ten minutes, without a spot on it. Also, when I was doing *Scaramouche*, I suddenly wanted a perfume whisk from the property department because I looked up and found out that ladies of that period would dip it in perfume and whisk it around them. Ten minutes later, they were down with five of them.

Dore Schary:

I get a little irritated when I read an obit on Audie Murphy and it said he was a hero who was exploited by Hollywood, by the studio system. Yeah, well, it's nonsense. It's a cliché. It's a cliché. Mario Lanza was another case when they cried exploitation. Good heavens, this man was catered to! He was given all sorts of thoughtful, believe me, very thoughtful training and thoughtful care. And somebody writes he was destroyed by Hollywood. He was not. He was not. It's within the nature of men and women to destroy themselves. I don't have to tell you that pictures, or the theater, any kind of creative work, really, has, within its disciplines and within its rewards, the seeds of destruction. You can be very spoiled. The secret is just not to believe it. Or at least to say it's true but don't kid yourself, it ain't going to be true all the time. Adlai Stevenson said it the best: "Enjoy it, but don't inhale it."

Joe Cohn (MGM Vice-President):

Mayer's main strength as a studio head was that he had an enormous respect for talent. He was willing to pay for talent. He thought you had to have young writers, young producers, young directors. It was just like a baseball empire where you have the [minor] leagues and the bigger leagues so that you could develop your own stars like we did in the Hardy series. We would develop people who could go on to important things. Mayer's big mania was that you had to use young people to develop, develop, develop, develop. He wasn't interested in making a picture that you could make money on if you didn't help develop people.

Gene Kelly:

The days in the 1940's and 1950's when I was at MGM were great days for all of those connected with the musical motion picture, because there was money enough and largesse enough that we could experiment. All the experiments that were made in the huge field of the commercial musical film were made during that period. The reasons are obvious; they were economic. We had no television competition. Movies were the number one entertainment, and musicals were making zillions of dollars. Couple this with the fact that we had, I can safely say now, from the vantage point of time, the best musical people creatively, as far as performance goes, at MGM. As a result, we turned out to be a repertory company. We had one thing that the American theater has been searching for for years—the same fellows in the Music Department, the same fellows doing the arrangements, and all of us doing choreography, directing, and so forth. As a result, you'll find on the credits pictures directed by Vincente Minnelli, or Gene Kelly, or Charles Walters, or Stanly Donen, and on and on and on. You'll also find us codirecting or cochoreographing pictures. Sometimes the names don't even appear on the credits—names of musical arrangers or composers who came in and helped out on a picture, like for one number, but couldn't take any credit because there was only one number—but, you see, they filled the gap.

Then, we all got to know each other. We even got to know each other in our bad moments, when we were difficult with one another, or when we got too important, or when we'd be too stubborn and say, "No, I can't do that." You see, we knew each other, and that's a marvelous way to create a musical, because you can't do a musical on the so-called *auteur* theory. That's impossible. Musicals were the product of a system created and developed by the studios, and at the time of *An American in Paris* MGM was at its zenith.

PART II

3

Prologue

Lowell E. Redelings (*Hollywood Citizen News*, November 10, 1951):

Gene Kelly plays a struggling painter—an American who loves Paris and seems quite content with his lot until two women enter his life. The one is a beautiful and rich patron of the arts . . . played by Nina Foch; the other is Leslie Caron, a pretty French shopgirl whom he meets in a night-club and immediately falls in love with.

The Wealthy Lady, too, has fallen hard for Gene, and she tries to help him get ahead. She introduces him to people of importance, builds up his confidence in his paintings, buys a swank studio in which he can work, and arranges for an exhibition of his paintings.

But all this is to no avail, for the girl in the night-club is the apple of the young painter's eye. They meet now and then for brief moments of rapture, until one day she confesses she is marrying someone else— someone to whom she owes a great debt. Thereafter the plot spins to its climax—with the help of a beautiful 17-minute ballet "dream sequence."

Variety (August 29, 1951):

Film picks up Kelly as the happy-go-lucky Yank who's the fave of the nabe in his poor Montmartre quarters. Miss Foch, as a wealthy Amer-

ican play girl, "discovers" his art talents and takes him on as a protégé
to add him to her retinue of lovers. Kelly accepts the idea warily but
then meets and falls for Miss Caron. She's a poor gal who is getting
ready to marry Georges Guetary, a music hall star, because he saved her
from the Nazis during the war. At the colorful Beaux Arts Ball she tells
Kelly about her impending wedding which sets the scene for the big
ballet (a depiction in Kelly's mind, told in terms of famous French
paintings, of his doleful situation). Guetary, however, naturally discovers the true situation and bows out of the scene for a happy ending.
Gershwin's music gets boffo treatment throughout.

Hollywood Reporter (August 28, 1951):

The yarn is simplicity itself. Gene Kelly, an American artist studying
in Paris, falls in love with a French girl, Leslie Caron, who is betrothed
to his good friend, music hall entertainer Georges Guetary. Nina Foch,
a beautiful, slightly neurotic American girl, takes Kelly in tow, adopts
him as her protégé and tries to make things spin. But Kelly persists in
his love for Leslie, discovers too late that she belongs to another. Sure
things work out at the finish but not until you've been treated to the
An American in Paris ballet, the most spectacular sequence of its kind
ever put on film.

Cue (October 6, 1951):

Thus, in quick out-line, this is a boy-meets-girl, loses-girl, wins-girl in
the spring, story.

4

Preparing the Book

Arthur Freed (Producer):

Well, pictures start in strange ways. Ira Gershwin is one of my closest friends, and I grew up with George Gershwin in New York when I was first writing songs. I used to spend a lot of time over at the Gershwins'. I still spend every Saturday night with Ira at his house, and we either play poker or pool. So one night I was with Ira Gershwin playing pool and afterwards, it was about two in the morning, we sat talking about pictures and I said, "Ira, I've always wanted to make a picture about Paris. How about selling me the title *An American in Paris?*" He said, "Yes, if you use all Gershwin music." I said, "I wouldn't use anything else; that's the object." This was the start of the idea. Now, I didn't know what I wanted to do. The only thing I said to Ira was I wanted to use George's compositions and his title *An American in Paris* and maybe do a ballet. I didn't even know who was going to be in it, but I knew it would have to be a dancer, either Fred Astaire or Gene Kelly.

We started a deal for the music with Ira and the Gershwin estate. The main thing, first, was to find characters. I remembered seeing a layout in Life magazine of the GIs studying in Paris on the GI Bill. I thought that would be a great character for our leading role because George Gershwin studied art in Paris. That made the character that Kelly would eventually play a little bit of Gershwin. So I had that char-

37

acter. Then, for the character played by Oscar Levant, who was, as you know, always very closely associated with George, I took David Diamond. Dave was a musician I know who always got scholarships and went to Europe but never had enough money to come back. He knew the Gershwins too. So that's the character we made Levant.

Now was the time to find a writer for the project. I talked to Vincente Minnelli about it and mentioned Alan Jay Lerner. Vincente was crazy about the idea, so I tackled Alan. I didn't think I'd get him, because Alan likes to write the songs. But, when I told him the idea and the characters, he said, "I'd love to do it," and he did. Then we decided on doing the ballet. Now, Gene Kelly is more of a ballet dancer than Fred, so that decided that. So we had all those initial elements. I told Mayer what I was doing. I'd have lunch or dinner with him every Sunday at his house. He loved the title.

Alan Jay Lerner (Author and Screenwriter):

Arthur had natural ties with Louis B. Mayer, and until Mayer left the studio that is who Arthur always went to see. What Arthur Freed was to me and to many people in that studio, Louis B. Mayer was to Arthur Freed. Arthur was Daddy to us, and Mayer was Daddy to Arthur Freed. Nobody respected Louis B. Mayer more than Arthur. Arthur was like his boy. He gave Arthur encouragement and that confidence Arthur gave us. Mr. Mayer was very involved in everything that was happening in the studio, and I think he was especially involved in things that Arthur did.

Dore Schary (Executive Vice-President in Charge of Production):

I think Mayer probably would have supported it because of its style and beauty. He would have understood it; yes, he would have. You see, the most difficult things he had to contend with, within his own personality and range of interest, were the harder pictures, the hard-fibered pictures. But he liked musicals and, in fact, they did very well for us.

How many we made a year depended on the number of ideas that came in. If we had ten good ideas for musicals in 1950, the year we made *An American in Paris*, we made ten. If we had one, we made one.

My feeling was, let's not count how many melodramas, or how many dramas or comedies, or musicals, let's just do the ones that look good.

We had kind of a musical stock company at MGM then. There was Joe Pasternak's company, which was kind of the land of "Pasternaky," including Mario Lanza and Kathryn Grayson and that whole group. Then there was Jack Cummings, who was a combination of Arthur Freed and Pasternak. Cummings's pictures were more pragmatic than Joe's. He had taste. He wasn't as imaginative as Arthur, though. He had, for instance, reservations at one time about *Seven Brides for Seven Brothers*, but then, when we got into it, he began to get excited. The Freed Unit was the most imaginative and the most skillful of the three by far. Probably, the group of people who worked for Freed, Cummings, and Pasternak (Roger Edens, Minnelli, Kelly, Donen, Irene Sharaff) were the best group of talent consistently making musicals that we've ever had. There's never been a group like that, nor will there be. One of the lost things you can look back on in that era and say was good was the system of patronage that enabled us to keep together a group of highly talented people and let them function rather freely and profitably.

My first memory of *An American in Paris* was Arthur Freed coming up and telling me what he had in mind. Gene Kelly and Vincente Minnelli were with him. They began to tell me about it, and I responded very excitedly. They didn't have the story line yet, but they had the title and the music. Gene even had the idea of some big, important ballet he wanted to do. He also mentioned the business of searching for a girl. There was some talk of Cyd Charisse, but Gene was not for that. He wanted to get a girly-girl, you know, a new, young, French girl. He loved Charisse as a dancer, but he said, "I want to get someone, and she should be French; there shouldn't be anything 'phony French' about her." Vince Minnelli (the director) and Freed also approved, and it all sounded marvelous. They also talked about Alan Lerner doing the script. I okayed that and they signed him.

Arthur Freed:

Alan and I were good friends; he'd done a picture for me. He said, "What are you going to do next?" I told him about the deal I had made with Ira and some of the ideas I had, and he said, "I'd like to write it."

He was good friends with Levant and with Ira. He monkeyed around a bit with *An American in Paris* and then told me some of his ideas.

Alan Jay Lerner:

I think it was in the late spring of 1949 when Arthur first mentioned *An American in Paris* to me. I went back East for the summer and then came back in September and began working on it. Arthur explained some further ideas, and we talked about them. At one time, we were thinking of playing the picture in the 1920's, about the time Gershwin had gone to Paris and was studying painting. That raised the question whether it should be biographical or not. I said that I didn't want it to be George, because writing a biography isn't something that I do. To write a biography of a flesh-and-blood character would be fighting the style of what I felt the picture should be. It had to be a fictitious character and situation so that I could establish the level on which people would be thinking, feeling, and seeing. If you have George Gershwin alive, you have to treat your story with a little more seriousness. He's flesh and blood. You have to keep in mind that there is no such thing as realism or naturalism in the theater. That is a myth. If there was realism in the theater, there would never be a third act. Nothing ends that way. A man's life is made up of thousands and thousands of little pieces. In writing fiction you select twenty or thirty of them. In a musical you select even fewer than that. But you cannot do that with a flesh-and-blood figure. Automatically you will be disemboweling him. So the idea of a Gershwin biography was discarded. A story line, therefore, using Paris and an American painter and Gershwin music had to somehow be developed. All I knew at this time was that I was going to write the story as if the Gershwin music had been written for it. I didn't want it to be just a cavalcade of songs. I wanted to write a story so the songs would appear because of the emotional and dramatic situation. I wanted them to seem like the original emotional expressions written for those particular moments in the film.

I started on it in September, and I remember that I went for a long time without an idea. When I say "a long time," I am speaking of California, where the days go slowly and the weeks go fast, especially for one who does not live there. During this period of six or eight weeks, I would go over to the studio a great deal. The great charm of writing films is that you are not alone. When you are in the theater, you are really alone. There is nobody to talk to. They don't have a whole operation functioning where you can walk and look around and see people doing things. Sometimes that activity will get you out of yourself. You can unwind a bit and it will head you into something. I would think about other stories. I would say to myself, "If I had written that story, would it be a good story for *An American in Paris?*"

When you are really concentrating on something, I think that you have another mind working. Time after time, people go to sleep and just wake up with an idea. Just the night before, that person would be faced with a problem that he didn't think he would ever be able to solve. That happened to me here, for finally I had one idea. It must have been some time in November when I finally got some notion of what I was going to do. And that was that a kept man falls in love with a kept woman. That was the problem that I started with and tried to develop. Arthur cautioned me that the girl could not be kept per se, so with this idea I began to write, and by Christmas I had the first act completed.

I wrote first, not unnaturally, the first scene wherein everyone is introduced—Kelly, Levant, Guetary, and Caron. I wrote it so that everybody has a false introduction first. I wanted to introduce the characters' voices on the sound track first while you see somebody else before seeing the person who is talking. This was done for two reasons: First, it allowed the camera an opportunity to photograph some atmosphere, and, secondly, and more importantly, it sets a style. Thornton Wilder once said, "More plays fail because of a breach in style than for any other reason." That is certainly true of a musical play. Musicals fundamentally have a style problem. In a film or on a stage, you have to establish a style within the first five or eight minutes. You have to establish it on the level that you are asking the audience to accept it. It is on that level that the audience will feel and laugh. The audience after that will know what kind of an evening it should expect. That is what I was most intent upon doing when I wrote the introduction the way I did. It was realistic but not quite realistic. It was fanciful, and so on.

As I continued to write, I indicated generally certain songs that I thought might work. I kept giving the work to Vincente and Gene, and they seemed to feel that I was on the right track. The script was developed so that a choice of numbers could flow from it. For example, with just a small change in the screenplay, I could have my choice of

"Our Love Is Here to Stay" or "Love Walked In." They could have the choice of either song and not affect the characters in any way. As I wrote, I automatically started thinking that at certain places I had to have music. My instinct tells me that it is right. Then I begin to think of the music, and it should all balance because the whole technique of writing a musical is to try to make the emotional requirements be such that they demand the kind of music that will balance the screenplay. If you have a romantic moment with a slow ballad, you cannot have another one right away. The whole idea is to make the story unfold so that right after that moment somebody will be feeling something that will bring in a gayer song. Also, you must balance the score from the standpoint of solos, duets, choral numbers, large numbers, small numbers, and so forth.

I got about forty pages done before Christmas, and then I went home for the holidays. At that time, I had no idea how that story was going to end. I came back to Hollywood and went through January and February without figuring out how I was going to end it. Meanwhile, Frederick Loewe had come back, and we began to think about another musical. Also, I was going to be married in March and go on a honeymoon, and still I had not gotten an idea about how I was going to end the story. The night before my wedding, I sat down at eight in the evening and wrote sixty pages. Somehow I ended it and I never changed anything. That is what is so strange about it. The answer to why I wrote it then is that I had to. Sometimes, when you have to, you do it. All of a sudden you say to yourself, "I have to put it down now. I have to do it." Very often I find I have solved my problems when I start putting it on paper. Often I am convinced that there is no solution and all the time I have found the answer and I didn't know it.

After finishing the script, I don't remember doing any rewriting except some minor thing when they started shooting. Vincente called me in New York and said, "We need one speech before the big ballet begins." He told me what he needed, dramatically. I wrote the speech and mailed it in. As far as I can remember, that was the only rewriting that I did. Small adjustments may have been made, but that was just a matter of editing. It required nothing on my part.

With the script finished, I turned it over to Vincente, who was, of course, responsible for making it come alive. After all, it was still type on a page.

Vincente Minnelli (Director):

Alan is marvelous at devising things like *An American in Paris*. The whole scheme he had for the book he got pretty much the first time through. It only needed the changing of certain things going in and out of numbers.

Because I've done so many of both, I've been asked whether I prefer directing musicals or dramatic pictures. Actually, for me, there is no difference at all. If you are going to do a musical well, it's just as difficult and just as real and requires just as much thought and sweat as doing a tragedy. Determining the human condition is just the process of motion that you go through, as you begin to live the characters and visualize them for either musicals or dramas. You say, "This could have happened this way." There has to be a way that it could have happened. There is nothing that is too banal to show dramatically, because in real life this is the way things happen. You say, "You won't believe this," and then you tell something that happened and it sounds like an old Fox musical. Or you will tell something else that really happened and it sounds like it's absolutely right out of a short story from the *Saturday Evening Post*. You see, to direct something, you have to believe it's happening. You have to find a way to say that this could have happened this way, within the structure of the story. I always try and find the element of verisimilitude in the story, and I'm miserable until I find it. The period before I find it is quite a dour period. The period before we solved the problem of the ballet, for example, or finding the right music, was dour indeed.

John Green (Executive in Charge of Music and Music Codirector):

MGM didn't own any of the rights to Gershwin's music. A blanket deal was made, and the licenses were acquired from the proprietors of Gershwin's copyright for *x* amount of money. The great bulk of George's music had been transferred over into his and Ira's own company, which is New World, even prior to George's death. As I recall, all the substantive and important stuff of George and Ira Gershwin was under one umbrella by the time we negotiated for the rights.

Arthur Freed:

I forget exactly how the money deal was split with the uses of the music, but it was about $300,000 for the title, *An American in Paris,* and all of George's music and Ira's lyrics. We also gave Ira an extra $50,000 as a consultant. He dug out all the old manuscripts and songs, and we played them up at his house.

Saul Chaplin (Music Codirector):

I remember the first *American in Paris* meeting we had to talk about music . . .

John Green:

. . . in Arthur Freed's office. Vincente Minnelli was there and Gene Kelly and Roger Edens. Roger was Freed's associate, but he had no credit association on this picture.

Saul Chaplin:

I think Roger was beginning to prepare *Showboat.* I remember, can't even tell you why now, having a yellow pad—I guess we were talking about something Chinese or something—and writing on the top *Amelican in Palis.* That was the heading of the page. No reason. When we were brought in, as I recall, Alan Lerner told us the sketchiest story of what we were going to do. I remember one other thing. There was a discussion as to whether to do a seventeen-minute ballet, and I remember what finally sewed it up. There was a picture called *The Red Shoes* that had come out that had a seventeen-minute ballet, and it was doing very well. That settled it. As long as they could do it, we *certainly* could do it, only do it better.

The Metro-Goldwyn-Mayer Studio in Culver City, California.
The Thalberg Building is in the lower left-hand corner.
George Gibson's Paint Frame is the tall building just above the
water tower.

The location of the street for *An American in Paris*, Lot 2.

MGM's executive staff: Standing, left to right, are L.K. Sidney, Nicholas Nayfack, Al Lichtman, James McGuinness, Eddie Mannix, Benny Thau, J. J. Cohn, Sam Katz, Lawrence Weingarten. Seated are Nicholas Schenck, Louis B. Mayer, Arthur Loew.

Preston Ames and Vincente Minnelli.

Leslie Caron as the Sphinx in the ballet *Oedipus and the Sphinx*.

Adrienne Fazan
and Gene Kelly.

Nina Foch and Oscar Levant
(at the black-and-white ball).

George Gibson.

The Paint Frame.

John Green conducting the MGM orchestra.

Georges Guetary
and the girls of the
"Stairway to Paradise"
number.

Dore Schary.

Leslie Caron, Gene Kelly,
and Vincente Minnelli.

Vincente Minnelli, Leslie Caron, Gene Kelly, Arthur Freed
being visited by Ava Gardner, who is working on *Showboat*.

Ed Woehler
laying out the
schedule for
*An American
in Paris*.

Nora Janney.

"Vincente . . . thought it would be good for a scene between Gene and Oscar at the piano in Oscar's room."

BYRRH

VIN GÉNÉREUX AU QUINQUINA

"We wanted to introduce the characters— the Frenchman, Georges Guetary, and the two Americans, Levant and myself."

"I'm going to work it in with the kids on the block,
and teach them the song."

"I'd like to sit down with a sketch man and do several
presentations of what I think this street should be."

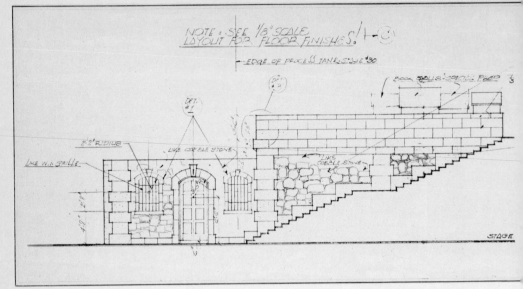

"These drawings might take . . . four weeks in order
to get a complete set of plans, elevations, and details."

The finished set piece of the stairway by the *quai*, built
from the construction plan in the previous illustration.

The Paris street on Lot 2.
Sacré Coeur, in the
background, is a
painted backing
strung across
the street.

"My family is in oil—
suntan oil."

Première photo
de Leslie Caron
à Hollywood

"In other words,
I was the gamine,
the pert little *Parisienne*."

"I was annoyed;
I thought it was
a great hairdo."

"The first big set we shot was inside Kelly's garret."

"By the time we got through rigging and changing . . .
it was a $10,000 bed."

"God! I rehearsed
longer on that than
I did on the whole
'Singin' in the Rain'
number! Then to
lose it!" A still
from the cut "I've
Got a Crush on You"
scene.

"A stairway . . . I had so real that poor Oscar Levant refused to go up and down."

"Not one little frame is haphazard; everything is studied." The kitchen set was eventually cut from the film.

"Perhaps one of the most challenging sets was the little café and the streets that worked with it."

Paris street
on Lot 2, with
unfinished
roofs.

The resulting shot of the
same buildings with
the matte shot inserted.
As can clearly be seen,
the entire third story,
including a photo of
Kelly looking out the
window, has been drawn
on top of the real building
and then matted in.

"Then, on either side of this stairway, Vincente had the idea that he would love to do a 'living chandelier.' " Al Gilks and his operator are in the lower right foreground. The stairs are in the lit position.

"Henry Greutert . . . was very instrumental in building . . . two shells of plaster that some poor girls had to fit themselves into."

John Green:

That settled it as far as the studio was concerned, but it didn't settle it with the ballet, nor did it settle it with the Board of Directors in New York, because everybody thought Arthur and we were out of our ever lovin' minds—that you could take a picture of this kind and suddenly, at the end, for seventeen minutes, make a ballet. So there was a real selling job on Freed's part with the money people from New York. But that happened much later.

Saul and I collaborated on this film, and people think it's necessary for two collaborators to hate each other on account of Gilbert and Sullivan, but I don't go for that. Certainly, on the kinds of things that you're talking about, which is a vast multimillion dollar project, you couldn't possibly have a successful collaboration such as Saul's and mine if there wasn't a concomitance of taste; it wouldn't have worked if what I loved he hated and vice versa. We like the same things musically, by and large.

Second is a great musical respect and the ability to delegate to one another and the willingness and—this sounds, you know, kind of "God Is Love-ish," but there's nothing wrong with that in the last analysis—no jealousy. Nobody wanted more credit then the other fellow. Each of us knows what the other fellow does; each of us knows why the other one is there and why we're both there. Saul had done many pictures without me, and I've done many pictures without him, but, when we're there together, there's a great reason for it which we both need and want.

Saul Chaplin:

That worked all kinds of ways actually. The problem of our collaboration on *An American in Paris* was Johnny was running the department. He was the head of the Music Department at that time. He had many other duties besides *An American in Paris*. I had nothing but *An American in Paris*. I was with it every day. When I needed him desperately, I would call and say, "Look, this is what went on today. Gene's decided he wants to do this," and he'd say, "Gee, this is a good idea!" We'd discuss all of the musical problems at least once a day. Now, when it came to final rehearsals, before anything final was done to any piece of music, of course John was a major part of that. Also, very often at night, I would come into John's office and explain what we had done musically. Often he would improve what we had done or we would discuss how we could fix it in different ways. In other words, I was with the picture actively all the time; John was with it, let's say, most of the time but also running the MGM Music Department, which was a formidable job at that time. I might add, parenthetically, at that particular time it was probably the greatest collection of musical talent ever assembled.

John Green:

. . . and ran like clockwork. It was incredible, because we all talk about it with such awe now. It's not the kind of thing you appreciate at the time, but, when you think back now who was in that department, it's overwhelming. To go back, the way we worked together on *An American in Paris* was just constant collaboration. At least once a day, and very often during the middle of the day: *"John, help!"*

My assistant, Chuck Wolcott, and the department manager, Hal Halpern, and I had coffee every working morning at eight, and there would be those days, as Solly [Chaplin] will remember, when at eight o'clock I'd say, "Chuck, it's your department; don't call me, because I belong to Arthur Freed and *An American in Paris* today. I don't care if the bloody place burns down." There were those days.

The first thing Solly did was go round and round and round with the songs.

Saul Chaplin:

There were endless visits to Ira Gershwin's house, going through every piece of published and unpublished material that George and Ira Gershwin had ever written. Going with me to Ira's was Gene Kelly, and sometimes Vincente, but mainly Gene, because he was also going to choreograph the picture.

Gene Kelly (Actor and Choreographer):

This selection process is always tricky. The screen itself is not conducive to good dancing, because it's two-dimensional while dancing is three-dimensional movement—it's kinetic. It's like sculpture as opposed to painting. It's also personal. So the best thing to do is to create a dance with an idea behind it which grows out of the plot or furthers the plot. It's not always able to be done that way, because often you are asked, in a commercial sense, the director or producer saying, "Here we ought to have another number because we're lagging. How can you fit something in here?"

What you do miss in motion pictures is, mainly, the kinetic force. On the stage you can do certain things, but I found out very early when I came to Hollywood that a dance I could do on the stage that would hold up for seven minutes would boil down to about two minutes on the screen. This is mainly due to the lack of physical or kinetic force. Also, the personality of the dancer is missing in pictures. You're with the audience in the theater. You look at them and you can embrace them and they can embrace you, so to speak, or you can hate each other. But you get no direct response from the screen. It is so remote from the empathy of the live theater.

I do feel that the best method for motion pictures is to relate the musical number in some sense to the story. Sometimes it doesn't have to be the narrative sense; that is, it doesn't have to be in the plot sense. If it can be, that's great, but, if it's just psychically or even mystically, in a sense, related, it helps. You just can't go out, dim down the lights, and do a specialty act. I'm afraid that's been done many thousands of times in Hollywood musicals, and I don't remember it ever working, even with great performers.

Now, on *An American in Paris*, Arthur Freed got a bunch of us together in a room, and I'll never forget it: There was Alan Lerner, Vincente Minnelli, Saul Chaplin, and myself. Freed said, "Now, here's the idea: It's an American and he lives in Paris." You know, it sounds very simple. Alan Lerner's job, which I didn't envy, was to write a very slight script which at the same time could incorporate the Gershwin catalogue of popular songs, including the symphonic piece *An American in Paris*. As he wrote the script, we found we did have to bend and twist it a bit to get some of the songs in. While Alan was starting the script, Saul

Chaplin and myself were going over the Gershwin music. Actually, we went to Ira's house, just around the corner, and we'd sit there all day and play right through the songs.

Saul Chaplin:

We were looking for songs that could lend themselves to staging in general and that we considered typically Gershwin. We were not going to take some real obscure, exceptional, outside song that he had written. We weren't looking for hits, however, so much as things that we felt were typically Gershwin. We'd take a stack of music and one of us would sit at the piano and we'd sing along and then discuss the songs, and gradually start to whittle them down.

Gene Kelly:

Saul Chaplin would find a song that wasn't so well known as, let's say, "I Got a Crush on You," and he'd say, "This song is one of the great songs and lyrics ever done; let's use it." We'd say, "Fine." Then, other times, we'd find a song that we just couldn't fit into the story— a song like "Maybe," for example. We all loved it, but the *modus operandi* was not there. Believe me, we were very lucky because of the breadth and depth of Gershwin's work. I mean, if you took a composer who had about six hit songs, Alan would have had a very tough time writing the story.

Saul Chaplin:

In other words, the story line was firm. What wasn't solid was the screenplay. The story line is about a painter who's in Paris, studying. He meets a woman who wants to keep him, but the painter falls in love with someone else. The bare bones of the story were there. The scenes could always then be slightly edited or adjusted to accommodate our musical needs.

Alan Jay Lerner:

I gave them the key dramatic moments—what I call the "pillars." For example, they would be whatever musical moments introduced people, whatever musical moments create the romantic interest or tear people apart. These are the pillars that hold up the roof. In between, they had a lot of freedom and latitude. I wrote a part where Gene comes up the stairs and sings an "up" song. Now, he could have done that alone or he could do it with Oscar [Levant] in the next room. Vincente decided to do it with Oscar. That was the freedom they had.

Saul Chaplin:

That's why the total thing was a collaboration in every respect. We found "Tra-la-la," you know, the song no one ever heard. We went over dozens and dozens of songs, and suddenly we came to that. I said, "My God, that's cute!" Vincente agreed and thought it would be good for a scene between Gene and Oscar at the piano in Oscar's room.

Vincente Minnelli:

Gene didn't know that song but was very struck with it. He liked it. I thought it would suit a situation with Oscar and Gene alone in Oscar's room and that Gene could clown it up or they could clown together. Lerner's script called for a scene in which this song would be perfect. It was the scene after he had met Lise and fallen in love and was high and giddy and almost drunklike. It was my idea to have Levant at that time working out a thing and being absorbed in a problem, not being interested when Gene comes in to start the scene off. That way, it wasn't written as an act of the Rover Boys, you know?

In another place, Gene wanted to dance with an old lady. He was always dancing with kids and old ladies. So we fitted "By Strauss" into that situation. It included the proprietor of the café and his wife and the big fat woman. We also got a dancer who was middle-aged and made her up to look older than she was. George and Ira had written "By Strauss" for a show of mine called *The Show Is On*, where we used songs by different people. (We couldn't get one composer who was at liberty.) The Gershwins were in Los Angeles at the time, and, because they were very good friends of mine, I kept asking them for a number. That's how they came to write "By Strauss." Ira kept calling me during the time it was being written, reading me certain parts they had just written. I flipped over the song. Marvelous also in *An American in Paris*. The trick there was not to have it look like a number. It had to look spontaneous in the café, with all these French people in it and the Americans; it had to look like it just happened.

Saul Chaplin:

"By Strauss," oh my God, what we went through with that! We needed a number because Gene had always had an idea of doing a number, or at least a part of a number, with an old lady. Well, if you think about dancing with an old lady, that's a waltz. So now you go through all the waltzes of Gershwin, and what do you come up with? Nobody knows any waltzes by Gershwin except the ones in *Of Thee I Sing* and things like that, but the one we found, "By Strauss," seemed so *Mittel Europa* and perfect. That's partly why it's in.

Gene Kelly:

We also made it serve our plot. We wanted to introduce the characters: the Frenchman, Georges Guetary, and the two Americans, Levant and myself. We also wanted to show their living quarters, the geography of the place, a sort of *La Bohème* kind of existence in which they lived, the free and easy atmosphere of how they'd half-pay, or didn't pay, the rent, also how they were well liked by the people who ran the building and by the people who ran the little bistro downstairs. This was a rollicking number, and when we all came across it we loved it at first. We didn't think, though, that we could get it in. But we made it fit, you know, and the way we made it fit was we pulled in Oscar Levant very early because he was a piano student, the world's oldest Guggenheim scholarship, or whatever you call it. From there, I went into the number with the old lady and drew the crowd. In effect, "By Strauss" was stuffed in—it was pushed in—but we trusted it felt like it belonged there. Sometimes we got to numbers that seemed like a sacrilege to leave out, like "I Got Rhythm." We had to get that in. You can't have a Gershwin show and not play "I got rhythm, I got music. . . ." You can't do that. Then Freed said, "But, gosh, Judy Garland and Mickey Rooney did it a few years ago, you know, in *Girl Crazy*, and so-and-so did that, and everybody's got it in their nightclub act." So I just sat in my old chair and thought for weeks about that one, about how to work it in. How to work it in. Well, I decided, I'm going to work it in with the kids on the block and teach them the song because it's so American, that's all, and it wouldn't be a song that the kids in Paris at that time would be singing.

Saul Chaplin:

Johnny and I had done a picture called *Summer Stock* before this, and in *Summer Stock* there was a song called "Dig for Your Dinner." Now, in "Dig for Your Dinner," I had written a patter, and the patter went "You gotta do so-and-so—you gotta do so-and-so—you gotta do so-and-so." So, in staging "I Got Rhythm" for *An American in Paris*, we figured out there would be a group of kids around and they'd all say, "You gotta . . ." and Gene would say the rest of the thing: "Do this, you gotta, do this." I don't know how the idea came up, whether it was Gene's or mine, but we said, "Listen what about with kids with "I've Got Rhythm" have them say, "I Got," you know, "I Got I, Got," and Gene can teach them English that way. That's how these things get born.

John Green:

An interesting one to talk about, because of the fact that it had an unusual personality leading into it, Georges Guetary, in "Stairway to Paradise," which came from the *George White Scandals*, one of George's early big tunes.

Saul Chaplin:

I remember we wanted to do a Folies Bergères number and "Stairway to Paradise" seemed perfect. You've never seen the Folies Bergères without stairs. I've seen them several times, and there are always stair-cases. They don't always light up the way ours did, but I must tell you one thing about the scene: I saw the picture recently on television, and the one thing which I don't think we'd do today is how we went from French to English. I remember the meetings about it: Here's a French music-hall singer singing in a French music hall, but we can't have him sing it all in French; he has to sing it in English. Now, how do we get from French to English? As I say, I'd never accept this motivation today, but at the time he sang the first eight bars in French, comes out on a runway, sees a friend of his who's an American, and says, "Ah, Johnny my American friend." Bang, the rest of it is in English.

Arthur Freed:

We heard a lot of music before the script was done, and there were certain songs that I had put down that were big favorites of mine. One of them was a song that wasn't a hit before, called "Our Love Is Here to Stay," and that was put in. I put it in as the love song and also for the wonderful dance Gene does with Leslie on the *quai*. We used cer-tain things that we knew were good (what I call "material songs") be-cause they were good for photography and business besides just being a verse and chorus. With the other songs, we monkeyed around—changed songs and switched them around, because the Gershwin cata-logue is phenomenal, you know.

John Green:

Arthur is a man whom I not only love very deeply but respect. In terms of both audible and mental articulation he fumbles along, but he knows what's going to come at the other end, and he is a great aesthetic entrepreneur and synthesizer. So *An American in Paris* was going to be *the* definitive articulation of the words and music of the Gershwins. He, Arthur Freed, was the one who was going to do it. So that kind of qualitative barometer, which was important, was put on it and that influence maintained throughout. In selecting the songs, an added facet was that we were picturemakers, which all of us, Thank God, in those days around the Freed unit, were. There were no (and, if this sounds a little disdainful or bitchy, it's only because it is) there were no amateurs around that unit. We were all "theater *Menschen*": we were all people from the theater, all of us, and, whether it's a tri-dimensional stage or a bidimensional screen, it's theater. So the *dramatic* values of the songs were most important to us. How do they apply to the story line? What can we make of it? Something that has both entertainment and good drama. For example, the decision that the *Rhapsody in Blue* would not appear in the picture but the *Concerto in F* would be the Levant vehicle, and that it wouldn't just be done on the concert stage somewhere but that it would be done with a Minnelli-ism, a device.

Saul Chaplin:

And in an entertaining way. If you remember, it was Oscar playing all the instruments of the symphony orchestra, playing solo piano, con-ducting, and applauding himself in the audience.

John Green:

And as it turned out it was Oscar's idea.

Vincente Minnelli:

Arthur had wanted him to play a medley of George's songs, which Oscar didn't want to do, and he came over to my office one night after shooting and said, "Oh God! If I could only convince him to play the concerto." A wild thing, he said, "Maybe if I play all the instruments." And I said, "That's a *marvelous* idea!" I called Arthur in the Thalberg Building just as he was getting ready to leave. We met him out front of the building, and I said, "Oscar's got a wonderful idea." I said, "I'll do it like the Dufy orchestra things, all in gold." So it ended up with Oscar not only playing all the instruments but being the conductor, the man in the box, and so on.

Saul Chaplin:

The point is, had Oscar not come up with that idea, there's every chance that the concerto might not be in the picture, because that's how the picture was approached. If it didn't have showmanship, the number wasn't in. There's not a single number in that entire picture where somebody just stands by a piano and sings. Everything was thought out clearly, and everything had showmanship connected with it.

I think something that should be pointed out here is Kelly's work on this film. He was a very busy fellow. He did all the choreography and was in the picture himself, but it was more than that. He's the one that found Leslie Caron and I suppose felt a great responsibility for her in the film. Also, choreographing her so she would look her best. Leslie's a marvelous dancer, but to just show what she does without going beyond that, you know, sometimes is difficult. Then, to choreograph that much dancing is a herculean task. Then Gene—and I'm sure he'll admit this—is always a little worried about his voice, about his singing. Gene has a very pleasant Irish voice; it's the most I can say for it; I'm serious. Gene approaches songs when they're rhythm songs like: How will they be staged? What will it look like? Fred Astaire, on the other hand, looks at a song as a song. His approach is: It's a marvelous song; I'll do the song.

Gene Kelly:

The public accepts lousy singers, you know. I'm stating it very boldly: I'm not a good singer. But, if you are, let's say, doing *An American in Paris* and you're talking about a girl and you're saying that she's wonderful, you sing " 's wonderful, s' marvelous, she should care for me." You're telling the other fellow about it; you state the thesis, you state the idea, and then you further it in dance form. "Singin' in the rain," you say, "I'm singin' in the rain, just singin' in the rain. What a marvelous feeling. I'm happy again." You state it; now you prove it. You further your thesis by dancing it. Also, what it does, which is very valuable to the dancer in pictures, very valuable, it bridges the gap between the spoken word and the dance.

Then there is something that's often overlooked, the one advantage that nonsingers like myself have over good singers is that we can almost talk what we have to say. We want the audience to hear the words. We're very particular about our lyrics. We say, "It's very clear, my love is here to stay." We make sure that the audience hears that. A lot of songwriters like dancers to sing. I'm not sure the music composer does; no, I'm not sure of that. But just for the average dancer to stop and sing a ballad usually doesn't interest the public. They are interested in staging—what he's going to do next—and I'm making it very mathematical now. It's amazing how well a song bridges the gap between the real and the unreal, because it is true that nobody walks out of their house and does a tap dance down the street, or a ballet dance, or whatever. To bridge the gap, to get from the real to the unreal and then back into the plot again, the song is invaluable.

Walter Strohm (Head of the Production Department):

One of the first things to happen on a picture is that it is given a production number. *An American in Paris* was assigned number 1705. It would first have a preliminary number that would collect all the charges on just the preliminary stages of production, for example, when the script was probably being drafted or the story discussed. As soon as the picture is given a definite go-ahead—"We're going to make the picture and sign people"—we give it a number. There was no numerology used; it was just given the next number on the list. The picture will carry that number for the rest of its life. Everything is charged against it. All the preliminary charges are thrown over to the picture number. That is the accounting number. The only function that number has is something to charge against. Then each department had a code, so it looks like 1705-25. That next series of numbers, 25, the subnumber, would indicate the particular department. This enables us to pull out a department's charges against the picture, the wardrobe charges, makeup charges, or what not and see who's spending what.

Alan A. Antik (Technical Advisor):

When Freed hired me, Minnelli was on vacation. I hadn't ever seen him. I only saw Gene Kelly, and he and I clicked very nicely. When

Minnelli came back, all of a sudden he was confronted with me. Minnelli is a very peculiar man; I think he's very talented as far as staging is concerned in a musical comedy style. But, as far as handling actors, he was nothing, just absolutely nothing. Well, anyway, when he came back, Freed called me in his office and introduced me. Minnelli always does a peculiar thing when he gets upset; he moves his mouth—how do you call this sort of an animal? maybe a crocodile—like munching. It's one of the peculiar things about him. I was very polite and friendly. Freed told him that he had put me under contract. Right off the bat I felt Minnelli had an animosity against me. He thought maybe I was an upstart. I also think he had somebody else in mind, one of his friends, for my job. But it was too late to change; Freed had hired me and that was that.

At this time we were beginning to get the script page by page. You study it more as you get closer to it, and you get more of an opportunity to visualize each setup, each scene, and combine them in your mind. The Research Department was at my disposal, and I asked them for some pictures of this and that for the Art Department, the Wardrobe Department, and for the Casting Office because there were lots of speaking parts that I would help to cast.

Dore Schary:

When the script came through, I saw it and thought it was a good, workable script. I didn't think it was a great script; if you see the picture today, you see it was lacking a kind of sophistication. It had a spurious sophistication, and some of it was really quite ordinary. It wasn't changed, because, number one, I think we were tuned differently; number two, Lerner and Gene and Arthur felt it was exactly what they wanted, and I always felt, as a production head, unless I was absolutely sure they were in for a bomb, I would say, "Okay, it's your picture ultimately." Sometimes I was proven right, sometimes I was proven wrong, but with *An American in Paris* they were right. I think the script was absolutely serviceable. More than that, it was a very distinguished picture. I would have liked, though, for the script to be just a little, well, perhaps, a little more mature, but Gene made some very valid points. He said, "It's a very light musical comedy. It's a flight of fancy, and the script should really be that way." As I say, I think he was proven right because it was just that. It was finished with a little air. So I had to conclude they were right.

Vincente Minnelli:

Alan Lerner completed the script, and I thought it solved the problem marvelously. The problem was: How do you make a picture using all of Gershwin's songs and finish with a ballet? That's quite a problem. But he came in with a very fresh idea and a wonderful set of characters, and it worked just right.

Then you make these characters come to life, but those are the things that you live with all through this preparation period and all through the making of a picture. Then you begin working with art directors and set decorators and all those other things that have to be prepared in advance.

Preston Ames (Art Director):

Actually, I did a lot of work even before I met with Minnelli. That's the way we used to work in those days. Cedric Gibbons handed me the script which was a "Temporary Complete" script. They'd generally print twenty to fifty scripts at a crack, and one of them was handed to me.

Cedric Gibbons worked very closely with me, as he did with all his art directors. The best way to describe our operation is to compare it to an architect's office. You confer with the head man, but eventually you are assigned an architect who works on your assignment. The office, however, is going to be very much aware of whether the architect's work is in keeping with the experience, the style, and the creativity of the head man. If there was bad taste, if there was bad composition, or if it couldn't be photographed, Gibbons would spot it right off the bat and you were in trouble. If you did something which you thought was the proper thing to do and the director came along saying, "This isn't right," Gibbons would defend you, or he might say, "It is a mistake." But if you were right you always had the support of your supervisor. He'd back you to the hilt. Gibbons had the background (I think that's the proper word) to have the great respect and admiration of the entire studio. He represented quality, and he represented good art direction.

In the preparation of a picture, I would go to him and discuss the problems. When I needed some help, I'd say, "Lets talk about the first set, the street." Mr. Gibbons would say, "Now, what is your idea of the street?" I'd say, "I haven't the slightest idea, but I'd like to sit down with a sketch man and do several presentations of what I think this street should be, because it is a very important set in the picture."

Then I would present him with all my ideas. God help you if you didn't, because, if you did something over his head or behind his back and you got into trouble, you'd sink! You would never even be allowed to swim. You had to play the rules. Nothing wrong with playing the rules. My God! I don't care what it's in, politics or playing tennis, if you play by the rules you can't get in too much trouble.

Gibbons was also responsible for the *décor* of the picture, and in those days the head of the decorators was a very charming, talented man by the name of Ed Willis. He had a staff of decorators who had been there for years and years, and Keogh Gleason was the chap that I worked with. So there were two supervisors and two unit men—Keogh Gleason, Decorator; Ames, Art Director—and we worked as a team, very, very closely.

Before *An American in Paris* I had never worked with Keogh, because I had always worked with little guys. Little guys worked with little guys. It was amazing; talk about class distinction, there were first-, second-, and third-class people, and I was, for a long time, a third-class guy. For each particular production, you were assigned your own class of guys to work with. This was fine and the way it should be.

Scripts were always handled exactly the same way. The expression "to break a script down" implies that you read a script over and over several times in order to get it thoroughly in your head. Now you sit down as an individual and work out those sets which are necessary to back up the production. In certain instances on *An American in Paris*, decisions were very specific. In other instances, they were very vague because everything had not been written down. There were two ballets in this thing, and they were slots left open. The book, however, was all there, so it was just a question of breaking it down and saying, "Okay, we're going to put this on a stage; we're going to do this on our back lot, and we'll go to France and do some second-unit work there." That's how we did it. Next, we sat down with all the people involved. We used to have great meetings about how we were going to do this picture.

Walter Strohm:

In the meetings, Gibbons would sit there and read scenes and discuss the acting. It was a general open meeting about making a picture. There were no restraints put on people as to what they could or could not talk about. Gibbons could say what he thought at any time, Freed said what he thought about Gibbons's idea, and I could say what I thought about both of their ideas. Now, we had arguments; don't think they were all tea parties. It couldn't be any other way with the personalities that you worked with, but most of the time they were pleasant. Very seldom did we have any temperamental outbursts, but we did have the freedom of exchanging ideas of how we were going to handle the picture.

Vincente Minnelli:

Having started as a designer, I used to live in the public library. I also have my own file of clippings, books, and things. I have millions and millions of clippings which I go through, which is a great help. It's a shorthand for working with art directors and set dressers. There are millions of books on Paris, so that was routine work for me.

I go through thousands of clippings because, you see, there's no way really of tabulating the clippings, because sometimes a thing that is Oriental will give you an idea for something that you are doing that is Parisian. First of all, you have a file for all the places in Paris, all the groupings and strange photographs that might come in handy. Then you begin to boil it down: This will do for that, and this street looks this way, and it's this kind of a street combined with this photograph and this clipping with this group of people. A film that means anything at all I always think is made up of hundreds of hidden things. Things that the audience may not be aware of unless it's pointed out to them but nevertheless help to involve them and haunt them a little. Otherwise, they see and forget as soon as they leave the theater, and that's what you're always trying not to have happen. It helps a great deal if you're relaxed with your characters as to their place in time and space.

Preston Ames:

Minnelli was the most difficult person in the world to communicate with, because he had everything preconceived in his head. You had to dig it out, literally just scratch it out. If you had a concrete thought, he was delighted because he liked concrete thinking. He didn't want you to go to him for problems. The thing that you would do with Vincente Minnelli would be, once you had developed a scheme, present it. You had to go through it step by step with every area involved, with sketches and continuities and layouts and photographs or whatever it took to sell your particular idea. Once he accepted you it was easier, but that was the thing that was very difficult with this man, because he either accepted you or he rejected you. It was no compromise, and in this picture there was one moment before the black-and-white ball when he absolutely rejected me like a bad blood cell. He just threw me out. But, for a good long while we got along very well because I came up with ideas and had the courage of my convictions.

Probably the toughest thing in the world to do was to sit down and say, "Okay, on a stage we will create Notre Dame, a bridge, and a *quai*, and Gene Kelly can do his dance number with Leslie Caron." Well, everybody thought I was crazy. But I had a preconceived notion that it would work, and Minnelli believed me, and we set out and did it. But, if it hadn't, God help me! I don't know what would have happened.

Vincente Minnelli:

We thought first of shooting the picture in Paris. I think we even went for our shots and passports. Then we started to think of the ballet. Gene and I saw a lot of location stills. The actual streets would be so difficult to control and so difficult to make a ballet in, so finally it was decided we could do it just as well here, and, with Preston Ames, I worked that thing out. So it only took a second-unit man for those few shots in the very beginning of the picture where they say, "This is Paris." So actually it didn't require going there. Preston worked this out so beautifully. It looked like the real thing.

Gene Kelly:

To begin with, I always believe that it's better to shoot on location. But I was quickly convinced on *An American in Paris* that the back lots would do fine. The reason for that was that Saul Chaplin and I found a piece of music called "Somebody Loves Me." The original idea was that I was going to sing it at the Tuileries, the Luxembourg Gardens, the Étoile, and every other place in Paris, and I was going to do it with Leslie Caron. We were going to go all around Paris singing "Somebody Loves Me" in a similar style to what I had done in *On the Town* with "New York, New York." This time we'd do it with more dancing, though, because I'd have a dancer with me. This was going to be our big ballet. As we got into that, however, I realized that we couldn't do this extended type of a number, because of Leslie's physical condition. She wasn't strong enough to shoot and dance a whole day, and, if you go to a city, you just can't afford to shoot only for two or three hours. So we agreed to drop that number.

Alan A. Antik:

When the decision was made to do the whole thing in the studio, my job really became monstrous. We had to figure out with Cedric Gibbons and Preston Ames what it would be like in Paris. Incidentally, in Paris I used to have a bachelor apartment up on the hill which is Sacré Coeur. There was only one modern building with four floors, and I had an apartment on the fourth floor, so I knew this section very well. At night, I used to go up and down the hill to the nightclubs and cabarets. We had to compromise somewhat on what the actual locations looked like, but I didn't want it to look like a set. I wanted it to look like the real thing, and this is where Minnelli and I didn't agree too often. As I say, he was a stage director who was used to spectacular musical comedy, and that's the way he visualized Paris. We had sessions every day with Cedric Gibbons and Joe Cohn and Strohm and Freed and Minnelli and Preston Ames and me. I was very careful not to say anything unless I was asked something. Considering my position with Minnelli, I did not want to put myself forward. But Joe Cohn was an old, wonderful man, and when they discussed something with Freed and

Minnelli they would put some questions out and Joe Cohn would look at me and say, "What do you think?" So I was forced to answer. He knew what I wanted to do. I wanted this to be representative of Paris as such. This, of course, was very difficult to do in any studio, but we managed.

Every day I would see Minnelli, I would come to his office and he was almost to the point of being rude to me, but I just swallowed it all the time and said, "That's all right." Minnelli visualized *An American in Paris* as a glorious musical comedy, that the streets of Paris were full of nothing but pushcarts with people selling flowers. Now, in Paris there were some pushcarts, but not to the extent he wanted. He visualized a sort of a Radio City Music Hall production with girls, and all the men wearing a mustache and a beret. The whole thing was too much, and in me he met a person who was extremely realistic in his approach to life. After all, I am a Parisian; I spent most of my life there, and the French as such are extremely realistic in their approach to life. They may not be very agreeable to some foreigners, and misunderstand each other, but basically they are extremely realistic and very independent. I did not, however, want to be independent in the face of Minnelli. I was just trying to make suggestions to the point of being helpful in the execution of my job so that the picture would become something.

Emily Torchia (Leslie Caron's Publicist):

We met her at the airport with news photographers. From the time she stepped onto American soil, Leslie Caron had not a minute to herself. Remember, also, it was a strange country. She spoke some English, but she had to perfect it. It was all very new to Leslie and it was hard. MGM realized her talent, so we were doing all the publicity possible. She was one of the "sweet little girls" brought over from France. Arthur Freed was very distinguished and always has been, and his productions were *the* big productions, and *An American in Paris* was no exception. You see, it was very important for Leslie to get a lot of attention. She had a lot of interviews, which left very little time for herself because when she wasn't working her luncheons were taken up with interviews. Then she had her English, her singing, and her dancing to study. Leslie had very little time for herself, so I can see where it might have been physically and emotionally very difficult. And it was all business with us. We loved her but it was still business.

Leslie Caron (Actress):

I think I arrived in L.A. on Saturday morning, June 3, 1950, and my new agent, whom I didn't know—little Harry Friedman—waited for me at the airport with some photographers and some studio executives.

From the airport, a limousine took my mother and me to a hotel, the Beverly Wilshire, and the agent advanced us a little money (I think about $500) and told us he would come and pick us up for dinner. Anyway, the next thing I knew was the dinner, at LaRue, and there was so much meat on my plate. I ordered like I would in France: *pâté* to begin with, then a steak, a vegetable, and salad. When it came, the portions were like for four people. I couldn't believe such wealth. In France, you could order *pâté* and a steak and a salad and some vegetable and a dessert and still be hungry because the portions were small, but here the steak hung over my plate. After the *pâté* I already had enough to eat. I couldn't bear to leave the rest, so my agent had to get a doggy bag.

Anyway, my mother and I spent the night in this plush hotel, and we woke up at dawn with the change in hours, and my mother, who was very aware of finances, realized that in one day we had spent one-fifth of my week's salary, a hundred dollars. So she promptly decided that we would go to a cheaper hotel. So, like 6:30 in the morning, we packed and left. My mother found a hotel in Culver City which was close to the studio. She decided that would be very practical, so we ended up in the worst dump in the history of poor displaced persons. It really was like—I don't want to say YWCA, because that's probably very nice—but anyway it was so lamentable. Then, around ten A.M., there was a frantic call from my agent, who had finally traced us and was panic-stricken that (a) we had moved and (b) we had gone to such an unglamorous place. We explained that we didn't have the money.

The next thing that happened is Gene Kelly invited us for the afternoon on Sunday. We arrived at his house and everybody was terribly nice. There were all sorts of movie people, and it was very free and very casual, which was very new for us. I was used to the formality of French houses, which is almost like in Spain, where someone is only admitted to the home after long knowledge of the family. But Gene's house was open and inviting and very hospitable. For a long, long time, I couldn't get used to this kind of informality.

Then, on Monday, I met Arthur Freed and Vincente Minnelli and

Alan Jay Lerner in Arthur's office, and they were terribly nice. I was immediately conquered by them. I thought they were very charming and terribly nice to me and very comforting. One of the discussions was: "We absolutely must not let Leslie take acting lessons." Sort of a plan of campaign was decided upon on how they would keep me from having to go to Lillian Burns, who was the established drama teacher at MGM. They wanted me to be very spontaneous in the film. They didn't want me to look like I had learned anything, so it was decided that it would be better for me not to go through any tutoring. They kept repeating this sentence (I didn't know what it meant): "You must be natural; just be yourself, darling."

The next thing is, my mother and I found another place to live. We started living in a motel, and that was even a worse *faux pas* for Hollywood budding stars, but my mother didn't know and didn't really care. She was very eccentric. It was a very nice neighborhood where we lived, and I met some bizarre women who ate candy all day long, and they were terribly interested in everything that was going on. There was a sort of family atmosphere, which I liked. They wanted to know everything that I had done and how it was going and who was there, and they were always gobbling candy. There were also some very charming kids, and I became sort of their Pied Piper. After three months, my mother left to go back to Paris to my father and brothers, and so I was left alone in this motel.

I started getting organized, but I was immensely lonely. I didn't have all my chums from the ballet and the cozy world I knew, but I took up painting and I started buying records. I think one of the first things I bought was a record player. Then I started studying at the studio. I took lessons in ballet, I took lessons in singing, and I took lessons in English. So my first days at MGM were taken up with studying, and then rehearsing with Gene and his two assistants. The first one, the most talented, was Carol Haney, who is now dead, and the other was Jeannie Coyne, who is now Gene's wife.

Gene had sort of told Carol Haney to see what I could do best. Gene was very clever as a choreographer. He would find out what the best points of a dancer were and make up a ballet around that. In other words, he suited the ballet to you, and not you to the ballet. He took advantage of my good points. Carol was helping very much with the choreography. She would sort of think up things and present them to Gene, and if Gene liked them he would incorporate them, and if he didn't he would change them—that sort of thing. She was truly an assistant.

And I had singing lessons with old Rosie [Arthur Rosenstein], but that didn't work out too well. He was marvelous, but I had no talent and no training, absolutely none. At first, they wanted me to sing in the picture, but there was nothing doing. I couldn't even hum. I have to admit I was completely baffled by it all, and it was still months before I went before the cameras.

I used to come to work through the gate by the electrical plant. I mean, that gate has never been passed through by a movie star since it was built. It caused such a flap.

Keogh Gleason:

At Metro, geographically, there's a back gate where the workers come in on the Culver Boulevard side. There is a little motel over there, and Leslie rented one unit with her mother so she could walk over to the studio. Can you imagine, from Paris to Culver City on that nasty little side street. Anyway, during the first couple of weeks, Freed came down, and here was this little French girl, and was there anything he could do for her? She said, in her accent, "You know, I used to be able to come in the gate that is so convenient to my house, but now they won't let me come in there any more; they make me walk way around the studio and come in through casting." He said, "What! Who?" She said, "The *gendarme* said actors cannot come in here." You know, the cop at the workmen's gate didn't know who she was from a bar of soap. So Freed gets on the phone: "Who's on that gate?" Freed roars. "Who's that dumb man that makes Miss Caron walk all the way around here?" By coming through this gate, she could go directly to the stages—simple. Instead, she was walking a mile around the studio to get in. Leslie said, "If you could do that for me, Mr. Freed, I would be very grateful." Here's the big star asking to be let in a gate that's convenient.

Rick Ingersoll (Office Boy):

At that time I was about twenty-three years old and Leslie was seventeen or eighteen, and I remember the office boys on the lot thought she was really different looking. We expected a Hollywood star to look like Lana Turner or Ava Gardner, and Leslie didn't look or act like that at all.

Vincente Minnelli:

Usually, at Metro, the way you'd get an assistant director is the head of the Production Department would call me and say, "We have available three or four assistant directors. Now, this is this type of man. I think he would work well with you. I think you would like this individual." We would narrow it down and finally I would choose one. I always had the best.

Walter Strohm:

Al Raboch, God rest his soul, was assigned out of my office. Generally, I assigned most of the key people on the picture. You have to consider temperament in making those decisions. It isn't just whether the director likes him, but it's whether he can function with the director. So you try to get Minnelli a person he can function with. With Minnelli, it was someone who could interpret his ideas successfully and get him to put them into motion so as to get a decision from him. Lots of times, directors are floating around with several ideas but they need someone to solidify their thinking or to help them make decisions. Raboch would say, "This is what we're going to do isn't it, Vince? Is this what you like or don't like?" or "This is the way you saw it in the magazine" and "This is what you want—fine," and that's that. Minnelli accepts that kind of authority. As for a unit manager, Minnelli was assigned Ed Woehler. He let him function in getting the sets ready and discussing the schedule and so forth. Eddie had a lot of schedule discussions with the director. I don't think anyone could top Ed Woehler as a unit manager. He worked with Cukor for years on big pictures so he was well qualified to work with Minnelli. He was a professional and knew how to get things ready and not come right down in the middle of a scene and say, "What are you going to shoot tomorrow?" which has been done by some idiots in the business.

The director has to accept the production part of making a picture as well as the artistic part, because nothing is going to be ready unless he cooperates with the Production Department. The name of the game is how you get it ready with the least number of headaches and least number of clashes. That's the job of the first assistant and the unit manager.

Vincente Minnelli:

We would have meetings with Woehler on the schedule, and this and that would be marked down. "Do you think you could do it in that amount of time?" So you would have to guess whether you needed less time here and more time there. It was pretty much a guess. When you actually get into it, some small scene that you thought wouldn't be difficult at all will turn into a problem, you know, like the black-and-white ball.

Ed Woehler (Unit Production Manager):

Scheduling is laying out how the picture is going to be shot. You look at your script. You know pretty well what the dramatic values are in the picture, and if it's financially feasible you try to keep in continuity as much as possible. You always try to give the director a 100 per cent break because I'm interested that Minnelli makes a good picture, even though he doesn't think so at times. That really happens.

Now, in a musical you have a lot of numbers. The script says, "She sings." Well, you know, how many bars is she going to sing? How long is she going to sing? Two minutes? Three minutes? Or what? So you have to get out of Minnelli how much of the number he's going to photograph. So you peck, peck, peck, peck, and then with that knowledge you kind of lay out the schedule. That's what a production manager does. He has to spread out all this knowledge. Now you've got to transfer that onto paper in terms of time, people, and money. Minnelli says, "I'm going to have forty-eight dancers and twelve men jugglers and a twenty-five-piece band, and we're going to have five bars of dogs jumping across the stage." Those are the kind of things that you have to lay out. You have to visualize it, and with your knowledge of production you figure out pretty well how long each one of those things is going to take. Lots of times directors disagree with you, but over a period of years you get pretty good at it. If the director shoots a normal day, the schedule usually comes right out on the budget. But lots of times they'll have a block, they can't get out what they want to do, and they'll sit around a couple of hours thinking. You can't project that in the schedule, because the director's not supposed to think on the stage. He's supposed to think ahead of time so when he comes on the stage he's ready for his performance. Then they get mad and say, "You didn't allow me enough time." But there's no way to schedule sitting around the set for a couple of hours, thinking.

You look at the numbers in rehearsal and see how they're progressing. Then they'll change it: "I don't like it that way." When you get up to what we call the final rehearsal you know pretty well what it's going to look like, and that's when we time everything. You then know for sure how long a number is going to take. Usually, a number takes three and a half minutes, but in *An American in Paris* the last number took about twenty minutes—a big number. So those are the things that you've got to figure out. In *An American in Paris*, I figured that we could get the book shot in forty-two days, and that's what it was budgeted for.

A director is in on all the scheduling. It is explained to him what the scenes are and the time allotted to shoot them. At that time he should speak up if he disagrees. If he speaks up, they usually give him a little extra time, but, if, from our experience, we figure that he's overestimating, then we try and stay with what we think is right. A lot of directors have a tendency to what we call "fatten their budget" out of their schedule. We can see through that, we're not crazy, and we try to be fair. If it comes to a conflict between me and the director, I take it to the head of the Production Department, Walter Strohm. He then becomes the arbiter. Lots of times, after we have budgeted everything, there's something that develops in a scene that the director wants to enhance. They want to put on a hundred people to do a certain thing to try and kind of bring something up. Well, that's all right. I just take that into the office, to Walter, and say, "Mr. Minnelli would like to do this on the end of this number, and it'll take about three or four hours to do this [or a day to do it], and this is what the cost is." Walter, in turn, goes to Mr. Freed, and Mr. Freed is the one who decides. He has to; he's producing the picture. He's responsible to the studio. Now, if he decided, "Well, I'm going to spend that money," then they would give it to him.

Walter Strohm:

Now, the breakdown is simplified to the point of making a board where you have all the sets listed across the top of the board and all the acting parts listed on the left, and then scene numbers down below, with a little scene synopsis. The unit manager or assistant then gets the shooting in sequence by manipulating this board. The x's go on to show you what actor works on what set. Maybe an actor works here and doesn't work way over there; that's a tremendous gap. The location, the sets, are another actor, in a sense. You may have a location here for an opening of a scene that won't show until three-fourths of the picture is shot. In the script, this kind of figuring is pretty difficult, but it'll show up clear as a bell on this cross-plot. They maneuver around with that until they get some semblance of order to the shooting. Now, maybe it would be changed as many times as there's ideas. All these elements then are floating around and are reflected on the board. You see an awful lot just studying that crazy cross-plot.

When ideas are fairly solidified in someone's mind and the producer and the director think it's right, you impose the time on it. Now, that's the big thing where the wrists are cut. How long is it going to take to shoot it? Sometimes you get a direct time allotted by the company. They used to say, "We're going to shoot this picture in six weeks, or eight weeks," because that was based on a money scale, but no more. The schedule now reflects how long and how much money they're going to expend. The management is also aware of these kinds of breakdowns. Joe Cohn could spit those out at you; he was that fast.

We know a musical is going to take longer because we're going to have many more elements. We're going to have all the rehearsing elements, prerecording elements, more rehearsing after you get the prerecording, the costuming that has to be built, and the shooting, which is another element in itself. Well, you do not only have boards for the drama; you have boards for the rehearsing and the shooting of the numbers, plus the wardrobe fittings. The wardrobe fittings also cost money. You can bring people in just so often for wardrobe fittings.

Once you get this all generally solidified, it's then turned over to the Estimating and Budgeting Department, as it's called. There the budget is determined, and they decree a final estimate, with the time allotted to shoot each segment. Sometimes this looks ridiculous, but it's determined by a mathematical division. There are eight hours in a daily shooting schedule, so MGM uses the one-eighth method. We work an eight-hour day, shooting from nine to six, with an hour out for lunch, so the day's shooting is broken up into eighths. Now, you may see on the budget an eight-eighths day for a certain scene. That is just one day. Then there may be three-eighths allotted for a scene and five-eighths for the rest of the day. That means three hours, three-eighths, before lunch and five hours, five-eighths, after. We had to somehow get it down and figure out how much it's going to cost for labor, which is a big item, on the hourly basis. We had to have something to measure by. This used to throw some directors right out of their minds. Well, I'd say, "You tell us what unit you want to measure by." We had to know how much it was going to cost. We had a hundred electricians on some of those big *An American in Paris* numbers. We have to know it's going to cost so much for those hundred electricians for one hour. How many days are they going to use a hundred electricians at so much an hour? So it has to be that way.

The budget estimate on the picture, when we get it, is broken into two elements: "Above the line" and "below the line" costs. "Above the line" we called "fixed charges." It made very little difference on the fixed charges whether it was a six-week picture or an eight-week picture. That figure includes the producer's unit, the director's salary, and the author's money or the price paid for the property. Time is not considered above the line. Those costs above the line are not affected by all the physical and material things you see below the line.

Ed Woehler:

"Below the line" is designing, the alterations, miniatures, construction, draperies, prop rentals, set drawings, production staff, extras, cameramen, operation, lighting, sound, cutting, still man, the film, the sound, the music, the wardrobe, makeup, out of hire, stock, meals, travel, and location. We would put the two elements together and come up with an estimate and say, "Well, if this picture was shot in eight weeks with the elements that we've talked about in the general meetings, then this is approximately what it's going to cost. If you want to try another way, we'll figure that out for you as well."

The budget for *An American in Paris*, not counting the ballet, was

$1,948,848. That's the book. With the big number that they put on afterwards, it went over the top of this figure by probably a half-million dollars.

Walter Strohm:

Now, there's one little piece that sits in here that's very important. I don't see how you can make pictures without doing it, and that is the timing of the script. Expert timers were one of the great things that we had at our place. They were capable of reading a script, and, knowing the director's style of shooting and how much film he shot, giving you a timing that generally came close to the footage of the actual finished picture. It's an incredible thing. People used to send over and ask to have a picture timed at our place because one timer was incredible, Nora Janney, Mrs. Janney.

Honore (Nora) Janney (Script Timer):

They were always in a hurry. Joe Finn, my boss, would give me a copy of a script, and he'd say, "Here's *An American in Paris*. I want it yesterday." And then you timed it.

I'd say it took about three or four days to get a script timed, because, in the first place, there comes an imagination lag, a brain lag. You can work just so long, and then pretty soon you find yourself going mechanical. Then you've got to put it down and go out and take a walk or go down to the commissary or do something, then come back to it fresh. You never wanted to get to the point where you're just reading, "he said," "she said." You have to make your mind a screen, and you see the characters and read their dialogue and react as you think they would react according to the story. You see, you use a stop watch, and you click it on when you start a scene, and you click it off when you finish. You do this automatically. You don't even think about it.

It's a very simple mechanical process, providing you know a little bit about people. I had an advantage in that I never read words per se when reading for pleasure. The words conjured up pictures. In other words, the characters came to life in my mind. The writer always describes locale, sets, props, notes to the Property Department, the art director, et cetera. From this information, you know the type of story, and you absorb these instructions and picture the sets. Now you are ready to read the dialogue aloud to the stop watch, remembering these are real people in real situations and not just characters in a movie. The people you are working with are artists acting, and they are going to make as much out of their parts as possible. Also, there is a lot of what I facetiously call "leering and peering" going on. You have to allow for it. So you read the dialogue aloud, then translate your minutes and seconds into footage. We worked in units of five feet for the sake of facility in adding the total. You divide your total footage by the number of pages in the script, which gives you a figure of so many feet a page, and this establishes the tempo. You also know drawing room comedies run pretty fast, and westerns are pretty fast. Musicals are very heavy, like, for instance, the shooting script of *An American in Paris*.

The first draft we had on *An American in Paris* was in February, 1950, and the book ran 9,290 feet. The script ran 104 pages, so that gave you 89 feet plus a page, which was too much book. They had another Temporary Complete on the eighth of May, and that, too, was cut down. So they knew they had a three-hour movie with a book that ran that long. That was too long in those days. Now, we timers took no responsibility for music. We simply asked the Music Department to tell us how much had been recorded for this and how much had been allowed for that, but we didn't show any music figure until later, because they hadn't decided on all the music yet. There were ninety-seven pages in that one draft of the eighth of May. That was the second temporary. Then the third one came along on the twelfth of June. You see, they were working awfully hard to cut the book down but keep the story line.

This draft was incomplete and it was 6,625 feet. By this time in June, we had music footage, 4,540 feet, which, when added to the book, gave you an average per page of 137 feet plus, which is not bad for a musical. Then, in July, on the twenty-seventh, they sent changes through which cut the book 320 feet. They added some numbers later, which brought up the total combined book and music to 11,610. That was in August. Later, the book was 6,320 feet and music 6,565 feet. Now, there's no date on that, but with final changes and revised music the book was 6,555 feet and the music was 4,230 feet. In my final timing, when I received the last revisions, the figure was 10,785 feet, which was a good figure, I thought. Well, the upshot of the whole thing was that the first cut was 12,122 feet, for an average of 156 feet per page, and it was released at 10,360, so they lost approximately 2,000 feet between the first cut and the release. My last figure was 10,785 feet and they released it at 10,360 feet, which is about 400 feet under my estimate.

After I timed a script, the figures were sent down to Joe Finn and Walter Strohm, and they looked at them and wrote memoranda to Arthur Freed, J. J. Cohn, and the head of the studio. The unit manager gets a copy and also the cutter.

The cutter immediately throws her copy in the drawer and forgets it. The unit manager looks at it, and he too forgets it. But the people who have to do with the formation of the story, the writing end of it, before it ever goes before the camera, use it. If it's too long, and if they want to know where to cut it, they can tell from my notes where the footage is. They can tell from this how long it takes them to make a point, and how long it takes to get to another story point, and whether there is a lot of lumber that isn't necessary and can be cut out. In other words, this is what it will run in film feet if it is shot the way the writer says it will be. J. J. Cohn and Mr. Schary would see the report because they were the ones who said "Yes" on budgets. They got the cost figures, plus the footage, and could then say, "Well, it's costing too much money to get from this point to this point. Can't that be done differently?"

Once they started shooting, I had no further responsibility—no matter how many changes they made after that. Very often, they'd put stuff back in that they had already taken out. They'd make changes and cut the script down and then, after the camera rolled, they started putting those very scenes right back in and got back to the original footage, which had been too long in the first place. This was common practice. It's like double-entry bookkeeping, but they'd always have an excuse ready. And, if the picture made money, who cared?

Walter Strohm:

Now, if you don't think Nora Janney was valuable. . . . We'd bring in the final cut picture and ask, "Where's her timing?" And it'd be only 300 or 400 feet off. You know, you believe in these things. This was an infallible and invaluable tool, and when you didn't use it you were rather foolish to say, "Oh, we're just going to go out and shoot." Wouldn't you rather know your script is indicating a 14,000-foot finished picture when you can release only 10 or 12,000? Based on her timing, you'd know you were going to throw out 2,000 net feet, and that's a waste of time and money.

Leslie Caron:

Two weeks after I arrived in Los Angeles I was taken into court. There was something so frightening about that. I was driven down to L.A. in a black limousine with my mother, and my case was put in front of a judge with my agent and . . . ugh!—terrifying. The judge explained some things to me. My English was not too good. Well, I didn't understand what the judge said, but my mother translated. He was explaining to me the terms of my contract. That's the law. For my contract with MGM to be valid I had to understand what's written in it. When you are a minor, your mother or father has to be there, and the judge has to make sure you understand the contract and are agreeable and are not being forced into it by your parents. This is the Jackie Coogan deal for minors. I was seventeen.

I suppose my contract looked very big compared to what I was being paid as a dancer in Paris. My salary as a dancer was $50 a month, and I thought it was a lot. Not that we were poor people—on the contrary, when one is always kept at home, pocket money of $50 a month seems a lot. MGM's money seemed an awful lot, but when I came here it turned out to be just what a workman got—I think $500 a week. Also about half of that was kept by the state because I was a minor.

Alan A. Antik:

This was something that was very funny. Once the casting department called me and said, "Mr. Minnelli wants to see you. We have certain people who we want to use for some speaking lines and we have 150 actors outside." They were all lined up when I got there, and they were looking at me with very hopeful eyes. Minnelli said, "Let's go walk and talk with them, and we'll see what you think." I said to Minnelli, "I'll bet they're all Greeks." He said, "Why, they look French." I was right. They were either Greek or Mexicans. Some of them tried to impress me. I'd ask them something in French, and they would mumble something in return. Out of the 150, we selected 6 or 7 who

FORM 72

METRO-GOLDWYN-MAYER PICTURES
C U L V E R - C I T Y
CALIFORNIA

INTER-OFFICE COMMUNICATION

To_____

Subject   Mr.A.kyan cc to Mr.Minnelli,Stroha,
           L.Ames
           AN AMERICAN IN PARIS

From_____ Date_____
           Alan A.Antik   May 22/50

Following information received from Paris,the cheapest
subway ticket-2 nd class is 20 Francs-one way.Consequently
the line " twenty francs" seems 30 :age 15 should be changed
accordingly,unless Mr.Lerner would expect Jerry Mulligan to
walk back home-which is quite a distance,possibly with his
pictures unsold.

                              Alan A.Antik

Memos from Alan A. Antik

FORM 73

METRO-GOLDWYN-MAYER PICTURES
C U L V E R - C I T Y
CALIFORNIA

INTER-OFFICE COMMUNICATION

To _
           Mr.Vincente Minnelli cc to MM.
Subject   Arthur Freed,Walter Stroha
           AMERICAN IN PARIS

From   Alan A.Antik   Date July 6/50

Dear Mr.Minnelli :

                Following your request and for the purpose
of saving time,I submit herewith all the observations referrin
to our script and details,which in my opinion could be easily
taken care of,thus avoiding mistakes and any complications.-I
shall proceed following the continuity.

Page 2   scene 6:Suggest modification of dialogue referring to
                 Left Bank,as "poorer quarter".-Not quite correc

Page 6   scene15:Brioches are never baked at home..always by the
                 bakeries (boulangerie,.Perhaps dialogue could
                 be modified in the sense,that the brioches
                 were just delivered-fresh from the baker.

Page 9 scene 18:As far as I know,there was a musical conductor
                 by the name of Felix Weingartner,don't know
                 if he's still alive.he was German or swiss.

same scene...   :Henri: "Poor Jacques,he was caught in the re-
                 sistance.-May not be very clear to audience,
                 unless added "resistance movement" or french
                 partisans,or"against Germans"....

continued:

Page 13scene 29:   Jerry to Therese could say "Bonjour instead
                    of"good morning".

Page 14scene 30:   The cheapest lunch in Paris is 300 francs.-
                    Cup of coffee 10-20 fros,while 1 brioche or
                    1 croissant(like a donut) is 20- fros.-.
                    sandwich is about 50-60 fros.-This speaking
                    of carfare,which is 40-fros.roundtrip and
                    lunch-we jave to consider the 100 Frcs. re-
                    quested by Jerry.

Page 18 scene30:   Fifty US , would be 17.500-francs at the rate
                    of exchange.-How about Milo offering 20.000-
                    instead of 15.000- ?

Page 25scene 41:   If Milo's hotel to be-is the Ritz,any adver-
                    tising posters on a kiosk seen from hotel win-
                    dows are out of question,for there are not any
                    on .lace Vendome-nor on rue Cambon.-The law
                    prohibits plastering of walls with posters,
                    unless it happens to be a construction fence.
                    Suggested either a vitrine in the hotel hall
                    or we could prepare a printed poster with
                    Laurel's face,paste it on a reel kiosk in
                    paris and shoot a scene with Gene pas ing it.

Page 25 scene 41 :   Should the amount of money given to
                       Jerry be changed-same here(dialogue)

Same scene....   :   Do you wish the maid to speak english
                       or would you prfer for her to speak
                       french? If so,I can give her the
                       lines.

Page 27 scene 41 :   May I reiterate my suggestion to
                       eliminate the word "Paris" from
                       Jerrys's dialogue.."guys in Paris"..

Page 28 scene 42 :   As a rule,waiters in such places as
                       the Ritz would speak english.-You
                       may add howver a maitre d'hotel-if
                       desired,transmitting orders to the
                       garcon.

Page 30 scene 42 :   Waiter(withdrawing) ought to say :
                       "XXXXXX "Merci Madame ! "to Milo.

Page 40 scene 53 :   I would eliminate the womans voice
                       on telephone "bonjour".-Just Maison
                       Duclos,spoken amiably and expectant-
                       ly-would be the proper form.

Page 42 scene 59 :   Do you wish Jerry to see the sign
                       with the name "Duclos" from the car?
                       It may be complicated to have this
                       sign placed in the vicinity of Place
                       Concorde.But if the perfume shop is
                       in the rue de Rivoli(collonnades) it
                       could be easily recognizable later on
                       when interiors are shot in studio.

continued :

Page 44 scene 61 : I have submitted six different imagi
                    nary names for the perfume.All in th
                    sense of the gag.Because NUIT D'AMOUR
                    exists.

age 46 scene 61 : Speaking of Cafe Bel Ami,perhaps it
                   would be wise to add"on the left bank
                   in addition to the "by the bridge" ?

Same page   63 : Is Jerry getting out of Milos car or
                     a cab ?

Page 48. scene 65 : Henri ought to say in French:
                     "Oui Maman "...not mama.

Page 49 scene 66 : The waiters lines should be:
                    " Messieur-dame. Vous prenez
                    quelque chose ? " and Jerry's
                    answer "I'll have a FINE "
                    (pronounced f-e-e-n)

Page 50 scene 66 : Suggest,to avoid english conver-
                    -sation of the waiter, for Jerry to
                    say " Rien-merci" to which waiter
                    surprised,but polite reacts and per-
                    haps in the following lines of Jerry
                    he may mention the word "amour"with
                    the waiter reacting understandingly.

Page 51 scene 67 : Reiterate suggestion to change
                    chestnuts to peanuts,because of
                    season.

Page 52 scene 68 : There just is not such a movement
                    like boats coming and leaving.All
                    we can have is perhaps one barge.
                    No row or sail boats.

Page 54 scene 72 : We have never cleared the Ecole
                    des Beaux Arts and while we may say
                    it in the dialogue,the question re-
                    mained always open where we were
                    going to shoot the scene.If it is
                    to be Beaux Arts,we must clear it
                    and find out about in a hurry.

Page 57 scene 87 : Suggest to use one of those known
                    on the Left Bank studio-duplex bldgs
                    while on location.Artists in better
                    financial situation customarily use
                    them.

age 59 scene 90 : as in 72,we have to establish where
                   and should Beaux Arts be impossible
                   I suggest either Cluny or perhaps
                   Tuilleries(Louvre) depending of the
                   circumstances.
                   As to the name MACROS,since we cannot
                   change it-lets pronounce it at least
                   in an inoffensive way.

continued:

Page 63   scene 97 :   Jerry to the driver should say:
                        "Ou est la demoiselle ? Que ce qudy
                        c'est passé ? " while the driver shoul'
                        answer : " Montez Monsieur,elle vous
                        attend "

Page 65   scene 104 :   Georges : " Tout de suite ".
                        (Observtn. can Adam have somethingelse
                        than coffee ? Red wine-soup de rouge ?)

Page 70   scene 1o8 :   Punch and Judy show is not in the
                        Bois de Boulogne,but in the Champs Ely
                        sees,below the Road Point.

Page 72   scene 112 :   as in 41 with reference to the sight
                        of the poster out of Mile(s room .
                        ~hatever you decide about.

Page 73   scene 120X : We have to obtain the clearance for
                   1 & 2   the Moulin de la Galette.

Page 74   scene 121 :   Would you like to use also a french
                        orchestra playing javas and valses in-
                        terchanging with the jazz ? Would be
                        very typical.

                        Yours sincerely

                        Alan A.Antik

FORM 73

METRO-GOLDWYN-MAYER PICTURES
C U L V E R - C I T Y
CALIFORNIA

INTER-OFFICE COMMUNICATION

To_____ Production Dept.
_____ cc. to Casting Dept.
Subject AN AMERICAN IN PARIS-Set Stage-dog

From____ Alan A.Antik   Date Aug.17/50

Okayed by M.Minnelli the following types :

6 of our chorus girls(NOT the same we have seen before !) all
in street clothes,but must bring with them another change of
either sport clothes or long skirts and bluses or sweaters as
well as low-heeled shoes.

2 elderly extremely elegant gentlemen("angel" types),but must
bring along another change of sportclothes or bus.suits.

3 young flashily elegant dressed frenchmen(age 25-30).-Must bring
with them another change of sportclothes or leisure clothes.

1 very fat comedian type.Street clothes,dark hat,bring along
a silk scarf possibly and second set of sport clothes(tourists)

1 very thin comedian type.Street clothes,bring along a silk scarf
(if any) and another set of leisure or sport clothes.

1 elderly-fattish vivacious actress type.Street clothes,summer
coat. Bring along a print summer dress with hat.

1 French traffic cop,with stick and cape.-also bring summer cloth
or sports outfit(jacket and slacks)

1 Young boy (age 8-10) short pants,high shoes,sportshirt,sweater.

Two small french cars (up to M.Koehler) parked.

All the above actors have to bring along this second set of
clothes as indicated to be used in our Montmartre-Montage shots
later on.

Alan A.Antik

were actually French. Most of the French actors in Hollywood were hams. Either they owned restaurants or they thought their mission was to be very French, and by being very French they were being ridiculous.

I went into so much detail, even though most of the details were never seen in the picture. But somebody's going to bitch, and I'll be responsible for it one way or the other. In other words, my responsibility was that it had to be covered, totally and completely covered. It was a matter of protection, of not having any consequences from silly letters coming in, "How could you do that?" After all, this was a picture about Paris which was shot in Hollywood, which is pretty damned difficult. It had to be authentic!

Walter Strohm:

For pictures like *An American in Paris,* we made models of some of our sets. All the master sets were made into scale models. First, you'd have a loose drawing, and Preston would come in and discuss it with Minnelli: "Does he want or does he need the bedroom joining the sitting room?" He'd draw the whole thing out. Then Minnelli would reread the scenes and say, "No, I don't need the bedroom; only use a wall to back it up." So those things would be discussed at later Art Department meetings. Now, after Minnelli okayed it, Gibbons and I would okay it. Then it would go into the final stages of drawing and then down to the mill for construction. Before it went down there, however, that final drawing would have an estimate made on it by the unit art director. He estimated the cost of the set, and, if something shocking showed up, if it was running over his master budget, we would have to decide all over again what we were going to do: "The set is just going sky high and we'll only use it for two days." So we then had to figure out what we could do to bring it back into focus. At this point, Freed could say, "Well, it's overboard but I want to see it." He's done that many times. He'd say, "If it's only fifty feet, I want the splash there, and we'll save the money someplace else." But we did have to save it someplace else. Even he couldn't go over budget. He'd have to get approvals because the money he's using is not his money, it's the company's money, and they've approved him making a picture for so much. All the overages had to be brought to the management, even Freed's.

PROD NO.	TITLE		ART DIR
1507	American in Paris		Preston Ames

ASSGN No / OUR SET No	SET TITLE	LAYOUT / APPROVAL OK / MODEL OK / WRKNG DG / DETAILS / APPROVAL / PROP. OK / CONSTR'N	BUDGET	ESTIMATE	COST
1 02	Ext. Pension & Street		12000	11933	10993
2 11	Ext. Lovers Room 2nd Fl.		500	225	319
3 04	Ext. Int. Pension 3rd Floor		3000	4133	4241
4 11	Ext. young man's Room		250	225	270
5 03	Int. Pension Stairs & Hall		5800	5989	6112
6	1st Retrospect Ballet	See Below			
7 01	Ext. Montmartre Sq & St.	No	6200	6062	4785
8 70	Int. Milos Limousine (P)	No	500	80	119
9 12	Int. Milos Hotel Suite	No	1800	703	939
10 04	Int. Hotel Dining Room		1200	1211	1103
11 16	Int. Café Florida		3500	3501	3405
12 06	Int. Perfume Store		3000	1200	1374
13 07	Int. Henri's Apt.		2000	1995	2109
14 08	Ext. Café Bel Ami & Street		3500	1155	872
15 05	Ext. River & Quai		10000	9719	9972
16 14	Int. Stage & Stair		4000	8863	9223
17 13	Ext. Stage Door Lot 2	No	1850	817	901
18 16	Int. Nicer Studio		1500	491	850
19 71	Int. Taxi #1 (P) Jerry's	M	100	35	78
20	Int. Taxi #2 (P)	Out	100		
21	Ext. Bow	out	3500		
22	Ext. Duel & Park Lot 2	out			
23	Ext. Moulin De la Galette (N)				
24	Ext. Entrance & Street Moulin		1000		
25 15	Int. Artists Ball & Bar		10000	10150	8614
26 24	Ext. Terrace - Artists' Ball		3500	2631	3004
27 23	Int. Henri's Car (P)		100	95	105
28	3rd Ballet - American in Paris	See Below			
29 19	Ext. Nicer Studio		500	310	343
30 21	Ext. Artist's Ball & Stair	No	4000	4166	2350
31 22	Int. Symphony Concert	No	4710	4710	2936
32 18	Ext. Perfume Shop	No	800	463	740
33	Int. Ecole des Beaux Arts		1000	1389	out?
34	Baroque		83010	80742	75757
35	Victorian			498	2884
36	Louis XVI	Retrospect	3000	488	786
37	Modern			497	
38	Jacobean			496	
39	Biedermeier			487	
40	Ext. Champs Élysées		3600	1467	
41	Ext. Place de la Concorde		9500	14506	
42	Ext. Place de la Madeleine		3400	3728	
43	Ext. Montmartre Street		4400	2792	
44	Ext. Eiffel Tower	out	3900		
45	Ext. Place de l'Opéra		3900	7672	
46	Int. Moulin Rouge		3900	3006	
47	Ext. Carnival		4400	6735	

Budget Form

Preston Ames:

You first made what we call a layout in designing a set. It might have been accompanied by a sketch, but it was at least an approach to the subject. Then that had to be approved by your supervisor, Cedric Gibbons, by the producer, and by the director. In other words: "This is what we're going to do for the *pension* on the street where Kelly lives." You got that approval, and that was ticked off on a form that we used. Then a model of this set was built and approved, and that was ticked off. From this point, working drawings were started in the drafting room. These drawings might take a day, a week, or they might last for four weeks, in order to get a complete set of plans, elevations, and details. Then you finally got the approval of that. The plans were presented next to an estimator, who gave you a realistic figure. For instance, for the street where Kelly lived, I had a budget, after all the drawings were done, of $12,000. I then took this estimate to my superior officer, and he signed it. Then I took it to the production office, and they signed it. Only then was it turned over to the mill for construction. Now, construction consisted of carpenters, painters, plasters, plumbers, and electricians. Each one of these departments had to be watched to make sure that they had all the necessary information, that they knew exactly how much money they had to spend, and that they didn't spend more. This is where you had control, and the studio respected that control very seriously. We were given a certain amount of money and told, "Don't spend any more than that, and, if you do, you're not a good art director." So we were very, very seriously disciplined in that way. It so happens that when I was given $12,000 for the street I spent only $11,000, which, for the street, wasn't too bad. There were certain other areas where I went over, but I was only 2½ per cent over for the total number of sets in the book. So, for that number of forty-odd sets, that was control and supervision.

Saul Chaplin:

Now, the continuing process is as follows: We're at Ira's house, and we find a certain number of songs that are going to go in certain places. We next go to a rehearsal hall with Gene and his assistants, Jeannie

Coyne and Carol Haney. We'd start in the rehearsal hall, and Gene starts doping out the number. Let's say, it's a number with Leslie Caron, then she is there and Gene choreographs a number. As he's choreographing, there's a rehearsal pianist, and I'm there, and we're fulfilling his musical needs. When Gene needed the music stretched or condensed to fill what they were doing, we would discuss it, and I would make notes, and the rehearsal pianist would play it. Often this required taking it home and doing it overnight, because sometimes you don't think of the proper idea at the moment. They had three rehearsal halls at Metro— A, B, and C—and they were all going like mad in those days. We also had pianos in our offices, and very often during lunch I would find out what they would want for later and say, "What about this?"

Besides all this, I would work with the singers in the morning and teach them what the material was that was going to be staged in the afternoon. Let's take the number "By Strauss." I would have Georges Guetary and Oscar and Gene in the morning teaching them the song, the basic words and music, so when they get up to the number they don't say, "Listen, what comes next?" They get to know it and become familiar with the music. Now they start rehearsing.

Vincente Minnelli:

For the role of the Frenchman, the other man who loves Leslie's Lise, we had originally wanted Chevalier. Alan had him in mind, but he was not available. He was doing one of his concerts or one-man shows. So somebody who handles foreign people submitted a lot of people, and among them was Georges Guetary. He had a lot of credits. I think we saw some films on him, and eventually we hired him.

Carol Haney, who was one of Gene's assistants, and who was marvelous, worked with him and worked with him to give him that style which is really American. She worked so hard with him. She just concentrated on him.

Alan A. Antik:

Originally, we tried to get Yves Montand. He would have been an ideal type, but we were told that he had sort of communistic tendencies,

you know, attachments, so Freed said that we would not use him, because we'd get into trouble. So they got Georges Guetary, who was a
nice-looking nobody with a nice voice. I never heard of him later on.
I kind of fought all of this, but there wasn't anybody else, as a matter of
fact. Chevalier would have been a bit too old. I think Guetary was well
known in Paris, but he was never famous. He was known as a singer
in what you call the music halls, but of no particular fame. He had a
certain reputation, but there were other singers who would be much
more popular than he would ever be.

Nina Foch (Actress):

My agent in Hollywood called me, so I came out to test for the part
of Milo in *An American in Paris*. That meant MGM gave me a per
diem like twenty-five bucks a day and flew me out from New York first
class. It was a serious test. Vincente Minnelli was a hot man; nothing
was done cheaply where Vincente was involved. I tested the scene
where Milo says, "Come to my house; we're having a party," and when
Gene gets there I say, "Yes, it's a party; it's you and me," and "My
family is in oil—suntan oil." That was the test. So then I went back to
New York and went on about my business.

Gene Kelly:

There were the usual discussions and conversations, and it was decided that Nina had just the right amount of *savoir-faire*, worldliness,
sweetness, and bitchiness. She was a damn good actress, besides. She'd
put on a Chanel suit and it looked like it belonged on her, and, being
a good actress, she could also play a slattern. In this case, we wanted a
lady who looked rich and spoiled, and a lady who got what she wanted
when she wanted it. It wasn't a tough job deciding on Nina Foch. We
were really delighted when she took the role. I wish everything was
that easy.

Leslie Caron:

You know, everything was sort of arranged for you to have a glamorous life, a so-called glamorous life. Now, if you didn't play the game,

if you didn't fit the mold, they were nice enough, up to a point, but there were things you had to do. I felt threatened. I felt I was an odd bird, not being what I ought to be. I played the opposite because I was so revolted by all their emphasis on pink and lace, and their idea of femininity, which was dumbness. So I didn't play the game.

One of the routines was that you had to be photographed throughout the four seasons following your appropriate image. In other words, I was the gamine, the pert little *Parisienne*. That was *always* on the bottom of my pictures, the caption "*oo la la*." I have a book of those nauseating pictures with "*oo la la*" written down there on every one of the pictures.

Every Easter, I would be photographed. I would be called by the Publicity Department and told to report next Wednesday at the Portrait Gallery, that they had "some darling Easter fashions" for me, and we were going to do some sweet and cute little pictures. So I would arrive there, and I was always handed either a basket of strawberries or a basket of eggs or a bunny costume or a hoop to jump through. And the inventions they would get up were just heavenly. For instance, Christmas you always had to have a red dress; then there was always red candles and those red winter flowers. Everything was red and gold. You would put Christmas-tree decorations on your ear lobes, and, the more you looked like a Christmas tree, the happier they were. That was Christmas. Then, in the spring, you were photographed wading in water, holding up your skirt, just showing the knee or the thigh, and flowers all over, or sitting in a field of flowers. Animals were very good, too—cats for me. And then the pictures were all the same; they were always trying to emphasize the bust, and those wonderful old men who were the photographers were anything but Richard Avedons. They really were sort of craft journalists. They'd started on the night staff of the *New York News* photographing murders, and they ended up at MGM studio under contract. The really good photographers, you know, wouldn't be under contract. So you had those really tough guys, whisky-drinking and so on, who would ask you to turn, and you knew what they meant: "Bust up, darling." There was this publicity girl who would come and sit and say, "Would you turn your shoulder just a little more; stand a little bit more straighter," and you knew it was a bust shot okay. Then there was the elbow shot for the cleavage, and then there was the pert three-quarters; you know that shot, the Mitzi Gaynor and the Debbie Reynolds. As a matter of fact, when I escaped that factory I got so fed up with smiling that I refused to smile for about a year, no matter how happy I would be. I said, "No, I will not smile," to the photographers. Of course there was the Ava Gardner style, you see— the shoulder forward and the chin up and the eyes half-closed—and, if your teeth were good: "Open your mouth slightly," and "Wet your lips, dear," and click. It was always "Wet your lips, hon." Oh God!

Emily Torchia:

We called it "holiday art," and I know Leslie did not like it. Very few of the stars liked it. We eventually stopped it, but every Sunday magazine in the country would use it, in color and in good papers. I sold a picture of Esther Williams, when she was just starting out, peer- ing from behind a barn with a gun and looking at this big turkey. She hadn't started big roles then, and this was just a way of familiarizing the public with her face.

"Holiday art" was very popular. With Leslie, I don't remember if she did, but, if she wanted to be treated in a dignified manner, we prob- ably set up the church with the colored glass thing with the Easter lilies, you see, or maybe she was in a swan pose, dancing. That was the dignified thing for Easter or something, but it was still "holiday art." On the other hand, no one ever forced anyone to do any of that. Of course, their innocence and naïveté may have made them feel they couldn't say, "no." There were those who said, "No, that's not for me." No one said, "You're on suspension," or "You're fired," but we were kind of insistent. We'd push it, but that's the job. I mean, there was never any reprimand or threatenings of lashings or whatever if they didn't do it.

Rick Ingersoll (Office Boy):

The other ways that Leslie Caron would be publicized were through the stories in the columns. Contrary to rumor, MGM never planted romantic items. At least I never did, and I don't think anyone else did while I was there. We never would plant a story saying that Leslie Caron was dating so-and-so at Ciro's last night. We never did that. That's something that columnists would pick up themselves. We were never allowed to do that. Many people believed that that's the function of publicity. Well, that may be the function of the press agent for the restaurant or whatever it is, but it wasn't our function at MGM.

Leslie Caron:

I know the girls in the press building would always try to suggest my going out with so-and-so. They'd say, very brightly, "Oh, honey, if you knew what a handsome man so-and-so is; he's just a dish. It would be nice to go out with him, wouldn't it? I mean, he's so nice to women." Or, "He's so continental. Oh, I hear he plays tennis so well. He's going to be a big star. I'm sure he'd be thrilled to take you out." You know, all that build-up, and I'd say, "No, no I don't want to. I don't know him, and I'm sorry, I don't have the time to go out."

Once a thing like that was organized for me and I let it happen, and it was a nightmare. I mean it was like two sticks having dinner together, not knowing what to say. Of course, all the press reported, "So-and-so was out with Leslie Caron last night." It was important to be seen at the right place with the right people.

Howard Strickling (Head of the Publicity Department):

I required a certain number of stories every week from my unit publicists. John Rothwell on *An American in Paris* was supposed to write three or four feature stories a week and two or three short items for the trade papers and columnists every day, and he'd indicate where he thought these stories should be placed. I would then read everything, and if something wasn't right I'd send it back to have it rewritten, or I might think that some other writer might have a better slant on it. We'd then also send these stories to New York, and they'd plant them there.

Every picture had a campaign. Just like *An American in Paris* had a script, it also had a campaign. Johnny Rothwell would have every national magazine, fan magazine, syndicate, press service, and an idea for everyone. We won't get the story in every one, but if we get three out of five we're okay. Also, in every campaign he has a list of the stills that are to be taken. We just don't shoot stills hit or miss. We sit down and decide what is the key to publicizing *An American in Paris*. We decide on lines that best describe that picture. It's a glamorous, big, musical extravaganza, with a romantic background of Paris. Once this is decided upon, we make sure all our stills and copy emphasize those things. That becomes our scenario for publicity. Every week Johnny Rothwell reported on the campaign to me. He showed me: "This is done. That's done. This is going to be done. This is in the works, and *Photoplay* is thinking of doing this."

Saul Chaplin:

Before the music got to the point of orchestration, which John and Connie Salinger did, it first had to be sketched. Sketching indicates what instruments are playing what, but it's not orchestrating. In other words, I would be at the rehearsal hall all day and, if any new music was required, either variations based on Gershwin's original music or arguing with Gene Kelly's saying, "You can't do a seven-bar phrase because it's eight bars," I would sketch out what we had decided on. Gene would try to tell me what he heard in his mind, and I would sketch that out on a piece of paper.

John Green:

There's regular so-called piano manuscript paper. It consists of blank staves. When Solly uses the word "sketching," he means he would probably brace three of these staves, and on three staves, sometimes two, he would write out the basic treatment, virtually playable on the piano, and he'd indicate strings, brass, woodwinds. Then he and I would discuss it. If I were going to orchestrate it, which in some cases I did, I would expand it for full score. The single staff where Solly wrote "strings" would now be converted to five staves: violins I, violins II, violas, cellos, and bases. That would be the end of it—Solly and me. If Connie were going to do it, it would be Solly to me to a discussion with Connie.

Arthur Freed:

In *An American in Paris*, I wanted to hear the real Gershwin sound. Connie Salinger did a lot of the orchestrating and Johnny Green did some. Connie had studied in Paris and was one of the greatest orchestrators we ever had. Johnny was a great orchestrator for Dick Rodgers and Jerome Kern in the earlier days. They all knew the Gershwin sound and were friends of the Gershwins'. Johnny had the same publisher when he wrote "Body and Soul." The sound I wanted in this picture was the *real* Gershwin.

Saul Chaplin:

Freed talked about a picture that really caught the Gershwin sound. I must tell you that's more Johnny than me. I mean I knew in general what to make it sound like, but, in listening the other night to the movie again, what struck me was one orchestration in particular that Johnny did for " 'S wonderful." That was some marvelous orchestration. I mean, if George had had that orchestra that day, I'm sure he would have written that note for note.

John Green:

How do you make a Gershwin sound? I'd have to say, frankly, I think it's years of experience. I have a picture over there signed George Gershwin and dated 1930. It says, "Wishing you a big musical success. Sincerely, George Gershwin." One of the problems for me on the picture, and it erupted one time into a confrontation between me and Arthur Freed, was the fact that, like Oscar, I too was brought up by George Gershwin. Oscar, however, as far as public image was concerned, spoke for Gershwin. All right, interesting, the way the chips fell. In 1950, Oscar was playing several Gershwin concerts with me on the podium. So, when Oscar and I would do the Gershwin concert with the L.A. Philharmonic, for instance, Oscar was the soloist, and I was the conductor. We had some pitched battles, Oscar and I. I would try to confine them to his dressing room or mine, backstage, but they sometimes occurred in front of the orchestra, and, as the conductor, I wasn't going to be intimidated by Oscar. Now, we get into *An American in Paris*, at the studio, recording the *Concerto in F*, and again I started being the maestro. Well, Freed hit me with every Sherman tank, every Louisville slugger in the place. Never was there a conductor so put in his place, because Oscar was *it*. Listening to a playback, I inadvertently

slipped over into being Johnny Green in front of the Los Angeles
Philharmonic.

At one point, the recording mixer had missed his cue, and all there
was on the track was piano spaghetti, without a trace of the thematic
content in the orchestra, to which the piano was but ornamentation.
I asked for another take. I didn't get it. *But,* when I ultimately recorded
the background scoring, I was sneaky: I slapped earphones on the upper
woodwinds and strings and added the missing element on another track.
Everybody loved the final results; no comment of any kind from Messrs.
Freed and Levant.

But then, going further, why did I get that Gershwin sound? I knew
Gershwin like Oscar knew Gershwin, and I knew what George loved,
and I knew what sounded well with Gershwin. Do you have any idea
how many performances of *An American in Paris* you can hear today
that must have George rolling in his grave? George taught me *An
American in Paris.* I learned it from George; I play it the way George
wanted it. The tempi and the sauciness of the times, the spirit, the
sentimentality, and the blues that sound like blues. The sound that
George got in his playing is characteristic of my orchestration of his
songs. Take, for example, the picture *Shall We Dance.* You know the
song "They Can't Take That Away from Me?" Well, in those days
there was no tape. (Fred Astaire and I recorded that.) We recorded on
those big, thick, soft masters, so you had nothing to play till three days
later, when you got back the rough pressing. I came to George's house.
His mother, Rose, and Ira and George were there. When George heard
my orchestration of "They Can't Take That Away from Me," I thought
I'd have to give him aromatic spirits of ammonia, because already he
wasn't well (but nobody knew how unwell he was), but he cried and
the nose was running. I don't know how to articulate it any better.
George is in my blood, that's all.

Saul Chaplin:

I also have to mention that besides Johnny there was Connie. It's my
considered judgment that Hollywood's major contribution to the American musical film is Connie Salinger. He's the most imitated, and was
simply the best for the kind of thing he did. Now, you didn't give him
a big jazz thing to do, but, for his orchestration of ballads, his ideas of

what went into them, and the eventual sound, he has been more imitated than I think even Debussy and Ravel by the guys out here who wrote those early scores. Connie was incredible, incredible.

John Green:

Connie, in the first place, had one of the most gigantic, monumental, delightful, delicious senses of humor that any human being ever had. He was hysterically funny, Connie Salinger. He was also a homosexual.

Saul Chaplin:

. . . but made no jokes about it. I mean he accepted it and he didn't care.

John Green:

He was not an alcoholic, because he only drank when he wanted to—which was not always but frequently. Often he drank too much. Connie Salinger could go literally weeks without having a drink. Connie Salinger also used to get into terrible scrapes, like getting beaten to a pulp by four sailors, but I mean picked up all over the street by ambulance attendants. Terrible.

I go back to 1929 with Connie, when we both worked for Paramount. We were the two assistants to Adolph Deutsch, who was, I think, the greatest single orchestrator per se of our time. Now, Connie at that time was miles ahead of me in terms of academic training. He had just come back from his years with André Gédalge in Paris; he's one of the few people who didn't study with Nadia Boulanger, but he studied with Gédalge, who was no slouch. Adolph Deutsch brought me up academically to the level that Connie was at when he got back from Paris. By the time Adolph Deutsch got through hitting me with a leather thong, he brought me up, technically, pretty close to Connie's level. I'm not talking about aesthetically, because Connie was unique. Anyway, I'm going back to those days when Connie and I became close, close friends, and way back in those days I said, "Connie, you gotta write; you have a composing talent." He always pooh-poohed this. We finally got to the point where I was able to say, "Connie, this is a rationalization on your part because you're a big, fat, yellow coward. Not that you *can't* write—your're *afraid* to, and that's terrible." I finally broke him in at Metro and badgered him into composing a picture. He was panic-stricken while he was doing it. I wet-nursed him through that, but I felt that this was one of my achievements, to get this man to compose. He wrote a damned good score, too. Then came television. Now I'm skipping, I'm telescoping, and Connie became a very successful television dramatic-music composer. But he lacked the one thing which is the *sine qua non* of a total success: He was never able to divorce himself from fright and the inability to cope with tension. Now, when I got into television composition I fully understood what tortured Connie. I was the composer of what turned out to be an unsuccessful show on NBC called *Empire*. You wrote seven original scores. You were then allowed to have six scores made up of the other seven, so for every thirteen weeks you wrote seven original scores. This meant you had twenty-seven and thirty-five minutes of music a week to compose and orchestrate. Murder!

Saul Chaplin:

When you consider that during those musical days at MGM—for example, on *An American in Paris*—we never had less than a week, a week and a half to do a chorus orchestration, which is thirty-two bars. Even then, I remember, we used to complain that we didn't have enough time. Well, if you put a man with that orientation into this TV milieu, you can see ... .

John Green:

I think this, with all the other tensions in Connie's life, is what broke him down. He never got over the panic of having to compose, and one morning he didn't wake up, and they found the empty pill box.

Saul Chaplin:

You know, it's hard to figure out what each of us did specifically on *An American in Paris*. Let's take "I Got Rhythm." John did a lot of "I Got Rhythm," I sketched a lot of it, and Connie did some of it. We all consulted on the whole thing.

John Green:

There was no proud flesh, you know. We would look and see that it was four o'clock in the afternoon on a given day and say, "Holy Jesus, this records day after tomorrow. I'll tell you what, Connie, I'll do bars so-and-so through so-and-so. You do so-and-so through so-and-so. Connie, we've got Solly's two-line sketch here. I'll expand it out to six lines, and you put it on the score paper."

Ed Woehler:

Now, we come around to two weeks before shooting. We've tested all the wardrobe, and if they have any special makeup they test the makeup. We would actually photograph it, because you have to have the movement and sometimes the makeup doesn't look good from a certain angle. So we watch all of those things. At the screening of the tests, the producer and the director okay the work of the hairdressers, makeup, and costume. Then, after the tests are made, everything is still-photographed and numbered, even the changes.

Adrienne Fazan (Editor):

I would normally be assigned to a picture a few days before they began to turn cameras. The head of the Editorial Department would mostly come in and say, "Here's a picture," and throw a script at me. That's how I first heard about *An American in Paris*.

John Green:

The next thing in the order in which things happen is that we would prerecord. In the theater, you have a whole day that's set aside for the so-called orchestra reading. The orchestra comes together for the first time, and they read the music. Now, in motion pictures, comes the day that you're going to prerecord such-and-such a number. When you go to the recording stage, there's no such thing as prerehearsal with the orchestra. They read, rehearse, record. Now, the artists are there, and, if Gene Kelly is going to sing, of course he's there. Say, it's a dancing number; now, you have at least Gene and Leslie there, and you probably record these things in sections to see if it's practical in terms of length. If you're in the live theater you have a rehearsal, and the choreographer may stop you and say, "It's too fast," or "It's too slow," or "Make that *fermata* longer," and then you do it. Even when the show opens, you can have the dancer come downstairs and say, "Jeez, you goddamned near broke my back tonight, holding that thing that long." The next performance you don't. Not so in pictures. Once that orchestra has been on that stage and that recording has cost you $12,000 for one number and the orchestra is gone, you've got a piece of inelastic celluloid that the dancers are going to mime to. Well, you just don't leave that to chance. The dancers are there on the recording stage, so you get a tape that you like and that Gene Kelly thinks he likes. Now you play it back and the dancers actually do it. In the case of big numbers, we have frequently all piled into a limousine and gone over to the stage, and they piped the recording down to the set. The dancers do it, and maybe you find out it's too fast. Then you have to go back and make another take.

Leslie Caron:

We would still be rehearsing all day, more or less, and I would say, "Listen Gene, we've worked four hours. I'm very tired; don't you think I could go home?" He would explain to me very cleverly, very diplomatically, that in the studio you have to look like you're working a full day. I'd say, "Gene that's absurd; everybody knows dancers can't work that way," and he'd say, "Yes, we know that, but they don't, so we have to fool around for a good part of the day and stay around; otherwise they won't be pleased." You know everybody has done that—Hemingway, Dorothy Parker, Gene Kelly, and Fred Astaire. Writers or dancers just simply can't work eight hours. So I was very surprised that a big man like Gene Kelly would have to fake the hours, but there it was.

There was a big, big rehearsal hall, very hot in the summer, with a tin roof and no air conditioning. We were in this hall with pianists all day long, and it was very nice and jolly. My rehearsal day was ten to five. I arrived late one day, and Gene was very stern with me. I said, "I'm sorry I don't have a watch or a clock," and he gave me this very simple answer: "Buy one." I was so amazed; it hadn't occurred to me that one could afford to buy a clock. It was like buying a chinchilla for a Mexican peasant, because during the war in France we just spent money on food and that was that.

Generally, I was pretty lonely, and my anemia wasn't getting any better. Anemia is so depressing: You just run out of strength—mentally, too. I mean I used to wish that I had broken a leg, because that's easier to bear than this physical lethargy and mental depression. At this point, the studio started taking care of my health, which was terrific. There was a studio doctor who would come and see me every day and who started giving me shots of liver and vitamin B, B_{12}, and B complex, but throughout the shooting of the film I had anemia. I was always so weak, and there was a time I even had fever every afternoon. That part of it was a nightmare.

There were only one or two people who were Europeans, or vaguely Europeans, that I had rapport with. One of them was André Previn, who had a French family, and he was nice; he took me out once or twice. Gene couldn't have been nicer, and all his friends were very nice, but they were all sort of football types—very, very familiar—and it just used to freeze me up. I became more and more shy and introverted.

Anyway, came the time to start the film. One of the things that used to be uncomfortable was this feeling that I was the property of this immense factory, and a specialist in each department would come and look me up and down and take measurements and discuss what could be done with me. Always very, very sweet, but this same personality used to drive me nuts. So, one day, just before we started to shoot, I was taken to makeup and I was put in this big chair. The head of makeup, William Tuttle, was there with his assistant, and the makeup man was there and Gene and Vincente. They were all looking at me and expecting some miracle to happen. Somebody came towards me with a pair of tweezers—they were going to shape my eyebrows like Ava Gardner's—and I said, "Not on your life!" and ran away from the chair. They didn't try that again, but there were tests made. There must have been some tests then, or maybe it was just flat photographs, but I remember being in the chair, being examined, being handed over, and being made up by an army of people, and I remember my nerves' starting to knot together. It took about two and a half hours, and I didn't have a thing to say. Everything was building up to the starting date.

Emily Torchia:

This was very unusual and unexpected to Leslie. She wasn't accustomed to anything like that. One thing I remember: When she first came from Paris, she had long hair and wore it the way girls do now—long, straight, and very pretty. A few days before they were to begin shooting *An American in Paris*, Leslie had a session in the portrait studio with Clarence Bull, who is a wonderful photographer, you know. And so we had one full day of lots of posing, which was hard on the gal. We didn't finish, so she was asked to come the next day. Which she did and which was a great blow to all of us because that evening she had rebelled and showed her anger against it. She had taken a bowl and put it on her head and chopped off her hair.

Leslie Caron:

I didn't like what they were doing; I thought it was too conventional; so the night before they started to shoot I had this big idea. They'd be thrilled when I came on the set with this. I thought, "Tomorrow I'm going to arrive, and they'll see what I mean," because I'd been explaining, "I'd like to have this new hairdo we have in Paris, started by Bettina." She was like Twiggy or Jean Shrimpton, and she started this new hairdo, what Mia Farrow eventually copied. I thought this would be great and modern, completely new, and it would be great for the film. So, the night before, I cut my hair, I was very pleased with it. I arrived quite innocently at the studio into the Makeup Department— and immediate consternation! Everybody was called up, and I remember I was taken from the little cubicle where you were made up to

William Tuttle's big office, and everybody came down—Arthur Freed, Vincente Minnelli, and Gene Kelly. They looked me up and down and shook their heads. It just didn't go down well at all. I thought, "Too bad, they don't understand," but I liked it.

I was completely innocent. Well, you can remember, in the days of Ava Gardner and Elizabeth Taylor, in 1950, they all had frizzies all around—it was flat here and then frizzy, frizzy, frizzy—so to see this little shorn wet cat just horrified them. They decided a wig wouldn't do, either, so a hairdresser was put to be my guard. She was really a guard, and her orders were to pull my hair out, to try to make it grow, and then to curl it. She literally pulled my hair and massaged it and put cream in it to see if she could make it grow. It was decided that they'd wait and see if it grew a little. So they started shooting with Georges Guetary and Gene and Oscar Levant, and they kept me on ice, pulling my hair. I was annoyed; I thought it was a great hairdo.

5

SHOOTING THE BOOK

Tokyo (AP)—The U.S. 1st Marines and an unidentified American unit landed in South Korea today as troops from the 2nd Infantry Division continued to pour ashore. The three outfits arrived to bolster sagging United Nations defense lines. . . .

London (AP)—Court circles speculated today that Princess Elizabeth's second child may be born about next week.

Washington (UP)—President Truman will accept stand-by Wage-Price and rationing controls if Congress insists on adding them to his economic mobilization program. . . .

U.S. Weather Bureau forecast for Los Angeles: Variable high cloudiness today and tomorrow. Warmer afternoons with high today near 78 downtown and 71 at the beaches.—*Los Angeles Times,* August 1, 1950.

Ed Woehler (Unit Production Manager):

We started on August 1, 1950. That's the day we began shooting.

Preston Ames (Art Director):

The first big set we shot was inside Kelly's garret, a student's quarters, small and yet big enough for the camera to get into and shoot. In

98

those days, we were shooting an aspect ratio of 3 by 4, known as Academy aspect. It was one of the requirements of a set to conform to this width and height so that the camera lenses used would not overshoot the set.

I also had to make sure that when you looked out a window it meant something, and in those days we were very prone to use nothing but painted backings, which were excellent. But I felt that the building next door was in such close proximity to Gene's room that if I didn't break it up with something it would not look real. So I used what we call foreground miniatures, which I don't think I've ever used since. This meant that the first plane outside the window was rooftops and chimney tops. Then that would be backed up with a painted background of Paris. In this way, as you walked by a window there would be a change of plane between the foreground miniatures and the flat backing, which would give a little more illusion of depth.

We then had to do a little ballet thing in Gene's room when he's first introduced, which was the breakfast set-up. All this had to be very, very carefully designed and laid out. It was tricky.

The room came first. Then Gene, being very inventive, said, "I'd like to do something which makes me look like I'm a pretty smart guy," and he laid out his routine and said, "This is the way I'd like to do it." So what we did was make a mock-up of the set and try odds and ends and bits of things, so that the action all flowed, whether it was a chair that slid, or table that moved, or a bed that rose, or a closet that opened. It was pretty well studied and worked out. He played with it, and, when we got all through, it looked like it was nothing, which was the way, obviously, those things should be. But it took two or three weeks to get this thing so that it worked.

Keogh Gleason (Set Decorator):

Kelly was only interested in the function of how it would work. Now, that bed that went up and down, with the rope and all that stuff, that was part of the choreography. The material cost, you know, $2.98. By the time we got through rigging and changing and doing it, it was a $10,000 bed.

Vincente Minnelli (Director):

In that little routine in his tiny bedroom, Gene was always doing something, pushing up something, and with his foot he was doing something else, and pushing another thing with his shoulder, so it was almost like a ballet. The only thing that I told him was "Do it as though everything was underwater."

Keogh Gleason:

That whole Paris street, where they did the opening number, was something, that whole street that Kelly was supposed to live on, with all those different vegetable stands, and stalls with everything alive and correct, and with the cats that didn't work. Minnelli had seen a French picture about Paris, and there was this marvelous little old woman feeding a cat, with four other cats waiting in line. Well, he wanted that as the camera came by. They spent all morning trying. He kept the cats hungry, which everyone does, so they perform. They don't feed them the day before. But nevertheless, the cats were gone the minute they had a movement of the camera. Minnelli didn't want to open on them; he just wanted to come upon them. Well, the cats were gone, no cats. They just couldn't get it. The animal man supplied the cats, but I had to supply the background for it. What kind of bowl was the little old lady to have? She was next to the vegetable stand, and the vegetables in Europe are a little bit different. So Minnelli had all sorts of research on this. He liked colors and various combinations, which he clipped from magazines. The woman would have on a red shawl with a gray apron, and there would be green vegetables framing her from behind, with the yellow lemons coming down. Every one of those things is important to Minnelli. Not one little frame is haphazard; everything is studied. We had a lot of preparation; we just didn't throw things in. You thought out every little detail. Everything had darned well better be French and true French. For example, the champagne glasses the French use you never see here, and ones here you never see in Paris. The ones with the hollow stem don't exist in Europe; they are American. Now, Minnelli knows this and I know this, but the audience doesn't care, but Minnelli cares. He said, "You get the tulip type, the type that the French have."

I went to the Vendôme restaurant and had them import some. Now, no one is ever going to know that. But Minnelli wouldn't sleep if he thought there was an American champagne glass sitting over there on his set that didn't exist in Paris.

Preston Ames:

There were certain things that I wanted to do which involved what I call "Mickey Mouse" details, but to Vincente and me they were terribly important. Just as a sample—grills. There's a kind of grill that the French use which is about eight or nine inches high, that cuts off the ground-floor window. And then there was another grill that works up higher. Then there's still another kind of grill that works on the doorways. Those are the little "Mickey Mouse" things that I worked like hell to make so that they'd look real. A fountain where you could turn on the water and have your dog drink. Whoever saw it I don't know, but we spent a lot of time developing it. A stairway in the *pension*, which was worn down, I had so real that poor Oscar Levant refused to go up and down the stairs. He said, "I can't do it," and I said, "What's the matter, Oscar?" Well, I realized afterward that he had sort of what you would call acrophobia, the fear of heights, or something, and he wouldn't walk down the stairway. It was too much for him.

Alfred Gilks (Cinematographer):

Perhaps one of the most challenging sets was the little café and the streets that worked with it, where much of the action took place. This was an exterior on Lot 2. A building was cleared here, and the café interior built in conjunction with a real street—in fact, three streets. Directly across from the wide entrance of the café, a street extended straight away for a block to another cross-street, parallel to our foreground street, which extended a full block from the café on one side and a half a block on the other.

Such an extensive layout was a far cry from a single small street or a backing tied in with a set on a stage. We had many sequences, both day and night, to shoot from the inside of the café, with the streets showing in the background; also, scenes starting in the café on closeups, and then, without a cut, pulling back with the camera to a full shot of the exterior of the café, then panning or rolling with the action on down the street into a long shot.

Both the day and night scenes were shot in the daytime. In addition, we made the other long process (or what we called Newcombe establishing) shots, and traveling scenes that were not tied in with the interior of the café. For these, of course, sunlight was most desirable. In lighting and balancing interiors and exteriors that work together, it is necessary to establish a marked difference between outside and inside areas of the set; also, one must stay within the exposure limits required to print properly. The new, fast Technicolor film was not available when we started the picture. Had it been, a great saving could have been effected—and I would now have many less gray hairs.

The usual way to handle a set situation such as this is to box in the streets and cover everything with black tarps, then rig it heavily with arcs, high and low. This would have been a whale of a job because of the huge area involved—and very costly, too. So we tried another method, which, by the way, is a very old one. The street sets already had overhead wires and white diffusers. To these we added black cloths, which could also be adjusted back and forth, as desired, to admit just the right amount of soft fill light for a day effect in the street. For night sequences, we reduced the amount of the fill light by means of the cloths.

Of course, we used a number of arcs on towers and rolling parallels to point up our day or night scenes, but we did not have to rig any of them high. We used a quarter of the light and crew that normally would have been required had we blacked in the set solid. When it was necessary to get long shots in sunlight, we pulled all the cloths.

The authenticity and the visual impact of the café interior in the beginning of the picture are due to the fact that the photography was planned to encompass the action, comparable to several scenes or takes, into one continuous take. Cuts were avoided wherever possible; also, the very natural action in the street in the background, such as people passing by, traffic moving in the streets, et cetera, added to the authenticity we were aiming for. This all had to be planned from the camera point of view in order that the full scope of both scene and action could be captured with a naturalness that frequent cuts cannot make possible.

The camera was mobile-mounted perhaps 80 per cent of the time. Thus, it moved from ground level in the opening of the picture to the second-story window of Kelly's room and moved in and out the window. In still another scene, where players climb a narrow stair to a third-floor room, the moving camera follows them as they ascend and, finally, as they walk around the stairwell rail. This narrow, three-wall set, over thirty-five feet high, with the Technicolor camera and boom almost filling the open side, always posed a bit of a lighting problem.

Ed Woehler:

Minnelli's crew would be about fifty-six people: electricians, grips, property men, makeup people, and all that. That's about the average crew. With the kinds of sets he had, he had maybe twenty electricians and maybe about six grips. And then, besides that, the camera crews with sometimes double cameras, so sometimes you had seven or eight people, two assistants, and so forth.

Minnelli had a quiet set. That's one thing about him. He sits in his corner while they're lighting a set, and he does his work, he goes over the script. There was no yelling or anything like that on the set. He is a very natural director. He doesn't make too much noise. Vince is a very mild person. He gets mad, yes, but I've never heard him yell at anybody. His eyes open and his mouth twitches. You could always tell when he's going to get mad because his mouth goes like this. He can't tolerate people who do stupid things, guys that don't think about what they're doing.

Adrienne Fazan (Editor):

I never had any trouble talking to Minnelli if I had a problem. He would sometimes sit in a corner of the set thinking about the picture. If he was interrupted, then he wouldn't like it. I knew that about him, so I'd wait until I saw him lighting a cigarette, which was every five minutes.

Leslie Caron (Actress):

Vincente's style is imprinted very much on the film, but Vincente is not somebody who talks to actors very easily. In fact, I can't remember him giving me more than one piece of direction in three films we made together. He sort of mutters and stutters and doesn't finish a sentence, which is unintelligible anyway. From that you gather that something is wrong, so you take it as a lead and try something else. But when the film comes out it's definitely a Vincente Minnelli film. He stutters and puckers his lips until you try exactly what he wants, but he's not going to tell you; he's incapable of it. He simply does not communicate; and so I have no memories of Vincente directing me, except to say, "Just be yourself, darling." That he did say, and of course I didn't know what myself was, so I couldn't help very much. But Gene had some hints. He was interested in acting and direction, and so he worked closer with me and gave me tips. I was his protégé. It was, in a way, his responsibility to see that I turned out all right, and he was incredibly conscientious in helping me. He was always ready to help me.

Nina Foch (Actress):

Vincente had very good taste. He didn't say very much. He didn't direct much, but he certainly had impeccably good taste. He's one of those few people who will just say, "I think"—you know how he goes with his mouth and eyes—"that's a bit much." That's it. Well, I'm sure he said things to me, but I don't listen too much. I say, "Yeah. Right," because I believe, as Ouspenskaya believes, that it's Pandora's box; you can't open it. I cannot tell you, when I'm working on something, what I'm doing, because I'll never be able to do it again. I'll cite you an example. I was doing a *Playhouse 90*, and there was a scene in which I was playing a fashion editor, a real tough broad. It was one of those castrating ladies that I play. Poor me, I'm a nice lady, with children and a home, but I play castrating broads. I think it's my nose. Anyway, this was a scene that happened after a fight we were supposed to have had the night before, and the actor that I was playing it with was an actor I had worked with all my life, and he was having a hell of a time with this scene. I said, "I'll tell you what I'm doing, darling, if it's any help to you. You and I didn't make it last night, you couldn't get it up, and that's what this scene is all about." And he said, "Jesus, that's good." Well then, he was marvelous in the scene, and I couldn't play it because I spit it out of my mouth. That's what I mean about not listening. I do listen, of course: If you tell me you want me to go over there, I'll go over there; I won't fight you at all, because it's my discipline to get what I want out of it and do it your way; you're the director, you're the boss.

Leslie Caron:

In filming, I thought it was incredible the amount of time you sat around not doing anything. I was used to things improvised at the last moment. In ballet, you would arrive in a country and have a stage that was half bad planks, and you had to change the choreography of the ballet because you couldn't dance in certain places on the stage. To me, filming was all preparation and not much real talent. I mean you never met anyone like Roland Petit, a tempestuous master, who would have squirts of inspiration all in a swirl, and then it was on the stage the same night. Here, everything was so prepared and tested and reprepared and slightly changed, and then there would be specialists who would come and change it again. I mean it was all committee filming. This to me was very laborious, and I didn't find it exciting at all.

So it really was very tedious for me; I mean to say that in all humility, because I realize what a tremendous opportunity it was and how helpful and kind people were, but it wasn't the fun I had had on the stage in the ballet company.

Preston Ames:

I think it was Gene who said, "I'd love to have this stairway working in such a way that the steps would light up each time Georges stepped on them." This was for the "Stairway to Paradise" number. Here I was, designing on a musical note, and in a theater. We were blessed with having a complete theater on Stages 5 and 6. This was a permanent set, so the question was one of adapting a runway and a proscenium and an opening that would give Georges Guetary a chance to do his thing. The stairway that we required was the kind of curved stairway that went off into nothing. It went, probably, twenty or thirty feet up in the air, at least, and it went sort of out of scene. So there were two or three things that we had fun with on that. Gene wanted the stairway to sort of open up electrically so that, as Guetary's foot was put on a tread, it would light up the riser so that it became a kind of series of light cues which lighted up in perfect time with Guetary's feet as he moved up and down the stairs.

Alfred Gilks:

The risers were made of glass, with a circuit of lights behind each one. Each riser was on a separate circuit, controlled by a mercury switch. All circuits ran to an ingenious master drum controller devised by Sid Moore of the MGM Electrical Department. During the takes, the controller was operated by Gene Kelly's dance director, Carol Haney. Because of her complete familiarity with the music and routine, she was able, after a few rehearsals, to operate the controller in perfect sync— as smoothly as a musician in the orchestra playing his instrument.

Preston Ames:

Then, on either side of this stairway, Vincente had the idea that he would love to do a "living chandelier" kind of thing, like they have in the Paris Opera House. My friend Henry Greutert in the plaster shop was very instrumental in building and designing two shells of plaster that some poor girls had to fit themselves into, so that the chandelier was in fact a "living chandelier." That's a story in itself. These poor girls went in to get fitted, and, of course, this was done in the nude. They'd get this wet plaster over them, and then they would faint, and the plaster would get all over them, and they'd have to start over again. They'd get, I suppose, some kind of phobia, whatever that phobia is, of getting wrapped up into a thing, and they would just pass out. Of course, that was the most horrible thing they could do, because the sculpture would then just go to pieces. But, like everyone else, we, and they, lived through it. And these were beautiful gals. They were gorgeous. That's the way we operated. Everything had to be a little bit different, a little more special, a little trickier, a little more expensive. This is what makes a Minnelli picture, period. Never deny the man. He's indefatigable, absolutely, and expects you to be the same.

Keogh Gleason:

Minnelli was concerned about every little thing or bit. He was very serious and worked hard. There was nothing else but that picture. He wanted every frame to be perfect, and every little bit actor was as important as the biggest star to him. There was no such thing as a throwaway scene. You never just walked out into the hall and turned left to get from someplace else to somplace else. No, this he doesn't do; he hated this, and the minute he began to move his lips, you knew he was furious and he was not about to do it.

Ed Woehler:

The company comes in to shoot at nine o'clock, but everybody concerned with the preparation of the camera would get there at eight o'clock. Minnelli picks the first setup for the next day the night before. When the camera crew comes in, they prepare for it. They take from eight to nine to prepare with stand-ins, going through the action and lighting it. Now the actors come on at nine o'clock. The first thing they do is rehearse the scene. Then, after rehearsal, they go in and check their makeup, and they put the stand-ins back in to fix the final lighting. Now the principals come in, and you run through the scene and then shoot it. That's the way a company should go. Now, a lot of times directors fail to give you the shot the night before, which is a great loss to the company, so we usually insisted that we get that setup. Minnelli, I think, is a kind of a dreamer, and I hope he hears this. He's always thinking. He's always trying to get something better in his mind, and, therefore, he's not really set on anything until he's up against the gun. Then he has to do it. I had to keep after him, you know. He disagreed with me lots of times, but there was no personality thing. It's my job. My job is to have the company function as efficiently as possible, so, if I asked him a question, I mean he should answer it, and he should prepare himself.

Minnelli shot about two and a half to three pages a day. I thought that was about what he'd average when I figured the forty-two-day shooting schedule. He's very meticulous and gives every scene gentle, loving care.

Gene Kelly (Actor):

You know, the acting role I had in *An American in Paris* puts tremendous demands on one. Anytime that a role is just lighthearted and gay you have more demands put upon you than if you're playing Hamlet, because you have less material with which to work. Dramatic roles are much easier to do than slight roles, much easier. There's an old bromide among actors: The ladies will say, "Let me play a prostitute or a nun and I'll win the Academy Award," and the men will say, "Let me play a junkie or a drunk and I'll win the Academy Award." It's much simpler to cry and moan and roll around than to smile and say, "It's been a nice day." This is much harder. What is also always overlooked, to my amazement, and by other song-and-dance men with whom I have spoken at length on the subject, is why people overlook all the good acting that's done while you're dancing and singing. Why is that? You know, everybody says we're not acting anymore. What are we doing? That's a very special kind of acting, and I think the hardest kind to do. You have to stay in that character while you are singing a song or doing a dance, but it is true that we'll never win that battle. "You're not acting; you're just singing and dancing."

Nina Foch:

One scene I remember particularly was when Gene gets in my car after he first meets Leslie. When he did the scene, Vincente said, "You're a Stanislavski actor; improvise it, because Gene is basically a dancer and a musical comedy man and this is really more or less a serious scene we have here. So what I want you to do is . . ." Gene didn't know what was going to happen, see; Vincente didn't tell him. In the first place, we had rear projection, so it wasn't as if we were going to have to break it up in any way. I think it's shot head on. He told me what he wanted, and he said, "Go, baby; do what you want." And if you look at that scene, it's really quite good.

Gene is really quite good in it, too. He's really shook because I'm really "aahg!" at him. That, I think, is a nice piece of acting.

Alan A. Antik (Technical Advisor):

Minnelli would usually sit there with a long cigarette holder, and the cameraman, Al Gilks, would talk to him, or Keogh Gleason would talk to him. I very seldom heard him explaining a scene the way he wanted it, unless it was very visual. He had a great weakness: He was always getting on those booms. He just loved to get on a boom high up. He loved that. He must have had a feeling of great power, being on top of everybody. It was a kind of spectacular something.

Walter Strohm (Head of the Production Department):

Minnelli loved to be on the boom and was very, very astute in using it, although it's a time-consuming and costly thing because you could take a whole day just to rehearse and shoot one boom shot. Sometimes he did a whole day's work in one shot, which is rather interesting. Some days he would be on the boom all day rehearsing, riding it, and, when the end of the day came, they would make a shot, and that would be the whole scene. Well, there are very few directors you could allow to do that, because they are not capable of visualizing and timing boom shots. They become very awkward and mechanical, and you become conscious of a boom and not of the action. Booms are deadly to most directors. In fact, we had a rule—people hated it, but we had to have rules because everybody wasn't Minnelli and everybody didn't know how to use a boom—so directors couldn't use the boom without my okay. You just couldn't have a boom put on a shooting schedule without my approval, and I didn't give it often. But, with Minnelli, some of his great boom shots were classic. I just used to love to watch his boom shots. The one that he did on "'S Wonderful," with Gene, is just a classic.

Gene Kelly:

That shot was routined so it would end with my leaving Guetary on the street. There was only one way to shoot it, so it was prerecorded weeks ahead of time to be shot that way, and the big Chapman boom, the only one large enough to accommodate this setup, was rented well in advance. These things have to be choreographed and prerecorded so far ahead because, aside from the number that I had staged and selected the angle for, Vincente had the problem of dressing the stage and keeping the people in the best spots at the best times, and all those other many thankless jobs the director is usually burdened with. In any case, that shot was another example of our constant collaboration.

Leslie Caron:

One of the biggest fights between the ladies was in hairdressing. Sydney Guilaroff was the king of that empire; he's on all the credits. He was a very colorful figure. He could be extremely helpful and also extremely cutting, depending on his mood. The actresses, to show their importance, had to be combed by *him*. So some mornings in hairdressing there were Kathryn Grayson, who was then a big deal, and Jane Powell, and Elizabeth Taylor, and of course myself, and then there would be one or two legitimate, real actresses, as opposed to the musical comedy stars. There was, for instance, Irene Papas, who was fresh from Greece. A great beauty, but of course she didn't have a little pug nose. She was a serious and a quiet girl, but she didn't wear pink, so this poor girl was a victim of the system. She didn't have plucked eyebrows, and she even had a faint mustache. She just wasn't the type, and so she was discarded. Then there were all the aspiring girls and the stars from other studios who were on loanout and who were very important.

The place was in the middle of this vast room with no cubicles, and the noise in the morning was like a chicken coop. It used to drive me absolutely crazy; all I thought of is not to be combed by Guilaroff and to just get out of there as quickly as possible. The hairdressers were all females; he never had a man there. Some actresses would, it was pointed out to me later, keep Sydney longer than others. We all had the same time in hairdressing, from 7 A.M. to 8 A.M., and they would keep Sydney longer by saying, "Sydney, this is not good enough," or "Look, my parting's too high; it won't match," or "Don't you think my hair's too curly today, Sydney?" So Sydney would have to fuss with that girl and couldn't get on to the next. That was the technique to capture Sydney for the whole length of time, so that some girls would have to go onto the set without having had Sydney's final touch. And then those girls who were neglected by him would whisper how unhappy they were to their private girl hairdresser, who was going to go onto the set with them. That hairdresser then would come to Sydney and whisper to him, "Sydney, you have to take care of Kathryn; she's really unhappy that you aren't combing her." So Sydney would then say to the difficult star he was combing out, "Sweetheart, I'm coming right back, but first let me finish off Kathryn before she goes on the set." He'd come to Kathryn and pretend to do something, because she was perfectly well combed anyway. It was hilarious. There was more acting going on in there than on the set.

Nina Foch:

I had long since realized you make your status in the studios yourself. You make them think what they are going to think about you. You make them think it because you insist on your chair, sweetly, you insist on your parking place, sweetly. If you insist on being treated properly, you will be treated properly. They must all be educated. They are children. Now, of course, you don't talk that way to Minnelli.

I feel you educate people to treat you well. I still do it, at Universal, for example. On the thing Dennis Weaver did this year, *McCloud*, I had a look at this dressing room they had given me. The production manager was having a logistic problem, I could see, but it's not up to me to be a Christian martyr; if I am, the next time they will kill me. I waited until there was just enough crew standing there, and I said to the production manager, "This, of course, is a mistake. You went all the way over to Columbia to get me this dressing room that I had in 1942, didn't you, darling boy, for old times' sake; isn't that why?" Well, in an hour it was fixed. So there you are. You can get what you want, but there's no point in wasting your time by being angry or saying bad things about Metro or Columbia, because it's futile. I have just so much emotion. I'm not going to waste it on the Thalberg Building. I want it on the screen.

Preston Ames:

The bridge, Notre Dame cathedral and the *quai* by the river were, I think, rather a truimph as far as execution was concerned. The idea was great, but sometimes you can have a great idea and the execution is disastrous. Sometimes Gibbons would say, "I hope that your set is as interesting as your sketch." He would needle you and bait you and make you work it out. The basic thing about the *quai* and the river was that it had to look like the real thing! It had to look like Paris.

George Gibson (Head of the Scenic Art Department):

I always worked directly with the unit art director, and, when we came to the phase where Gene Kelly and Leslie Caron did a number by the Seine, it demanded Paris, and nothing else would do. It had to be done down by the river bank in Paris. So Preston designed a set that carried a scenic background on which my team of artists and myself painted one of the bridges of Paris with Notre Dame on the right end of it. We had the Seine three inches deep on the stage floor, and we made it a night shot, which further aided us in the illusion. So on our stage we created the bridge, the *quai*, and Notre Dame. We painted the bridge and the cathedral for night, and illuminated it from the back so that the lights on the painted bridge would light up. The first thing that was a little bit more out of the ordinary was the size of this painted backing. I think it ran 160 feet long and about 35 feet high, so the bridge was darn close to being full size on this two-dimensional muslin backing.

It was a very important set because Preston had really plugged and said, "Now look, we don't have to do this kind of thing in Paris. We'll do it here!" Then we got into the problem of the reflections in the water and how to get them. Preston came up with a picture, I remember, of a long reflection in the water from the light up above on the bridge. Well, of course the light up above in the picture was way back really, but here we were on our backing on a vertical surface, so the light wasn't beginning to occur until it was right in our foreground.

Preston Ames:

The lighting of this set was a preliminary problem that was extremely difficult because we were doing something that needed balance like you can't believe between backing, water, stone, the actors, and camera movements. The set stood on the stage waiting for something to happen.

Vincente Minnelli:

I've always gotten along marvelously with cameramen, but I didn't care much for Gilks's work. He disappointed me in a lot of things because there wasn't enough mood. When we got to things that really needed mood, I really laid on him, like the scene on the *quai*. That sort of thing must, must, must have mood, and he wasn't getting it.

Ed Woehler:

Gilks was a very methodical cameraman who knew his business. During the picture, he and Minnelli didn't, what I call, become great friends. Minnelli is the kind of a guy who likes people to dream like he dreams. Well, Gilks was the opposite. He knew what he was going to do, he knew how he was going to do it, and he did it. It was a matter of personality more than anything else. I think Gilks was very flexible. Of course, John Alton, the other cameraman, who shot the ballet, was a different one. He was what I called a suave smoocher, a kind of baloney guy who played up to a director's ego, whereas Gilks was the opposite sort of guy. That's why I don't think Minnelli liked him. I know during the picture I heard a lot of conversation about how they were going to get a different cameraman, but it never really came to pass until the ballet.

Walter Strohm:

Minnelli wasn't happy with Gilks, and I wasn't happy with him. We had several problems with him. I just thought, bless his soul, he was sort of not a top man in the sense of [Hal] Rosson or [Joseph] Ruttenberg. I think he overlit everything. Everything was lit from the top and looking like there was a skylight in every room. It's hard for me now to go back, but I never was great on Al Gilks.

Preston Ames:

Al Gilks was a charming, delightful man who, like I did on the black-and-white ball, when lighting this set down on the *quai* fell flat on his face. He didn't do a proper job according to what we were after. We tested it cinematographically with his lighting, and unfortunately it was nothing. It was just flat and uninteresting. So Ray June was assigned the job of lighting the set. John Arnold, the head of our Camera Department, assigned him. Ray was available, and John just said, "Ray, go down and help the boys out." It was the old story: Don't spare the horses. If you have to do it with sixteen guys, do it with sixteen guys.

June was a joy to work with. He was a dedicated, wonderful person who finally killed himself just by sheer fatigue of wanting everything to be perfect. He was never so happy as when he could call up the laboratory at three o'clock in the morning and ask them whether or not there was anything on the film, when he knew perfectly well it would be a beautiful thing. So Ray went in there on our Stage 12 and spent three or four days backlighting the backing so that we could get light through windows of the cathedral at night, and lighting the *quai* and getting reflections of lights in the water that were up on the bridge. We had to cheat these and build little lights in the water that would look like what the lamps had reflected. What this was doing, then, was giving life to water which was three inches and which should look like it was thirty feet deep. We made some photographic tests and then made some small corrections.

George Gibson:

Ray June shot the tests. He did one thing that I felt uneasy about. We had the bridge, and the light was directly up over the parapet on the bridge, and he had a spot on the wall of the bridge, hitting down as though it was illuminated from that light. I said, "Ray, this couldn't happen; that bridge ought to be just black; you can pick up the details of the piers and so on but not the wall itself." "Oh gosh, I guess you're right," he said. But the goddamned things were lit so that when they shot the test the reflection was on the wall. There shouldn't have been any reflection, but it was left that way. But these were things that, oh, I don't know, we sometimes get a little fussy about, things that really don't matter. Who would know that, anyway, except me? Nobody else seemed to realize it. Cedric Gibbons felt the test was great, so I just let it go.

Preston Ames:

Then Minnelli came back with Gilks and the two actors, Caron and Kelly; the stage was lit; and they were ready to go again.

Diverting a half a second, maybe ten or fifteen years later I went to Paris to do *Gigi* and one of my friends said, "I'd like to take you someplace and show you something." So we went to the Quai de la Tournelle, which is at the back end of Notre Dame, and the bridge there is known as the Pont de l'Archévèque, meaning the Archbishop's Bridge. There before me, exactly, was the very set I had designed ten years before for *An American in Paris* but had never actually seen, only felt. It was a great moment.

Leslie Caron:

One day, something happened which is all part of Hollywood's history. Hedda Hopper came on the set, and it was like Queen Elizabeth was coming. There were whispers, "Hedda Hopper is coming. Where are we going to sit her? We don't tell her this. We don't show her this. We're going to show her this. We're going to do this scene for her and tell her this and tell her that and don't tell her this." It was a great hullabaloo. So this extraordinary creature arrives, with an umbrella for a hat. There was more hat than you needed to shade an elephant. It was an enormous thing with fringes, and there were jewels, and there was lipstick and shining glitter and scent, and she had rings and varnish and so forth, and they sat her in the director's chair, and then I was brought up to her. You know, I was still a convent girl, and I was still used to curtsying to people, especially to elderly ladies, and I curtsied to her. That was my education, but everybody thought it was so quaint—this quiet little girl who curtsied. So there was the whole afternoon that Hedda Hopper came and gave her blessing. Everyone flirted with her and brought her coffee, I mean it was a big deal. Once you were big enough to tell her to go to hell, she was perfectly all right. You could then be very sharp with her and tell her, "Oh Hedda, get off it; that's none of your business." But, for beginners, she was a terrifying bird of some other plumage.

Adrienne Fazan:

On a Tuesday I would receive the Monday dailies. What we call dailies is all the film shot the day before. My assistant would sync the dailies Tuesday, during the day. Arthur Freed would mostly run the dailies in the afternoon, and then we would run them at night for Minnelli, the assistant director, and Gene Kelly and his assistants. If either Gene or Minnelli would have a suggestion to make, they'd tell me. If not, they'd keep their mouths shut. Mostly, I hoped they would speak up and tell me what they wanted.

The following day, I would start cutting if it was a completed sequence or if there was enough film of one sequence to start work on. I like to start cutting as quickly as possible. On and off, the producer would run the cut sequences. With Minnelli—especially Minnelli—the minute that I would have a sequence completed in the first cut, I would run it for him right after the dailies, and he would make corrections. I would then make those corrections on the film before starting on a new sequence.

Keogh Gleason:

I was always being called on the carpet, because Minnelli was asking for the moon on a silver platter. He'd say, "We'll have this," and I'd say, "Yes, we can do it, but it's going to be expensive." Then he'd say, "Well, let's not bother about the cost." So there'd be J. J. Cohn, who'd tell me, "God, don't give him everything he wants, only the essentials." One thing, though: You saw everything on the screen. He was not like Cukor and a few others I can mention, who did all sorts of details and then shot it all in two shots. Minnelli was very production-conscious. He did the composing of all the scenes through the camera. This is why he'd study it through his hands. He'd say, "Keogh, let's bring this in and move this around." He'd compose it like a frame. He would make sure I'd get the essentials so he could compose.

He's a great clipper. He reads every magazine, and he has his little scissors, and has anything, from a pot handle to a bowl of flowers to a chair, researched and catalogued. His secretary was always busy with this. Now, to talk to him, you wouldn't think he was that organized, but he is. For instance, he had one whole file of just mirrors. When he had some business in front of a mirror, he'd say, "Use this type of mirror or one similar to that in feeling." He'd never say, "Use exactly that same mirror." Sometimes that feeling was a poor man's version of it. I don't think Vincente ever understood middle class. See, he came from a circus, a tent show; his mother was a French actress, and his father was part of the Minnelli Brothers Tent Show out of Chicago, and from that background Vincente went on to be a huge success, designing stage shows at the Music Hall in New York. He therefore thought everybody dined with candles and a crystal chandelier. He'd say, "Is that expensive?" and I'd say, "That's terribly expensive, you know, for what it is." And he'd be very surprised and say, "Oh, it is?" He didn't understand the value of anything.

Walter Strohm:

You had the daily shooting order to determine the time the company was called, and different departments were all listed. Each department was given a special order—what time they were due and what specific thing had to be ready at what time. Ordering the crews was involved in this order, too. We called it the "planning order." When a company was shooting, all the departments of the studio got one of these orders each day, and that determined the size of the crew needed and the length of time this crew would be on the set. Sometimes they didn't need a crew member all day; a prop shop man might be needed in the morning for one company, and, if they knew that, they could then use him in another capacity or another area in the afternoon. All the activities were listed and thought out so that there wasn't confusion. We always tried to avoid confusion.

Then the "three o'clock" went out to wardrobe, casting, and makeup. A "three o'clock" is what they call the actors' report. It calls the actors in for the next day. For instance, if it's Oscar Levant, it tells him to be in the Makeup Department at a certain time, on the set at a certain time, and to wear wardrobe number such-and-such and have makeup number so-and-so on. It also indicates what scenes are going to be shot. Basically, the "three o'clock" was for actors and the "planning order" covered everything.

Both orders were mimeographed and broken down by messengers

FORM 47

THREE O'CLOCK REPORT

DATE 7/27/50

PROD. 1507   DIRECTOR Minnelli   TITLE .n .merican In Paris

DAY Fri. DATE 7/28 HOUR _____ WEATHER CONDITIONS Rain or Shine

1ST SET	Fittings and Showings	SC.	LOCATION OF SET	
2ND SET		SC.	LOCATION OF SET	
3RD SET		SC.	LOCATION OF SET	

CALLED	NAME	CHARACTER—WARDROBE—DESCRIPTION	WARDROBE	MAKEUP	ON SET
	Call for fittings and showings -The following				
	ask them to dress as indicated below and bring a change of				
	similar type clothes for selection -- .ll Clothes				
Suit the frc.p.n.unts are	.lbano Valerio	Baker (Dumelle) Business suits			1PM
	Chas. Millsfield	Man at book stall- Business suits-			
		Not as good as he wore Wed. Felt Hat			1PM
M.y	Capt. Garcia	Shutterman - Slacks, Vest, Shirtsleeves			1PM
	Carli D'Elnor	Sells veg.to nuns - seedy suits			1:15
ever ox	Ray Deravenna	Tricycle Delivery - Dark pants, Jacket, Cap.			1:15
suit the fc'cay	Wm. McCormack	Street Sweeper-Old work clothes, scarf,			
		work jacket, heavy shoes, cap.			1:15
	Carlos .lbert	.rtist casual clothes - French flavor			1:30
	Walter Findon	" " " " "			1:30
.ax	.lbert Petit	" " " " "			1:30
	Dan Foster	Poss-smiling boy- Casual			1:30
	Louise Colbabet	Cat woman - Early Morning Clothes			1PM
	Panchit Costa	House Wife- House Dresses, Sweaters			1PM
	Lupe Chaves	" " " " "			1PM
	Catalina Cruz	" " " " "			1:15
	.lice Partugal	" " " " "			1:15
	Nina Bourget	Office worker- Business Suits or Dresses			1:15
	.atian Mosick	On top of wagon. Old work Clothes			1:30
	2 Blond boys- as selected for lower and/or smiling boy				
		Bring own casual clothes 2 Chgs.			1:45
ore	Don Davin	Lover.			
	Blond - cardran.	Smiling boy.			

REMARKS _____

MAKEUP _____

TIME OF YEAR _____   PICTURE—B AND W [ ]   COLOR [ ]

ASST. DIR. .l Rabock _____   UNIT MGR. E. Weehher

FORM 47

THREE O'CLOCK REPORT

DATE _7/28/50_

PROD. _1507_   DIRECTOR _Minnelli_   TITLE _An American In Paris_

DAY _Saturday_ DATE _7/29_ HOUR _9am_ WEATHER CONDITIONS _R or S_

1ST SET	Recording	SC. Narration "Strauss"	LOCATION OF SET #1
2ND SET		SC.	LOCATION OF SET
3RD SET	Rehearsal	SC.	LOCATION OF SET Hall "A"

CALLED	NAME	CHARACTER—WARDROBE—DESCRIPTION	WARDROBE	MAKEUP	ON SET
X	Gene Kelly	Record narration	Stg. #1		9am
		Record Strauss	Stg. #1		2pm
X	Osca Levant	Record Narration	#1		9am
		Record Strauss	#1		2pm
X	George Geutary	Rehearse with Fogler	#1		10am
		Record Narration	#1		11am
		Record Strauss	#1		2pm
X	Mary Young	Rehearse	Hall "A"		9am
		May record	#1		2pm
X	Martha Bamattre	Rehearse	Hall "A"		9am
X	Eugene Borden	Reharse	"		9am
X	Jeanne Coyne	Rehearse	"		9am
X	Carol Haney	Rehearse	"		9am
X	Leslie Caron	Rehearse	"		10am
after X	Leonard Mazola	Mirror boy - to show ward.			10am
	Call Interview young girls - 18-25yrs - as discussed				10am
	Call Junaita Badt(Marie) - wear own street clothes				
	& bring change for s lection - as Paris Show girl				10:30am
	Call For fitting & showing - wardrobe - push cart vendors - Selma Resaw.				
	Mini Perolio, Teresa Testa, Toby Green - wear own dark				
	heavy shoes				10am
	Call for fitting & showing - workmen - heavy work clothes				
	Chas. Wagner, Robt Johns, Antone Northpole, Jack Santoro				
X	Carlo Albert	Ward. fitting & showing			9:30a
X	Walter Findon	Ward. fit ing & showing			9:30a
	Call Capt. Garcia	Shutterman fitting & showing			9:30a
	Call Carli D'Elnor	Vendor - fit ing & showing			9:30a

REMARKS

MAKEUP

TIME OF YEAR

PICTURE—B AND W   COLOR

ABST. DIR. _Raboch_   UNIT MGR. _Woehler_

5:05pm/darrell

and delivered by bicycle, as fast as they could get them to the various departments. If you put out a corrected "planning order," or "shooting order," as we sometimes called them, then you had to make a whole change and then that had to be distributed. If it was after six o'clock, you had to phone all the departments to see if it was possible to change a crew call. It was planning that made it work. If you haphazardly guessed and came in, called the Makeup Department, or called the Prop Shop, and said, "Look, we need two men tomorrow," well, we couldn't operate that way. We had to have a record of everything that was ordered in a big plant the size of MGM. Thousands of people were sometimes involved. There was always a heavy drain on the departments to keep their personnel working and to move them smoothly between companies. This paperwork is what facilitated the daily operation.

Then there were the eleven o'clock meetings, the production-office meetings. The eleven o'clock meetings were generally attended by the department heads or their assistants, somebody from the Budgeting Department, and the unit manager or the assistant director, who would represent the shooting company. So all the key people involved in the functioning of the departmental aspect of the lot came to this meeting. There'd be about thirty people at each meeting. Each unit manager or assistant put in a strip for a projected week's work. These were all read off then and discussed.

Ed Woehler:

We would read off what we were going to do. For instance, I'd say, "We're going to work interior Kelly's apartment. We're going to do sequence number so-and-so, scene so-and-so, special effects so-and-so, with lighting effects. We would tell all the departments about it then. That's why, when the companies got on the stages, they'd have everything they needed to work with.

Walter Strohm:

Even though it's tedious each day to go through the same thing, it helped us to forestall a calamity. And it would be a calamity if there was one thing we didn't pick up on.

Preston Ames:

One of the big sets we had to contend with was Oscar Levant's dream when he finally plays the *Concerto in F*. He imagined himself always terrified to play a concert, so he imagined this was the way a concert should be played. So he fantasizes that he is every musician, the conductor, and the audience, as well as the soloist. Minnelli came forward and dictated what he would like to do, and some of the things he wanted to do were absolutely contradictory to the norm of things. He wanted all the musicians in silhouette, but he also wanted shadows of the musicians on the wall. I said to myself that Vincente had asked for something which didn't make any sense, but I wasn't going to argue with him. You have to realize that you never said "no" to this man. You always thought, "How do you do it?" The top row of musicians were bass-fiddle players. So, to create the shadow, you had to put other bass players down below the players you could see, who were standing on risers, and project their shadows from a hot light onto the cyclorama behind so it looked like the men in silhouette were casting their own shadows, which, of course, was physically impossible. This was really Gilks's problem.

Alfred Gilks:

To achieve the effect that the whole orchestra was composed of Oscar Levants, we lighted the whole set without actually lighting the faces of any of the musicians, the conductor, or the audience. They all appeared in silhouette. Thus, Levant could be placed in any of these positions as a dark figure, preliminary to making a close shot, during which he would lean slightly one way or another so as to bring himself into a closely controlled key light, and thus disclose himself to the audience.

The multiple-image shots of Levant in this sequence were made by Irving Ries's Optical Effects Department.

Vincente Minnelli:

When we did the orchestral things with Oscar, I promised the studio that I would do it in one day. They were beginning to get nervous about the cost, and that was one number that they weren't sure about. After all, it was one man playing a concerto, which was kind of high-hat Gershwin. So I said, "I'll do it in one day," and I did; I finished it in one day. I said, "Just give me this kind of a set with mist and yellow lights and I'll do it."

Walter Strohm:

They had a cost system so that every day you knew what the picture cost. Every day, the previous day's work was all tabulated, and the producer would have his cost sheet delivered to him. That's why he was in on all that preproduction estimating and budgeting, so he would know both the cumulative costs and the daily costs. Whether it went over or under, it was all presented to the producer and the management in these report cards. The progress reports went out every day, and they would tell whether the shooting company was ahead or behind, and by how much. There was no guessing on what the picture was costing. You had that right there, cold. Once you started running over, then the management got into it at the executive meetings. It has nothing to do with down in the picture area. This was upstairs in our executive meetings, which were just cold and calculating. You had to figure out: "How are we doing, kids? You're running so much over a day, and what are we going to do?"—because they couldn't continue this nightmare. But Freed, if he wanted something, or if he felt Minnelli wanted something so strongly that he couldn't sacrifice it, would try to figure out how we could work it out or cheat it somewhere else. In the case of the concerto, Minnelli said he could do it in one day, and he did it. If he hadn't that scene or some other would have had to have been cut.

Leslie Caron:

I remember once Louis B. Mayer making a speech on the steps of the Thalberg Building, and we were all down below on the street. It was the weirdest scene. He was very short, so he needed a few steps to put himself on the same level as everyone else. This was in the beginning of the McCarthy era, so the whole studio was asked to come and listen to Mr. Mayer speak on how we had to be good Americans.

There were other, equally extraordinary happenings that occurred each day on the set. I know, for example, that some of the women attached to me personally absolutely reported to management. I was very closely watched. I had one woman who practically saved my sanity—an Indian woman. She was my body-makeup woman and was very loyal and very honest. She would tell me whatever could help me. You see, it was very like being in a military state: You didn't quite know what you did that was wrong or that displeased or what you should do that was right. The assistants were the worst. I have intolerable souvenirs of assistants; they always reported you, whatever. Your ballet-shoe ribbons broke in the middle of a number, and there was this embarrassed silence, and somebody would tap their foot and then you knew you'd be reported because your ribbons had broken. Then someone else would be reported because the thread and needle wasn't right there. The good chums would cover for each other. Some people would cover up and say, "Well, her thread was on the other side of the set because she was sewing a button for the understudy." There was always a lot of whispering—you know, gossip—about who got into trouble for what. For instance, there were stars who would insist on putting on their own makeup and who did it badly; therefore, so-and-so would get into hot water because they hadn't been able to tell her to take her hands off her face. Or so-and-so had eaten too much and gained weight and her costumes had to be let out, or "Don't do that, dear; the director wouldn't like it." There was always a lot of intimidating. "You'll be reported" was the usual phrase used. The script clerks, they were the big SS agents, and the assistant directors, too. They probably did have a tough time, but if you were not ready you were reported; if you were late in the morning you'd be reported; if you went out for a walk or for a pee and you didn't realize that you were holding the company up you'd be reported.

I mean there were like fifty people who were involved with presenting you as a movie star, from the hairdresser to the press agents, from the clothes people to the car people. Every itemized event in your day was the direct responsibility of somebody who would get into trouble if you had done something that didn't enter into the frame of what they thought a movie star should be like. I mean there was an absolute scandal when Marlon Brando arrived at work on a motorcycle.

Ed Woehler:

We had a daily log kept by the script girl. She keeps all the logs of whatever transpires on the set. Now, that isn't to peek in on Minnelli's ambition or the actors' private lives or anything. It's just to see what delays we can prevent under similar circumstances on another picture. Let's say, Minnelli shoots fifteen takes of Scene Ten and prints takes nine and fourteen. That's the end of that scene. Now, rehearsal for the scene by the river on the *quai* is next. They rehearse it with the cast. Now they go back and touch up the lighting from 10:20 to 11:20. Now, if there's any delays, maybe Minnelli says, "I don't like this water; let's change it." Well, that's all written down: "Minnelli discussing water" and the time. You see, he okays all the Art Department sketches. Now, there shouldn't be any trouble after that at all. Lots of times directors get second ideas, which I call production delays, because they should have thought of that in the first place. So that's a lapse of memory or something. Or, another example, an actor called for nine o'clock shows up on the set at 9:30. That's an actor's delay. Once we have two or three of those, the producer talks to them right away. Now, in the days of Mr. Thalberg, whenever lateness would happen two or three times, he would call the actor in after the day's work and would have an understanding with him. He was a very honest man, and when he'd talk to them there wasn't any kidding around about it. He pointed out the reasons why they had to be on time and why it was costing the company money for their delays. So that was straightened out beautifully. But later on, after Thalberg's death, the producers became a little lenient. If they wanted an actress in their next picture, they would kind of, you know, let her do things. Well, the first thing you know, the actresses weren't getting there for an hour, and that made for production delays. So the purpose of the log isn't meant to be detrimental to anybody. But, if you were responsible for the delay, naturally, you got the beef. But, you see, you've got to have integrity in picturemaking. That's what the log's for, to see exactly who or what is causing delays. It's above-board. Anybody can read the report. It's no secret. Therefore, a lot of people didn't want their names on the report. Well, if they hadn't been late, they wouldn't have had their names on the report.

Vincente Minnelli:

Towards the end of this period, when we were shooting the book, one thing bothered me tremendously. We had decided to have the ballet at the end of the picture. Just before that, however, in the book, there is a very long sequence we called simply the masquerade ball, which bothered the hell out of me. I thought masquerades were horrible. It was just a terrible problem. It was a very long sequence, besides, and it would be followed by the ballet, which was all based on color. So, when I got the idea of doing it as a black-and-white ball, it was the greatest moment of my life. I called Freed immediately and said, "I know what to do with it! We'll make a black-and-white masquerade with wild black-and-white stripes and checks and polka dots. There will be no color in it except the flesh tones. Even the serpentine confetti will be black and white." I thought this would give the eye a rest, so that when the black and white turned into color it would be so much more dramatic.

Preston Ames:

Here I was, the naïve graduate student of the École des Beaux Arts, who had been to the Artist Ball and had seen what it looked like. I was saturated with what it was and how it actually operated. It was a very colorful, crazy operation. When I presented Minnelli my colorful sketches, he threw up his arms in horror! That I should even dare consider this kind of a thing! He knew what he wanted later on for the ballet, but at this point he could not tell us how he wanted to build this ballet to a crescendo of the ultimate in color. You have to realize, at this point, the ballet hadn't even been planned. Well, I kept falling flat on my face. So, getting nowhere fast, Minnelli brought in Jack Martin Smith, who had worked previously with Vincente. Jack was asked to design something for the ball. Then someone, either Minnelli or Smith or Walter Plunkett, another clothes designer who was consulted here, came up with the idea of a black-and-white ball. Well, just those three words were the key to the whole thing. The costumes were designed as black and white, the set was designed as black and white, and Minnelli was delighted with the concept.

Keogh Gleason:

Everything was black and white. I had to get in thousands of various branches that had a "feeling for rhythm" and then paint them black and white. We played on that set for days, trying to get a "feeling." He had something in the back of his mind but couldn't verbalize it. I remember Minnelli saying, "Just everybody go away. Keogh, get your staff and we'll play around with this." Eventually, we got it to his satisfaction. There was a balcony, and I had branches all over the place. Well, all you have to do is see the picture and you know it doesn't come off at all. His one fault was in not realizing that people are also a part of the *décor* of a set. So you allow for that, but, by the time we got the people in there and the other things, it was like spaghettiville. There was just no sense or rhythm or design to it. It was just a mass of black-and-white moving things. Sounds like it might be a great idea, only it didn't come over in the film that well.

He was also trying to throw in sexual things here that are now tame as hell. The censor was a Mr. Vogel. Minnelli wouldn't even talk to Vogel when Vogel came to the stage. He ignored him. He turned him out as if he didn't exist. They really were ridiculous about cleavage and the whole thing, absolutely ridiculous. I got a big call one day about a nude painting on the wall in Kelly's studio. It was a nude by Modigliani which all the students would have a print of. If anything is less sexy than a Modigliani nude I'd like to know what. Now Renoir, all pink-and-white flesh, that's sexy.

In the black-and-white ball, I'll never forget looking at the dailies. My God! There was just no design; it was just a mess; it was over, over, over! I think that was why he was so mad. He's still mad about it. It didn't come off. It just didn't come off. He sweated more on that just trying to make it come off. Then they cut it and cut it and cut it.

Gene Kelly:

We were all groping there. It was shot way overlength. Adrienne did a superb job cutting the black-and-white ball, because, if you'd seen the mess of film that was shot on that, it would gag you.

Adrienne Fazan:

I think the black-and-white ball was never exactly laid out properly. I don't know the reason why, but that's the impression that I had from the film they shot. I say "they" because Gene Kelly had quite a bit to do with it. Minnelli would always ask Gene Kelly's advice. They shot quite a bit of film on that black-and-white ball, and, I remember, nothing matched. We had angles but no matches. In that one scene they shot the most film. When Minnelli shoots that much film it is mainly proof that he isn't quite certain what he wants. So I just cut the film according to the script and then worked it out after that. I would take the film and study it and try to cut it exactly like the script read. Well, if it doesn't work one way it has to work another way, somehow. It just has to work. We ran the film on the movieola time and time and time again, till finally we saw something that went together.

Vincente Minnelli:

I picked extras to be in the ball, because I wanted them to look natural. I got hand-picked people and told them what the ball was about and for them to form groups and do crazy things and work out things by themselves. I said, "Now, you are all very good, and you are all professional, and this is the way it's got to look, and it's got to be real. Let me see. Put yourself into groups. Work with people. Try different things. Put that there, this here. You come in at this time." We had to keep the ball hot and keep the audience excited.

Alan A. Antik (Technical Advisor):

Every time that Minnelli was setting up the black-and-white ball scene, he would rehearse with the actors, seldom saying anything except "Give it a little more of that." He wanted a certain amount of exaggeration. Each time that it happened I felt kind of funny. I said, "Oh, oh." But I kept my mouth closed. The only thing I did was to talk to Strohm about it. Every day I was sending memos and production reports about what happened: "This is what I suggest"—all in private of course. It never got to Minnelli, but I wanted Joe Cohn and Strohm to know. Copies even went to Freed. I covered myself from the legal point of view. Anything that came up later on, they couldn't say, "Well, why didn't he do that?" Then they would see this note from Alan Antik.

Keogh Gleason:

Keep in mind, this was before *My Fair Lady* and the whole black-and-white bit in that, which was so sensational on Broadway. I saw the opening of *Fair Lady* with Oliver Smith in Philadelphia and the black-and-white sequence brought the house down. That was the Derby Day sequence in *Fair Lady*. Now, Oliver Smith took that straight from *An American in Paris*. But with *Fair Lady* it was so stylized and so great—Cecil Beaton's clothes—it worked; it was sensational! There was no color on that stage. Minnelli's idea was sound, but he was ahead of his time. In *An American in Paris* it was just too much.

Alfred Gilks:

Another lighting problem involved the closing scene of the picture, in which Kelly, on the balcony outside the black-and-white ballroom, watches Caron and Guetary running away down a long stairway to the street below. This was a night shot made in daylight. We photographed only the lower part of the scene; the upper part, representing the sparkling Paris skyline at night, was later filled in by a "Newcombe process shot," a method of special-effects photography devised by Warren Newcombe.

Our part was to mask off the scene before the camera in an irregular line on the top, corresponding to the area to be filled in by the Newcombe process, and to photograph the lower part of the scene to give the illusion of night. Shooting day for night with Technicolor film, we drastically cut exposure and used exceptionally strong practical light globes in the lamp standards lining the stairway. In addition, we had decorators paint the light effects on the walls of buildings to our left to further the illusion of night illumination coming from the lamps. The real key to effectively lighting this set was shooting it with the soft light of low, late-afternoon sun.

Ed Woehler:

During the final weeks of shooting the book we had left the Nina Foch stuff for last, since we didn't need her throughout the whole picture. Well, one morning she came up and said, "Something's happened to me." So we got the doctor and found out that she had chicken pox.

Nina Foch:

I always say that I got chicken pox from one of the kids in the "I Got Rhythm" number. The reason I say that is because . . . Can't you see some rotten stage mother saying to her poor kid, "I don't care if you are sick, goddamn it, you're going to work today!" And the poor little kid goes to work with a rash on his tummy, and there I am, sitting on the set, getting his chicken pox. I had it so badly. To have it as an adult you have to take Demerol, you're in such pain. You know, it's not like kids at all.

So there I was, sick in bed. I was in this little house that I had rented, and Benny Thau and the cameraman are outside the front window, looking at me through the window to see if the spots have healed up enough so that I can come back to work. They've shot everything, they've shot inserts, they've shot hands and faces, and they've run out of stuff to shoot, and there I am holding the picture up. They started pressuring me so terribly, you know, "Fuck you, this picture is going to get finished and you're holding us up. You're costing us $5,000 a day." For three weeks I was sick. Well, they docked me the time that I was holding the picture up. In fact, I lost money on *An American in Paris*. It cost me more to make it than I earned. It was a total failure for me financially. The three weeks or so I was in bed I was not paid. So they weren't very gracious about that.

When I got back into the picture, I had lost so much weight that my waist had shrunk to nothing. Every day that I worked I would get thinner. So every morning everything that I put on would have to be fitted again, because it was falling off me. Not only that—several makeup men with little Japanese brushes were putting makeup into the pox marks because, you see, they were still there. They were still on my face, with the result that I still have several scars that I wouldn't ordinarily have otherwise. The extras didn't know what the hell was going on, because we weren't going to tell them that I had just had the chicken pox.

No one knew or realized then to what advantage Minnelli had used the days he was shut down, waiting for me to get better. Afterwards, he came up to me and told me, "You really did me a favor with your chicken pox." Well, they finally finished with me and closed down. They had shot the book and needed time to get the ballet ready.

Saul Chaplin (Music Codirector):

In the particular case of An American in Paris, we shot the entire picture, then closed down and rehearsed the ballet and other dance sequences separately. The economic reason for that should be fairly obvious. The ballet required the services of just Gene Kelly and Leslie Caron as principals. We didn't need Oscar Levant and Nina Foch hanging around, and there was no reason to pay them. If you do the ballet in the middle of the picture, there's five or six weeks where you're paying them when they're not doing anything. So you finish with them and get them off salary. Then we got to work on the ballet and some other numbers that fit into the book, like Leslie's introduction, which had also been saved for the end for the same reasons.

Vincente Minnelli:

Just prior to directing An American in Paris, I had done Father of the Bride. We did it in such a short time, and everybody concerned got along so well, MGM decided to do a sequel. They were writing it while I was shooting An American in Paris. So, when we started the rehearsals for the ballet, I began shooting Father's Little Dividend, the sequel to Father of the Bride. It was play because it went like the other one did. If it had been a difficult film, something devious and difficult to work out, it would have been very difficult to work on both it and the ballet at the same time, but this fortunately was not. The Hacketts [Albert and Frances (Goodrich)] had written it very well; they had written the original one, too, and it was fun to do. We shot it in something like twenty-two days, so that left a lot of time for the ballet, because the ballet was in rehearsal about eight weeks.

Gene Kelly:

As the wheels ground on at MGM, Vincente Minnelli had to fulfill a commitment to direct *Father's Little Dividend*. So I was left with some numbers to shoot and to choreograph, plus working on the ballet. One that we did with Leslie was when Georges Guetary and Oscar Lavant are in front of a mirror and Guetary tries to explain to Oscar what she's like. This was the scene that introduced Leslie.

Alan Jay Lerner (Author and Screenwriter):

I wrote into the script the basic idea that Guetary at this point describes Leslie to Oscar. It was Vincente's idea, not mine, that, in describing her, Guetary and Levant misunderstand each other. But, in terms of the script, I indicated that Leslie should be introduced in a dance at this point, and left it open for Minnelli to figure out how precisely to do it.

I wrote that Guetary starts to talk about her and that there was going to be a mirror, and you would see her. She was a dancer. It was important, therefore, to show her dancing before we showed her doing anything else. Stylistically, that was very important. The audience had to accept her as a dancer. We weren't worried about people accepting Gene Kelly as a dancer, because nobody is surprised when he dances. But, if there is some character that you have never seen, and all of a sudden you see that person dance, it may shock you. You may have seen the character on the screen for twenty minutes, and, if they then suddenly break into a dance, the audience might say, "Hey, wait, who is that? What's happening here?" With Leslie Caron, who was a beautiful dancer, I felt that it was important that you see her dance before you know anything more about her.

Saul Chaplin:

Minnelli took me to lunch one day—that's no big deal, because we went to lunch often—but on this particular day we went to a Chinese restaurant in Culver City. When we sat down, he said, "Listen, I have an idea of how to introduce Leslie Caron at the beginning of the picture. What if we went to a mirror shot, and we go through it while Guetary is talking about the girl, and we see her in different settings while he's describing her?" He asked me, "What song could we use for that?" He said it should be a pop tune, and I remember saying, "Look, if we didn't want to sing "Embraceable You," that would be a good song." At that time I thought we should sing it. The musical thing and the choreography was later amplified by Gene and myself.

Gene Kelly:

Oddly enough, these little vignettes were the most difficult for me to visualize in the entire picture. Let me explain why. Just a year or so before, I had codirected a film called *On the Town*, and Betty Comden and Adolph Green had written in a similar idea, where a sailor on the subway, in this case myself, looks at a poster and, as he reads it, it describes the girl in contradictory ways. I kept wondering and wondering how I could make the scenes with Leslie not look like a rehash of the ones I had done for Vera-Ellen. Then Vincente came up with a marvelous plan for the *décor*, which threw me into a whole new line of thought. He designed each room in one complete color, and each room had its own period furniture. It sounds terribly simple, but it was a brilliant idea, the kind that choreographers can really use.

Vincente Minnelli:

In staging Leslie's introduction, I thought, "Wouldn't it be interesting to do it monochromatically?" Each vignette would be staged in a different type of room. I had decided on doing each room in one color: a Jacobean room all in yellow, a Biedermeier that's all pink, and so on. Leslie's costume would be the only color contrast. Since the situation was such that Guetary was trying to explain this girl, and Oscar would take him literally at his word, I felt the scene called for this type of treatment. I had done that kind of thing before, on the stage, treating rooms in one complete color, painting everything the same. It's just a way of doing it. If you're trying to visualize one person from a description given you by another person, you don't see it very well; you see it distorted. "She's very studious." "Oh, she reads a great deal." "Not at

UAD: Preston Ames

October 4, 1950

"AN AMERICAN IN PARIS"
RETROSPECT OF LESLIE CARON SEEN IN CAFE MIRROR
BY GUETARY AND LEVANT

REVISED

Budget   Cost

1. She is Beautiful

    Baroque ultramarine blue $ 498.00   1153

2. Sexy

    Victorian silver gray   395.00   671

3. Old Fashioned

    Louis XVI Brilliant greens   488.00   948-

4. Jassy

    Cork and aluminum, modern crimson   500.00   743
    proj color to intensify

5. Studious

    Jacobean room, sulfur yellow   496.00   898
    saffron

6. Gay and Happy,

    Biedermeyer, dusty pink   487.00   788-

             Total Budget $ 2,864.00   5,201-
                                                Cost

These notes were made at a meeting in Miss Sharaff's office
with Messrs. Minnelli, Kelly and Ames.

over Budget 2,337
(±100%)

Budget and Cost Memo for the Leslie Caron Introduction Scene all—she's very gay." Staging that kind of a scene the way I did suits that situation. The colors were poster colors, absolutely like from a child's paint box. I then asked Irene Sharaff to design the costumes and the color combinations.

Irene Sharaff (Costume Designer):

The costumes were brilliant things, but I must say it was Vincente's brain child. I forget the sequence except for one bright saffron yellow dress I did for it. This was just a little present that I gave *An American in Paris*. It was done as a gift. I think Vincente and I talked about it as being done in very jewel-like colors, very sharp prismatic colors, so that you got it as one sharp thing against another, compared to the subtleties of the ballet itself.

Preston Ames:

This scene was done in the little café that we built on the street, and Mr. Minnelli was very anxious to have a proscenium screen to frame the vignettes that was actually a baroque framed mirror. He said, "I want to photograph this thing so it looks like the real thing." In other words, "I want it to look as though we are photographing right into the mirror." I said "okay" because you never said "no" to this man. We always came up with something, and if we ran into real difficulties we went to him and said "Look, Vincente, I'm sorry, but we're going to try something else because what you are asking for is actually a physical impossibility." If you had a reasonable answer for him, that was fine, but, if you didn't and just said, "I'm sorry but I couldn't do it," then you were scum. "No" was a dirty word. We never used it. We never even knew how to spell it.

So, to be able to shoot right into the mirror and not see ourselves, we first photographed the mirror with a still camera and then rear-projected that image, so we could then create a trapezoid with a false shape. In other words, the reverse of what we saw on the screen, so that the foreshortening of the mirror frame became a rectangle rather than a trapezoid. We reversed perspective in this case; the vanishing point went the opposite way so that it corrected itself to having no vanishing point. The lines became parallel, where on the actual thing they diverged backwards.

It was a challenge that was thrown at us: "Do it!" The typical Minnelli thing. You know, "Why even ask? Why question it? Do it!" This is why you loved Minnelli or hated him.

Leslie Caron:

That sequence of introduction numbers was particularly hard for me to do. I was frightened to death—little me, all by myself on this big stage with all those men. First we got rid of the book, the acting sequences, then we did all the dancing. The other big numbers, "Stairway to Paradise" and "Tra-la-la," the ones that were less balletic, were shot with the book.

The series of my introductory numbers were all rehearsed perfectly, and I had great, great support from the two girls, who were just terrific, Jeannie Coyne and Carol Haney. Gene was really the director for those things. He'd say where to place the camera, which was the best angle and the best cuts, and so on.

When he got down to actually shooting the introductory vignettes, I did it one day in bed, one day shooting, one day in bed, one day shooting. It was about like that. Those days of shooting were so horrendous. You know, in the legitimate stage you practiced one hour and then you danced on the stage what amounts to ten or twenty minutes at the most. You don't dance all the time in a ballet. When I was filming, however, I danced for practically eight hours. Those days were just exhausting. Now, there were two numbers that I liked very much. I liked the Charleston; that was very amusing for me. I'd never done anything like that. Jeannie Coyne was best at that; she was very jazzy. The other number I liked was the modern dance with the chair, what they called the "sexy number." I remember it was a blues, sort of heavy, nearly bump and grind, and that to me was great fun. It was all American jazz, and I thought it was terrific. We did this number once, and then I started hearing rumbles about it. It was shocking, and it was going to be censored. There was trouble. So onto the set came the censor, a very sexily dressed female censor, and she was shown the number. Then I remember the whole performance that went on: Gene practically seducing her on the set and she being thrilled with all the attention. Eventually, she decided, if we trimmed it a bit here and a bit there it would be all right. So we reshot it and made it a little less provocative. But the appearance of this censor lady was just the wildest thing. Everybody was sort of giggling in corners, and Gene was doing his whole number with her. It was very funny.

Ed Woehler:

During the rehearsal period of the ballet, I went to France to shoot all the footage of the real Paris that would be used in the picture, including the footage used for the process work when we had to go to rear projection. Peter Ballbush was the director of this second unit in Paris. We shot all the famous landmarks of Paris. We used an all-Parisian crew, but we had an exceptionally good English cameraman. While we were there, a very funny thing happened to us at Notre Dame. We had to go down and shoot the gargoyles all over the cathedral. So, as we walked into this huge church, the first area we came into, there was a wedding going on. As we went back a little further, there was a man confessing. We went back further, and there was a couple of other meetings going on and a prayer service with different people. Then we went further back, and there was a man back there with a big long scooper, like a rake, and he was raking out the tills. He was literally raking the money and putting it into big bags. It was the funniest thing I've ever seen in a church.

Before I left MGM for Paris, I knew what shots we had to get. We knew we had to have right to left cross-light on Sacré Coeur when we shot it in Paris so it would match the lighting of our Sacré Coeur back on Lot 2 in Culver City. For the footage that was going to be used for rear screen projection, we knew what our horizon had to be. That meant the height of our lens from the ground in Paris had to match the height of the lens on the Mitchell camera that shot the master at MGM two months before. You see, that's all laid out in the technical blueprint. It told us the height of the camera; it told the times of day we're supposed to shoot and how wide and so forth. The whole thing was worked out. My shots had to be an absolutely perfect match to the shots made in the studio.

We shot in Paris, I'd say, about 10,000 feet, of which they probably used 500 feet. But film is the cheapest thing you can use. Really! Plus the fact that all that film was put in our stock library and used many times by other productions. So the $20,000 spent on getting those shots was not what you call lost money.

Now, while I was in Paris I got a cable from Freed, telling me to go to Natchez, Mississippi, to take over George Sidney's company there on *Showboat*. Freed had begun this other production, and I was assigned to work with the second unit, which was shooting all the stuff on the river, the townspeople going down to the water, and all the tie-ins which we did later in the studio. So, when I finally got back to MGM in Culver City, the *American in Paris* ballet was nearly completed. You see, the ballet was like a new picture; it was handled separately. Al Shenberg, who has passed away, replaced me and was the unit manager on the ballet while I was in Paris, France, and in Natchez, Mississippi.

Arthur Freed (Producer):

Toward the end of shooting the book, we started filming *Showboat*, which I was producing, with George Sidney directing. *Showboat* was an easy picture to make. The tough thing was to find the right person to sing "Ol' Man River," because the song had been murdered to death on everything else, by everybody else. It stopped the show, however, in the picture. There were some other little things, with Georgie Sidney, of shooting stuff through shadows in the water, and a lot of crap like that, which we got rid of. But the picture was very successful, with that great music of Kern and Hammerstein. *Showboat* was easy to make because everything was there. But—oh God!—with *An American in Paris* we created everything new, especially the ballet. There we didn't have anything to go on. I mean it was just fantasy!

6

The Ballet

Vincente Minnelli (Director):

We had no definite plan for the ballet all the while we were shooting the book. We knew in a vague way that it had to incorporate parts of Paris that artists had painted, but we had no time to figure this out until Nina Foch came down with chicken pox. There was nothing left to shoot whatever, so Irene Sharaff, who I had hired to design the costumes, and Gene Kelly and I locked ourselves in my office for hours and hours and hours on end. We worked out the entire ballet during those days. It was the luckiest chicken pox I've ever known.

We started out by racking our brains on all the material that we had. We knew we wanted to do certain things. Gene had this idea that he wanted to do Toulouse-Lautrec's *Chocolat*, so we tried to work that in some way. Well, you know, I had done several ballets in the shows I'd done in New York—the first surrealist ballet with Balanchine, in one of his shows, a thing called *Death in the Afternoon*, so they rather looked to me for a synopsis.

You had to have a central idea, because the ballet went on for a long time. Gene thought you had to have a story. I said, "You can't have a story, because, if its a new story, that's bewildering. It wouldn't work at all. You're at an emotional crisis here, and, if you retell the story we've been telling, it becomes redundant." I said, "It has to be something to do with emotions, the time in his mind, the way he feels having just lost his girl, and a whole thing about Paris." Everything had to become a jumble in his mind, a kind of delirium because Leslie's leaving him hits him so hard. When she leaves, he has already drawn a black-and-white sketch, rather like a Dufy, and he's explained to her that Paris can not only be exciting, warm, and wonderful, but it can also be very cold, that the color would go out of everything if she left. It wouldn't be the same city. He loved Paris; he painted there; he loved the men who had painted Paris, greater than he would ever be— Rouault, Van Gogh, the Impressionists. Then you slide into the ballet, keeping in mind his delirium. This is, of course, easy to say, but the first problem we had was how to go from the black-and-white ball into the color of the ballet. We felt there was no sense of continuing into the ballet until we had solved the question of that transition.

Gene Kelly (Actor and Choreographer):

In effect, the problem was: Leslie has left and I'm very sad. I'm on a balcony looking out over Paris, and I'm thinking about what the city means to me, my life, what it's done for me, and what I am in respect to the city and to painting. Then, we had to somehow get into this ballet. Once we got into it, it was just fun, but it was torture trying to find a way to slide into the thing. Here's a case where we didn't have a song to get us into it. It's easy if you have something to sing, like "Here is a ballet about a painter who lives in Paris." If George Gershwin had still been around, we probably would have asked him to write it. It's always a little tougher without the song.

The solution to our problem was very much like a dance I did with a newspaper and a squeaky board in a picture called *Summer Stock*. One night, I was having drinks with a fellow who's dead now, Nick Castle, choreographer, and he asked me to listen to a sound that he was making with a newspaper. I said, "My God! It's perfect for a number. Would you mind if I used it?" But I needed another sound to complement it, something to give it dramatic contrast. For days I went around walking over sewer gratings and kicking things around the house, but I couldn't find the sound. Finally, I found what I needed, the sound of a squeaky board. So Nick found one thing and I found the other. Well, with the transition to the ballet I remembered a rose that Leslie had dropped as she left, and Vincente came up with the charcoal sketch that I tore up. The two together gave us something to invent with.

Vincente Minnelli:

It had to start off in black and white—that was the charcoal sketch—and then we had to introduce color into it, and the rose was perfect. Then it had to go to total color. I didn't want to do things that were done at the lab. Months later they turn up with something and show it to you and it's horrible.

Preston Ames (Art Director):

Vincente wanted to do the resolution of black and white to color in the studio. We were aware that we had a rose dropped by Leslie and a sketch made by Gene Kelly of the Place de la Concorde. Then there were to be splashes of color introduced, and we were to be aware of this same sketch in color and not in black and white. Again, that was, and I probably use the word ill-advisedly, thrown at us. All the things were challenges on this picture. How do we do it? Everybody had a different idea until the head of the Camera Department, John Arnold, was brought in, and he said, "I don't think this is too difficult if you have the right tools," and he introduced to us a photographic mirror, or black-glass mirror. This gave you an opportunity to either see through the mirror or to photograph a reflection. So what we did at first was to see this sketch reflected into our mirror in black and white. Now, the color was in an identical sketch on the other side of the glass, and that at the moment was not lit. As you took light off your black-and-white sketch and lit up the colored one on the other side of the mirror, it became a perfect match dissolve, until all you saw was the colored sketch. So we solved the transition by taking light from one image and putting it on another image.

Vincente Minnelli:

Gene picks up the rose, they turn on the spotlights, and the color splashes in. Once we solved that problem, we returned to the bigger

"He was always ready
to help me." An MGM
publicity still.

"It's much simpler to cry
and moan and roll around
than to smile and say,
'It's been a nice day.'"

"I'm really 'aahg!' at him.
That, I think, is a nice
piece of acting."

The end of the backing clearly seen, as effects men at the water's edge wait to put ripples into the "Seine."

"Just give me this kind of a set with mist and yellow lights, and I'll do it."

"I had to get in thousands of various branches that had 'a feeling for rhythm' and then paint them black and white."

"He sweated more on that, just trying to make it come off."
Minnelli, partially hidden by operator's shoulder, riding
the Number 8 camera boom.

"Those days
were just
exhausting."

The Jacobean set.

The Biedermeier set.

The Baroque set.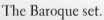

The Charleston.

"As you took light off your black-and-white sketch, . . ."

"and lit up the colored one . . . it became a perfect match
dissolve, until all you saw was the colored sketch."

"The Rousseau section I definitely based on
The Sleeping Gypsy, and the carnival from his *Notre Dame.*"

"With Renoir
I used the
Pont Neuf."

Artist's
treatment
of the
Rousseau
section
of the
ballet.

"We also needed something that gave a color palette which was red, white, and blue. These, of course, are typical Dufy colors."

The Greutert Fountain. "That became a battle royal that lasted a month . . . to say, 'This looks like Dufy painted it.'"

"This was the only possible way we could operate with the dancers." The *pompiers* are entering from the right frame.

"A great deal of work was done right on the level of the water, which . . . was a stage."

"We want a Rousseau zoo . . . and one enormous painting became another and another and another."

"The little girls came out with . . . little white gloves, which we tried to make look like white doves."

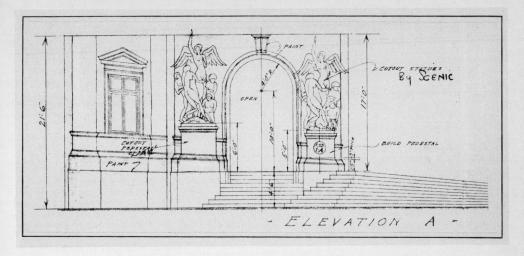

The development of the Van Gogh Place de l'Opéra.

"This was a monochromatic transition, which was very difficult to do."

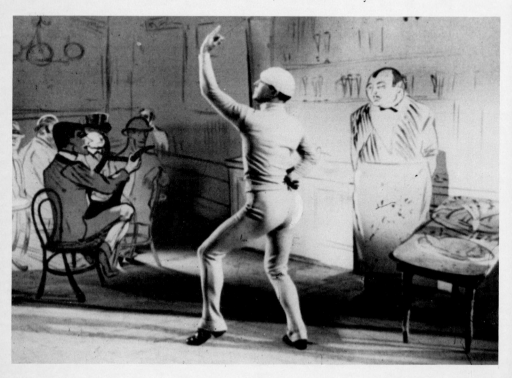

"We had built some cement stairs for our version of *Kismet* . . . and here these stairs were, sitting on our back lot."

"On the screen, Kelly and Caron run up three flights of stairs and embrace." The two levels of stairs on the left, next to Kelly, are a painting that is matted into the picture to give the illusion of three flights. The steps that the men are standing on are, of course, real.

"You have special programs printed up."

"My name was called and I was alone."

Saul Chaplin and
John Green, with
their Oscars.

Preston Ames, Cedric Gibbons, and Arthur Freed looking at the
Argentine "Club Gente del Cine" Award for Art Direction.

MGM's poster for *An American in Paris.*

problem of what to do with the ballet. The clue to the ballet was the emotions, and we knew we had to start high. You see, the music dictates a lot of it because you start with "yum de dum a yum ta ta," which is Paris and traffic and policeman, the people, the Orientals, and ever-body. It's Paris that is gay; it's Paris and it's wonderful. Its traffic is frightening, and Gershwin actually uses auto horns in the music. Gene catches a glimpse of a girl, who is Leslie. By the time he crosses the square, she's gone. Then the lights fade and the scene turns into a flower market. The girl is still on his mind. He dances with her as if she is a ghost, and finally, as he is slowly turning with her, it becomes just the sorrowful flower market, and he is alone. Then, for the next section, I had a clue from Deems Taylor's original program notes for *An American in Paris,* which was that section of the music where the American is wanting his own roots, lonesome for his own rhythms. That's where the servicemen come in. Then the American is happy, gay, and goes to the zoological gardens. It's very gay, and they imitate Americans, and they are all very happy until . . . What he can't forget is the passion that's under it. Then comes the long, passionate dance on the fountain that turns into the Van Gogh Place de l' Opéra. Now the dancers are part of Paris again. They see the sign of the exhibition for Toulouse-Lautrec, and Gene imagines himself as Chocolat. Then it erupts into the whole city of Paris, the music reaches its climax, every-thing is up, wonderful, gay, exciting, and, bang, everybody disappears. He's alone again.

So the ballet goes from highs to lows, as you do in deliriums like that. You had to keep the story going, so you knew at the end of the ballet that the girl had gone. So it had to be a thing of emotions and vision—then a very quick ending to the story and picture after that.

Gene Kelly:

Sharaff, Minnelli, and I met for several days in Vincente's office to try to "lay out" the theme of the ballet. As for myself, I was only adamant about one thing: We must not use the paintings of Degas. I had a strong feeling for Toulouse-Lautrec because one section of the music cried out for him, especially the character of Chocolat. Because it was postwar Paris, I saw only two very clear ways to make an Ameri-can look *really* American amongst all those French Impressionist paintings: The first was to incorporate servicemen in it somehow, and the second, to find a place where we could do some tap dancing, as opposed to classic ballet. Now, tap dancing is almost always done as a rhythm accompaniment like drum beats, but here I put it right on the melody. It worked, and it looked as American as a hot dog.

Two of the scenes in the ballet, the Dufy opening and the Van Gogh colors of the Paris Opera, were done completely by Irene Sharaff. I'm afraid Vincente and I just threw those at her and said, "Flood us with costumes and we'll make it work." The rest, of course, came out of the choreographic plan.

Irene Sharaff (Costume Designer):

There was nothing when I came out that had been written down on paper about *An American in Paris* except that it was to be a ballet about painters. There was nothing on paper for the ballet except Gershwin's score for *An American in Paris*, the concert piece, and the fact that Arthur Freed and, I suppose, Vincente and Gene, wanted it around the painters of that time.

One must give tremendous credit to Arthur Freed, who is a very peculiar man with a great love for painting as well as all the other creative arts. He is an inarticulate man and not one who is full of great knowledge, but his instinct is extraordinary. Arthur fell in love with the Impressionist painters, and, as *An American in Paris* was a story about Paris, I think he felt this was some way of showing his love for nineteenth-century and early twentieth-century painters.

Vincente, Gene, and I first jotted down a whole series of sequences into which we could incorporate the different painters. I also did the scenery for the ballet. Now, that doesn't mean I sat down with a T square and triangle, did the mechanical drawings for it, or constructed it, but I did do the basic springboard for the *décor* of the ballet.

It was extraordinary that a studio like Metro was so generous in allowing us this kind of freedom to do the ballet. There were no holds on what we did. The ballet was based on the painters Raoul Dufy, Toulouse-Lautrec, Utrillo, Henri Rousseau, Van Gogh, and a bit of Monet. Of course, nobody can reproduce a scene exactly like a Raoul Dufy; this was to be an impression of something.

Keogh Gleason (Set Decorator):

Sharaff was something! Minnelli wouldn't do a picture without her, but she used to drive Freed right up the wall. She made lots of demands, like her own car with chauffeur at her disposal and "Stand by; I'll call you; don't call me, but be there." And don't call her a costumer; she is a designer. Someone called her a costumer once; well, that's like a wardrobe woman. Boy did she blow!

Saul Chaplin (Music Codirector):

At another studio, the sudden introduction at this point of Irene Sharaff into a team that had been working on *An American in Paris* for six months might have caused problems, but not at Metro. There you didn't have to worry about getting to know each other's personalities. We'd worked with each other before and so knew and respected each other. We didn't have to waste twelve meetings on trying not to offend somebody.

Irene Sharaff:

I chose certain things mainly because it had to become a continuity. I played the *An American in Paris* score constantly while I was designing it, and certain characters in Gershwin's scores came out. For example, a costume that I did for a black dancer came out through my subconscious as I listened to the music. It was a jazz thing that my ear caught that Gene utilized. I dressed the dancer as a spahi with a white turban and a blue burnoose. I was completely open in the characters I invented at my drawing board, and let my subconscious come out listening to the music. I don't say that I have that direct connection with my unconscious to let it work that way all the time. I would be silly to say that. I mean there was a plan. For example, the group of *pompiers*, the firemen, that run through it were obviously the leitmotiv for *An American in Paris*. I can't sing the tune for you, but it's a very marching, lilting kind of music. I thought it would be marvelous because at that time, certainly, the *gendarmes* were a little more romantic looking than they are today, and so were the *pompiers*. Everybody's uniform was a little more dramatic than the kind of utilitarian uniform that you see on servicemen today. So I made a dramatic form out of the uniforms. They wore brass helmets, and they had an awful lot of brass shining around. They never walked singly. They always walked in groups, like the *gendarmes*. So then it was up to Gene to decide how to use them. All I did was feed him certain characters that he would then utilize.

The Rousseau section I definitely based on *The Sleeping Gypsy*, and the carnival came from his *Notre Dame*. With Renoir I used the *Pont Neuf*. The Von Gogh section, which was placed in the place of Place de l'Opéra, found its style from the pattern of his *Cypresses*, painted at Arles—all the yellows and sunflowers. There I tried to get the Van Gogh palette. With Toulouse-Lautrec, I used Lucite figures of actual characters that he painted, like *Chocolat at the Achilles Bar*.

Gene Kelly:

Other times Irene would just feed me a background and I would stage the scene around it, as was the case for the Utrillo street scene in Montmartre, when the GIs jump out and dance with me. Irene decided that she would wash their GI uniforms as if Utrillo painted them. She took a brush and painted the marine, sailor, air-force, and army uniforms right on the dancers.

Preston Ames:

The ballet became a series of meetings with a number of people because, obviously, Gene had his choreography to do, Sharaff had her costumes to do, the music people had their things to do, and I had the sets to do. We went off into various groups to try and figure out how this would be done. After a few weeks, it was resolved that some Impressionist paintings, which we were going to create in a third dimension, were to be the background for Kelly to do his choreography in. Now, we did several things. We came up with a multitude of sketches and models to show Minnelli how we could photograph it. With the models, he was able to look at it through his little finder and see whether or not it gave him the kind of fluidity he required. When we got all through, we had a couple of dozen models and a multitude of sketches to help him decide whether this was the right thing or not. We were always interrupting his shooting of *Father's Little Dividend*. But he loved it. It gave him an audience of his crew there, and he was never so happy. He was really the king on his throne when this all took place. He had suggestions, but he was giving us our head. He wanted us to come up with something, and he wasn't going to destroy this creative quality.

We got to a preliminary point when we finally got to the great meeting with management and all of our people. We sat down with them and said, "Okay, here is our ballet—x number of dollars, x number of days to shoot, x number of people that we need." It was a monumental request. We were asking to do something that had never been done before, and for big money. There was only one little humorous moment, when it was decided who would emcee this meeting. Everybody had so much to say that if you loused it up by too many words or too much description you could have thrown the whole thing in the garbage pail. Dore Schary said, "Excuse me. I think I'll go out and come back in again because I can see somebody has to take the floor on this thing," so he made a little humorous moment. It was Vincente who finally said, "Okay I'll do the honors." After that, it was all seriousness. Vincente took the floor and described the whole thing the way it was, what we would do, and how it would work. Nobody knew really what we were doing, much less ourselves, but we had a pretty good idea of what we wanted to do. My God! It was so big that it was a little bit beyond all of us, and yet we weren't afraid.

Dore Schary (Executive Vice-President in Charge of Production):

It was quite a shocker at the time to be presented with a ballet that was going to cost us this amount of money. It was to be very costly. You know, in those days to be talking about a ballet that might run a half a million bucks, wow! You know, *An American in Paris*, a symphonic piece of music, no less.

Of course, I knew the Gershwin piece and loved it, and I was on their side. I saw all the sketches that Irene had done and Minnelli had worked out, including the camera angles. I just fell in love with it.

Everything that Gene was doing was so imaginative. He even had the sketches of Chocolat and how they would use them. So I said, "Fine. Go."

Preston Ames:

He could have said, "Trim it a little bit, restudy it, and cut it down." Then we'd have all looked at him and said, "You do it properly or you don't do it at all." There would have been words, and there would have been sulking and all kinds of things. Eventually, we'd have done it anyhow. But it was the greatest morale builder that you could imagine to have management say, "Job well done—go!" That's basically what it amounted to.

Dore Schary:

Then we began to run into trouble. The budget which came in was extremely high for a musical at that time. Particularly in the era I was there, because I cut down the cost of musicals enormously. We began to hear from New York: "Expensive picture. Ballet? Whew! Half a million dollars for one number. *An American in Paris*. Dore, it can't sell." Nick Schenck, President of Loews, Inc., our parent company, had Joe Vogel in charge of sales. He was a Schenck man, and he and I had had many disagreements before and after that. He just said, "Dore, you're making a terrible error. Nobody's going to see it; we'll cut it out of the picture." I said, "No, you won't cut this out, because we might as well junk the picture, and we're not going to do that." It took a lot of persuasion. They came out at one time during this period, and we showed them the sketches and models. Howard Dietz, the head of promotion and advertising, began to get enthused by it, and he had some clout. I'd be going to New York, and they'd come out to California, and we'd have a go-around. Sometimes they were heated, but mostly they were not, because generally things were running very smoothly. They stated their warnings, and I politely answered them. I argued that this was the most expensive picture we made. You see, the average cost of our films by then was down to about $1,400,000, and for it suddenly to be going up well over $3 million made them very panicky. And Freed had muscle because his record in musicals was very, very good indeed. He also was a man of taste, style, and certainly talent, and they took that into consideration. The argument which probably was the strongest, and which probably carried the day in favor of us doing it, dealt with our European potential. For musicals it was always considered important because your costs on musicals were larger. You therefore wanted to make musicals that would sell in Europe. At that time, the percentage we needed to get back on our European distribution was somewhere between 35 and 40 per cent. For instance, *The Great Caruso* had the kind of built-in European audience which we needed. *Lili* had an appeal much greater than New York believed it had, and so would *American in Paris*, which is the argument which prevailed. This New York understood.

Alan Jay Lerner (Author and Screenwriter):

At that time, the idea of spending $500,000 on a ballet was a very adventurous decision, to say the least. In terms of this ballet, Mayer played a key role in making the decision to keep the ballet in no matter what the cost. As a matter of fact, that decision was probably one of the last major picturemaking decisions he was to make. I remember that Louis B. Mayer left the studio sometime before *An American in Paris* was previewed. All during the time of the making of the picture, there was a lot of animosity between Mr. Mayer and Dore Schary, a lot of in-fighting. It had to do with Dore working more closely with the New York office. I never really understood all of what was happening, nor did I care to get involved. Anyway, I remember very clearly the day that Arthur Freed went up and discussed the whole thing with Mr. Mayer. Freed then came right down and told me that it would be all right. Louis B. Mayer had okayed the money for the ballet.

Preston Ames:

Concretely, we needed first a set that would give us a big area, which would give Gene space to choreograph in. We also needed something that gave a color palette which was red, white, and blue. These, of course, are typical Dufy colors. Consequently, combining these two elements, we came up with a treatment of Place de la Concorde which, incidentally, Dufy had never painted. But that wasn't important. The fact was that he contributed a color palette which gave a whole pattern to this opening scene. Arthur Freed describes Dufy as a calligraphic painter, which means the background was a mass of color in which line drawings give you the details.

George Gibson (Head of the Scenic Art Department):

Raoul Dufy is essentially a water-color painter with a lot of calligraphic strokes and a lot of color. So Preston said, "I know that we can't get anybody in the other departments to do this, so could you make a sketch for the model of this thing?" I made the sketch of the Place de la Concorde à la Raoul Dufy. I'm a water-color painter myself, so it was no great problem for me. Then Henry Greutert, who was the modeler and the sculptor down in the plaster shop, modeled up a fountain that was as much Dufy as you could make a three-dimensional object. It was very difficult to do this kind of thing. He had to make it so it could be seen through—penetrable, you know. It was all disrupted by shapes and forms within it, while it still retained the feeling of the fountain that exists in the Place de la Concorde.

Preston Ames:

The third-dimensional thing, where Henry Greutert came in, was creating a Dufy-like fountain for the Place de la Concorde as if it were a calligraphic thing. That became a battle royal that lasted a month at least, to say "This looks like Dufy painted it."

Vincente Minnelli:

Greutert designed this marvelous fountain in miniature first. There was a bad time for a while about that design. Cedric Gibbons, who was head of the Art Department, wanted to make it a different way. He said, "That's not in the style of Dufy. Dufy is with lines; therefore, make it solid and paint in these lines." He just got this idea in his head.

"You have to do these kinds of figures, and then you make broken lines." I said, "But, Cedric, that isn't going to work with the light changes, because, when you silhouette it, it'll look just like a Henry Moore, you know those doughlike figures. It will just look like a blob, nothing." He was rather stubborn about it. All he saw was how it wouldn't be like Dufy. Finally, I convinced him this was the only possible way we could operate with the dancers and still get all these changes of mood in.

Preston Ames:

To trace the complete genesis of the idea for the Place de la Concorde, you have to go right back to that sketch by Sharaff. There was the fountain and there was the Dufy background. Now, Place de la Concorde in Paris has two fountains. It also has an obelisk. It has all kinds of things, and in my first designs I introduced too many of these real elements. The result was that I was out of scale for myself and for what Gene wanted to do. Gene at that stage wasn't too sure what he wanted to do, but I knew that he needed acreage, and that's where the model paid off. Looking at my first model, they said, "What's that?" I said, "Well, that's an obelisk." They said, "What's that for?" And I said, "Well, because that's what's there." They said, "It's going to be in our way." "They" meaning Kelly and company. Vince realized it, too. So we had to weed out the garbage. Our big set piece was the Greutert fountain, which took a great deal of design just determining whether it would be full size or not. We settled on building it three-quarter size. In any event, it served as a stage of operation. A great deal of work was done right on the level of the water, which was not water but a stage. That had to be designed to satisfy Gene's bit with Caron, because there was a great deal done up there. Then a backdrop would be hung behind that which was at least 300 feet long. Then there was to be a cove that went up to it so that it would tie the floor into the backing. It was meant to give a feeling of going from the floor right up into the air into the backing. It was tremendous in that sense because there had to be a lot of people on that set. On the other hand, there was one moment when Gene would be there entirely alone, and he wasn't too sure what he wanted to do, so he said, "Gee whiz! I'd love to just run over this whole damn thing." It was crazy, like only Gene can do. He made this tremendous run right around the whole thing. Now, if it had been too small, it would have been ridiculous, but this gave him, with the right-angle lens, the opportunity to do that wonderful kind of strange, wild run around the fountain.

All these decisions are taking place at the model stage. Nothing has been built or painted yet. But these models were pretty good size, probably six feet long and three feet wide. Even at this size, Greutert's fountain was a kind of strange, decadent thing.

Then Vincente said, "I want water to play over the fountain." I said, "Vince, for Christ's sake, this thing is, you know, water!" He said, "Well, can't you figure out some way of doing the water and not have it water?" Typical response. So we developed a dry-ice technique, where we had steam and dry ice which came out with fans and wind and whatever we had. It really looked like the fountain was playing, and nobody got wet.

Irene Sharaff:

Once our ideas were accepted by Dore and the rest of management, we all proceeded from there. Vincente went on and finished his direction of *Father's Little Dividend*. Gene did what he had to do, which was to choreograph the ballet. The scenery had to be built, and the costumes had to be designed and then made. I had photographs made of the sketches after the general meetings were over. I then fed them to Gene and his crew so they were constantly aware of the different characters that came out of my drawing board. Now, if an impasse came, and if one didn't know how to shift one thing to another, a general meeting was called. Otherwise, we were on our own.

When I sketch I use gouache, which is a tempera. It's an opaque paint that you use with a water base, and you can get the vibrancy in color that you can't get with any other medium—at least I can't. Oil is too laborious, doesn't dry, and is pretentious to use. Now, these wonderful acrylic paints which dry immediately are superb. When I do a sketch, this is actually the most pleasurable part of designing; the color is there for anyone to see. The color that I choose is down on my sketch. When Vincente and Gene and Preston and Cedric saw the sketches, they saw what they were going to see on film.

Keogh Gleason:

Then there was a little thing—Cedric Gibbons always had a few strange quirks about red and green, the bright Christmas colors. He felt they should never go together. Well, we come along with Minnelli and that went out the window pretty quick. Minnelli showed me a color combination of a Williamsburg green wall with a bright cherry red sofa against it. I thought, "Oh boy! Here we go!" This is exactly what Gibbons disliked. By this time, however, Gibbons wouldn't touch him, so we did it, the first red and green in MGM Technicolor. Before that we were in the beige stage. I use to call them the "er" colors, everything was a littler "er." There was darker or grayer or bluer. There were no pure colors.

Irene Sharaff:

Each one of the painters that I used had a palette that was very much his own. I mean, after all, painting is a very personal thing, isn't it? Certainly a painter with the stature of the painters we used in this picture had his own style, his own sense of color, and his own sense of light. In designing the colors for these balletic settings, I used my senses. There is no theory about this. This is the thing that only people sitting behind closed doors worry about, thinking that there are theories. There are many books that have been written about color theories, and it's a lot of nonsense. If you have a great passion for color, as I do, you do it with your instincts; you do it with your guts. You don't sit down and say, "Oh, red has a certain amount of white things compared to green, which has certain other things." That to me is sheer nonsense! I love color and I understand color. My whole springboard is color. I'm a visual person, and I use color from my guts, I don't use it because of theory, and I don't think one bloody painter, a great painter, uses color in any other way. I'm not interested in a technical class of why green and red do certain things. I know it instinctively; I don't have to know it technically. I feel certain colors to me have happiness; certain colors to me mean sadness. You can't have a theory about that. I don't say "I can't use that because it's against the rule." If there's anything in the world that's free, believe me, it's color. All you need is some tubes of paint.

An American in Paris was probably one of the largest ballets ever done. It was equivalent to a full-size Broadway show. I did something like five hundred costumes.

This is one of the strange, dreadful things about time and the fact that, at times, very few things are planned—planned in advance, the way when building a building an architect would have blueprints down to the finest detail. But, as time is of the essence in both the theater and the movies, you really improvise three-quarters of the time and feel lucky that you can get things done on time. Gene choreographed as quickly as I designed the costumes. Everybody was working on a terribly tight time schedule. Sometimes it's kind of marvelous when a movie works and when people get on the same beam. The real magic is how you can work quickly with the kind of collaborative forces that allow you to use that extra degree of energy that people always have stored away and can conjure forth when the occasion is needed. I worked around the clock, literally, because, when I wasn't at the costumer watching the costumes being made, I was at the drawing board designing them. I didn't sleep and I didn't eat and I would work at home on a board propped up on a desk, because I knew by a certain time I had to have certain costumes into the costumers to be made. It's fascinating. Sometimes, however, I would love to be given the great present of being able to design something not casually but leisurely.

Preston Ames:

Irene Sharaff came up with a presentation of costume sketches which incorporated a very interesting treatment for the background. She was saying, and rightly so, "I just cannot give you a sketch of a costume and not show you how it works and where it works." So there was a little professional jealousy on everybody's part. But it did no harm, because she has a way of doing things her way, and in this particular instance she made the whole thing possible. She felt that the various painters should come into the picture, and she tried to give her sketches that treatment. She gave a color key which was invaluable that ran through the whole ballet. Maybe they were only suggestive things, but they were there, and, when you got all through with it, there was a completeness to it.

The art director, me, has the right to say, "Look, you have a color thing, and I'll work with you colorwise, but my background is going to be my background." But, in this instance, it was a correlation between the color of the costume and where it was to work. Now, needless to say, this didn't take me off the hook at all, because, when we finally agreed that this was it, then I had to take all of this stuff and make it work, and that was not easy. It's one thing to have a pretty sketch—and in this case they *were* pretty sketches; they didn't intend to be anything else—and another thing to then take those sketches and put them into a three-dimensional set and have them painted to look like Dufys and Renoirs and Van Goghs.

George Gibson:

The first one we tackled was the Dufy Place de la Concorde. We thought we could do it, but we didn't know. There were all kinds of technical problems inherent in the techniques of the various painters that had been chosen. You see, when you do a water color it's essentially a washy thing, and much of a water color becomes a sort of accidental happening which you take advantage of and use in the development of your painting. Dufy, of course, is no different from anybody else in this respect. He likes to put on a big splash of a wash and drop color into it, a splash here and a splash there, before he starts all these calligraphic delineations of buildings or whatever. This is all right, doing it on a sketch which might run 40 inches long and about 20 inches high. But, when we got into painting the backing proper, you realize that we couldn't rely on these happy accidents. It all had to be done on this huge scale because, you see, this darn backing we painted on was 35 or 40 feet high, maybe 250 feet long. The happy accidents that existed in the original sketch had to be painted absolutely on our enormous canvas. All the accidents had to be literally drawn. The feeling of watery wash and all of these things had to be consciously done.

We were on Stage 27 with that. Then, of course, we asphalted the stage floor. They used to put paper over the wood and then lay asphalt and roll it, a thin inch-and-a-half–thick topping of asphalt, which they ran right up to the backing. Well, we picked up with little profile balustrades, painted à la Dufy, and carried the color off the backing right onto the floor so that the whole stage became a complete painting. Of course, this astounded everyone. I remember Preston saying, "Minnelli walked in and saw all this going on, and he was astonished." He'd never seen this type of thing before. Well, this was something that Ames and I had talked about: "We'll do it this way, carrying the color down on the floor, and we'll get it so that it has a vertical appearance, although it is a three-dimensional thing as far as the set and the backing are concerned."

Of course, once we proved it could be done, we had to go with the whole thing. All the sets had to be done on this gigantic scale. "We want a Toulouse-Lautrec, we want a Utrillo street, we want a Rousseau zoo, we want a Van Gogh opera house," and one enormous painting became another and another and another.

Meantime, along with the design of the Place de la Concorde, Preston would have people designing the Utrillo set. Then, that would be fed into us as it was finished in the design stage. There is no problem for us as far as construction is concerned. All we have to have is the sewing room put the muslin together and we can start in on the backing. We would maybe be working on the backing for the Utrillo set two weeks ahead of the time that we would get the flats for the Utrillo set from the mill. By the time it would be delivered, we would have everything pretty well keyed and anchored. That way there were no delays.

John Green (Executive in Charge of Music and Music Codirector):

Simultaneous to the design and construction of the sets, a similar process was happening to the original score that Gershwin wrote for *An American in Paris*. Namely, we were arranging and orchestrating the score to fit our dramatic needs. "Arrangement" meant for us the adaptation of *An American in Paris* to the needs of our ballet. For instance, there is a trombone theme that comes in early in *An American in Paris*. The next substantive motif that you hear in the picture George Gershwin never wrote. Saul Chaplin wrote it. Before this picture, it didn't exist.

Saul Chaplin (Music Codirector):

One reason why we had to do it was because we did one painter at a time. We did Dufy first, and we decided certain things fit with Dufy. Then another piece of music fit with Toulouse-Lautrec, like *Chocolat*, the jazz theme—that's perfect. Well, that comes early in the music, but we couldn't have Toulouse-Lautrec up early and then come back to him at the end, so that's one reason why the ballet music was changed to fit the needs of the separate dramatic sections.

John Green:

That's arrangement—now about orchestration: If you look at the printed score that you buy for $25 or $30 of *An American in Paris* you will see "edited by F. Campbell Watson." F. Campbell Watson was an English orchestrator, arranger, and music editor–type fellow. Gershwin, as you know, didn't get around to the larger and extended forms of music until comparatively late in his life. George started writing *An American in Paris* in the fall of 1924. The previous February was that famous first performance of *Rhapsody in Blue* on Lincoln's birthday in Aeolian Hall, with Paul Whiteman. The following year (1925), George was in Boston with a show called *Rosalie*, of which he was a collaborative composer. He and Ira wrote a song for this show called "Oh Gee, Oh Joy." You know who copied the parts? At night? Me! I was satellite number one hanging around Gershwin. If he would smile at me, this was already a joy. I copied the parts because the reading with the orchestra was the next morning and there was no other copyist available that night. Between the time of *Rosalie* and 1927, George wrote *An American in Paris*. At that time, he was not a master orchestrator; he literally wasn't even sure of the transpositions—B flat clarinet, B flat trumpet—and he was shaky about the viola clef, things of that nature. Consequently, he lacked orchestral courage. He was also a compulsive doubler because he didn't really know the orchestral sonorities. He ultimately began to learn them and would have, if he had lived. What I'm getting at is this: Something that would have been perfectly fine by itself in solo bassoon he'd double in the viola. That would be one double. Then, for safety's sake, he would put it also in the celli.

Everything was all doubled up all through the orchestra, which made for great weight and often thickness.

We were using this music for a recorded medium, the microphone, in terms of our recording techniques as of 1950. Also, money for us was a consideration—speed. What Connie Salinger and I did was make that stuff foolproof for the recording stage. If we had used Mr. F. Campbell Watson per se, the printed thing, the recordist in there would have been frantic with the dials and moving microphones. We made it foolproof recordingwise. The sound as you hear it on the track, that's what you've always heard, except that we wrote it more practically for recording. The same registration, the same color, but effective for the microphones the first time down. That's why we reorchestrated it. If George had been alive and on the picture, I can assure you that neither Solly nor Connie nor I would have done any adaptation. George would have done it. But he would have done exactly what we did; I know it.

Recording sessions are set up in three-hour units. As I recall, we recorded the ballet in three days, meaning that there were six sessions and some overtime.

Saul Chaplin:

I remember one session was at night. I think one day we had three sessions, so I think it took five sessions, or fifteen hours, just to record the 17-minute score.

Gene Kelly:

In the beginning, I tried to describe what I was doing to everyone with whom I was working, including the assistants, the costume designer, and the music men. You start working out an idea in a chair. You just don't get up and dance on the floor; your feet don't work it out; you work it out first in your head, just like the guy who writes the story. To chaps like Saul Chaplin or Johnny Green, who have this kind of eye and feel because of their theatrical background, I'd say, "Well, I like this, but this I don't know about." So in the initial stages you always had some help. We were also here every night with Jeannie Coyne and Carol Haney, just working out costumes and colors and things like that.

The days we really had to use for rehearsals with Leslie and the dancers. If I had composed something, I'd turn it over to one of them. Then I'd compose something else and turn it over to the other one and say, "All right, drill them on it." There again the repertory idea came in. Carol had been with me six years, Jeannie not quite that long, but she had been around studios. Jeannie had an added thing: She had great inner sense about dancers' clothes. That's a very important thing. For example, in one scene we might have three dresses made for Leslie— one knee-length, one knee-length but cut completely different, and one cut above the knees—and the audience would never know they saw three different skirts. One would be for the dance, one for the scene, and one for a section of the dance where we'd want her leg extended. You see, this is an item itself, just knowing what costumes will move well on dancers.

Carol Haney's training of dancers was fabulous and continued to be so after she became an independent choreographer. She was that good because I was always so mean. I'd say, "It has to be right! Go back and do it again." Her precision, you know, her eye for seeing that everybody did it on the beat, was wonderful.

Leslie Caron (Actress):

Arthur Freed would drift into the rehearsing studio quite often. Always his hands in his pockets, always jangling coins, always on a diet, always fat and completely inarticulate and monosyllabic, but a genius for what was good and what wasn't. He knew how to put talented people together, and he knew when the combination was good and the result was good. He also knew when it wasn't good. He couldn't tell you why. He cannot articulate why it's not good enough or why it does work, but he knows when it's on the right path. He was very shy, too.

Saul Chaplin:

The interpolation in the ballet, where the five dancers do a tap dance, was Gene's idea. Because he felt that the thing was full of girl dancers and all kinds of costumes, he wanted to do a section with five men.

Gene Kelly:

When we did the Rousseau, the zoo thing, I purposely had the fellows do everything the way George M. Cohan would do it, like an American would do it. In the middle of that Frenchy scene, and that's as Frenchy looking as you can get, I wanted to do something immediately identifiable as American. The little girls came out with their hats and had their hands up in little white gloves, which we tried to make look like white doves, Frenchy as could be. But the American men were to be as American as you can get. Don't forget, this is an American looking at Paris, so we had the canes and the straw hats and we walked like Cohan and we did a tap dance. Now, you could go into the jungles of Africa and you'd know immediately that those fellows were Americans. That's what I wanted.

Also, tap dancing fit the music exactly. You can tap dance to practically anything in *An American in Paris*. Gershwin's beat is perfect tap music. I don't necessarily like to tap, and if I hadn't felt I needed it to portray the Americans I probably wouldn't have done it. None of us ever like to tap that much because you always have to synchronize those taps in a postrecording session. Because of leakage on the sound track during the playback of the music, you have to wear earphones and look at yourself on the screen and then somehow synchronize your taps. It's the worst chore in show business, and everybody who's had to do it hates it!

Preston Ames:

We went from the Dufy setting into a flower market in the style of Renoir. We created the style of Renoir in what we needed to tell our story. Then we went to the Montmartre street, and we felt that nobody ever did Montmartre streets like Utrillo, so that was painted and built as if by Utrillo. His palette worked itself into the costumes of the men. They started in military uniforms and then changed into their George M. Cohan costumes. The next transition took us into the Henri Rousseau carnival square and zoo. This was the kind of thing that Rousseau had painted. Van Gogh was next, and this was the Place de l' Opéra. This probably, as far as George Gibson and his Scenic Depart-

ment was concerned, was the most difficult to do, not because of th
painting but because of the actual physical job of using paint that was
15 per cent plaster. Those poor guys went home exhausted at night from
just toting buckets of plaster. Then, from there we went to a frozen
frame of Gene Kelly in one of the little sketches of Toulouse-Lautrec's
called *Chocolat*. This was a monochromatic transition which was very
difficult to do because it was color without color. This then dissolved to
a wildly brilliant, colorful section with mirrors, back in the Van Gogh
Place de l'Opéra and ended with a return to the Place de la Concorde
and a huge finale.

Irene Sharaff:

The scale that these things were done in was staggering. Just to do a
painting as a backdrop is a bore, but trying to catch the feel of these
painters in this grand form was a very tricky thing.

Vincente Minnelli:

Preston and myself got Gibson very excited about this. He made the
paintings of these backings almost like a game, a competition among
all his men.

Preston Ames:

George Gibson was the unsung hero of this entire film, especially
of the ballet. Without him there would have been no ballet as we did
it. We would have had to settle for something a lot less.

George Gibson:

We got into the problem of painting à la Utrillo when we started
painting in pastel. Here, as with Dufy, we had the problem of scale. It's
one thing to take a half-inch brush and lay in pastel on a canvas; it's

another thing to lay on impasto on something that's twenty or thirty feet high and two hundred feet long. We had to paint it first as a sketch, then take that and paint each brush stroke on the backing. Each brush stroke became something maybe two feet long and a foot wide. To paint this in relief, we augmented our paint with the aid of Textone or filler material so that when it dried it would dry actually looking like pastel. When we shellacked it, it would have the quality of an oil painting, and naturally we also used this technique throughout Van Gogh's Place de l' Opéra section. You know how Van Gogh used to paint with those great strokes, so we're up to our ears in bags of Textone getting this oil quality on this overscaled painting. Normally we would paint these paintings on our frame, but the impasto effect was so large you couldn't get the damned stuff to hang on the walls. The Textone and the paint would become a viscous fluid. On a vertical canvas you couldn't get it to hang up and stay there, so we put the canvas down flat on the floor, and we would paint the heavy, viscous impasto paint on the cloth of the floor. Then, after it dried, we would set it up for the glazing or the breaking up or whatever was necessary to develop the idea of the drawing.

We would start one of these gigantic designs by getting the research together. Preston would say, "Well, look, maybe we could make one wall with this treatment of the street. Then they go into a store and come out of it. I think here maybe we should use a church on the backing. The church in this painting is good; let's use it." So, at times, if we could take the research and use it directly without going to a sketch, that's all we needed.

My people working on the backings, the artists, Coakely and Wayne Hill and Harry Tepker, Ben Carre, Clark Orovins—all of my people who were leading this parade would also come up with ideas. The motion picture industry has a notorious reputation for always being a one-man deal: "Here is the man who does all this." Well, in point of fact, there wasn't any one man who did all this. Everybody did it. I had a department of men on whom I relied to a point that nothing could have been done without them.

You have to remember that these fellows working on this thing were the end result of an extremely selective process. We were working here on the ballet with perhaps twelve or fifteen people. They were the end result of a selective process in which maybe a hundred people were involved during the years. I knew talent when I saw talent. When someone came in with extraordinary talent, I always contrived to hang on to him if I could. Of course, through the years a lot of people came in and a lot of people left, and there would always be one that I would hang on to. So this was really, you might say, the cream that we had skimmed off the top, working at this time.

We did the Renoir sequence with the flower stalls, and we actually did a duplicate of Renoir's famous *Pont Neuf*. We were copying it from a reproduction of Renoir's painting that was maybe twelve inches long and five or six inches high, and we had to put this on something that was one hundred feet long and thirty feet high. Naturally, everything had to be drawn—the minutest brush stroke, the assimiliation of a brush stroke, all had to be drawn so that what Renoir had done with a four-inch brush we had to copy so that it would be three or four feet long. We would have to reproduce all of the nuances of color that creep into the paint, you know, the process of Renoir taking his brush and picking up a little blue and a little white and a little yellow. Putting it together gets the fusion of these colors. We had to duplicate all this.

Problems of scale would always arise. Let's start with the Renoir flower market. When we draw it we enlarge it. We would have to decide the scale of it. Was it too big, for instance, or was it too small? We'd enlarge through all sorts of processes: the old square-by-square enlargement method or just through straight drawing, by just division of the canvas and the reproduction of a few areas.

You have to remember that time was of the essence in these things. It had to be on a stage at a specific time; otherwise everybody else couldn't get their work done. There would be seven or eight artists working in different areas of the backing, or phases of it, because you'd have several flats going at once. We'd have a couple working on one line of flats, and two or three others working on another line. In addition to a lead man, we'd have journeyman scenic artists, and the assistants who were doing all the carrying and the heavy work of mixing. Then the pieces of the canvas would be taken to the stage and assembled.

Once assembled, there would be corrections. We'd rediscuss things; some new business would develop. Kelly in his rehearsal would want to go here, where there was no door. We'd then have to revamp that flat and make a door and then tie it in to the steps and the stairs and all of the other various things of the flat.

Vincente Minnelli:

As I have mentioned, I wasn't too well pleased with Gilks's work as a cameraman, because every single little thing was lit, and there were certain things that had to have mood. So when we got to the ballet, we laid off to rehearse, and I insisted on using another cameraman, someone who had never worked in color, John Alton. I'd made *Father of the Bride* with him. Before that, he'd only done melodramas and some very fine black-and-white things at Eagle-Lion. He was disliked, however, by the other cameramen because he had written a book called *Painting with Light*. They all thought he was egotistical. But he was so fast and used so few lights. I got along just wonderfully with him. I felt that the ballet needed someone who would live dangerously. We had to take chances because in the ballet there is nothing that was done afterwards in the lab; everything you see was done on the set. So I decided it needed John Alton.

Joe Cohn (MGM Vice-President):

I remember I saw something of Alton's which I was greatly impressed with. He used one light and threw it against a building with enormous economy, I think it might have been in *T Men*. I got him to the studio and I hired him. I had to pay him $800 a week, more money than I was paying any other cameraman. I gave him that salary because I wanted to hire him and he wouldn't work for less, and I wanted to shake up the other cameramen. I thought our cameramen had become too complacent, and I felt we needed a cameraman who would shake the hell out of the place, and I thought Alton could do that for me. In lighting, he saved a lot of time by lighting only from the floor. This made him very unpopular with the other cameramen.

Walter Strohm (Head of the Production Department):

Most people hated him. They said, "How can Minnelli put Alton on the ballet?" I said, "Because he knows how to light." Believe me, he knew how to light! I'll tell you a director who's difficult to get along with but who was crazy about Alton: Richard Brooks. He thought

Alton was just great. Alton had a technique for a production man—and now I'm talking about my side of it—that was very helpful. I know why they didn't like him, and that was the thing that we liked about him most: He had none of this old studio technique. Some cameramen used the same lighting technique every time to light a set, because, the more units they had up there to light with, the more electricians it gave jobs to. Alton didn't give a damn about any of that. He was interested in getting an effect, and he could get an effect like that. He was very fast. Of course, that killed them; he was too fast for them. They didn't like that. He was ready, and the director was left holding the set. He just said to the director, "I'm ready." The director wanted to take two hours while they rehearsed and fussed around, and Alton said, "No, I'm ready. Anytime you want to."

Ed Woehler (Unit Production Manager):

Minnelli would suggest something, and Alton would "yes" him right away. Gilks wouldn't necessarily do that. I think Alton probably married some very rich woman; that's the type of guy he was—Wore spats and gloves and everything. He was a kind of go-getter, a society man.

Gene Kelly:

Vincente suggested a lot of the light effects. We'd say, "Wouldn't this be great?" but often they took a lot of time, because cameramen can get very stubborn. But we found Alton willing to try anything. We'd say, "Can you do this?" He'd say, "Yeah, that's easy. Yeah." And for the first few days we were sort of worried because we'd been used to a lot of cameramen saying, "You guys are nuts. You can't do that." It seemed that about every picture we'd try something new and the person with whom we'd be working would say, "No, you can't do that," because they had never done it before.

Preston Ames:

Sometimes there were petty corrections. Sometimes the corrections were warranted, and sometimes they weren't. For instance, the Van

Gogh set was probably the roughest to do, because here we had something that was just unbelievable. It was so beautiful and so hard to do, and everybody had to work so hard on it. John Alton, one day, set yellow light filters on all the lights, and he said to Vincente, "This is the only way you can shoot this thing, you know." And I looked at him, and I said, "What? What are you doing?" And he said, "Oh, this is the only way it can be done." So I had to get a hold of Kelly and say, "Kelly, do you want a bright yellow face when you're dancing?" And I said to Sharaff, "Do you want this bright yellow light all over your costumes?" She was furious, and there was a battle royal about it, you know: "Rip those lousy goddamn things off," and that's what happened. He started to get smart. He was working his way and not our way, and our way had been studied. He just came on the scene and thought this was very clever. He did the same thing on the next set; he put some purple filters on the Toulouse-Lautrec thing. It was horrible. It was just horrible. But he was painting with light. He loved to use that expression. This fellow was doing a petty thing, and he was destroying everything we had worked months to get, which was the perfect matching of everybody's thing clicking and working together. All of a sudden, he was saying, "I'm going to show you really how it should be done," and he loused it up, but royally. We corrected it, and in spite of everything it came out all right, but you had to be very careful that somebody didn't pull a fast one on you and really do things wrong. You just couldn't let them.

Leslie Caron (Actress):

The ballet part of it was the hardest. It was very unsatisfactory from a dancer's point of view, coming straight from the stage. First of all, I was forever struggling with the floors. They were too hard, and they had a mania for painting them bright colors. Some very conscientious prop man would come and shine them with dust cloths, so that before we started rehearsing they were like mirrors. Now, everybody knows that you can't dance on a mirror. It's got to be rather unslippery; otherwise you just fall all the time. Gene would always take me to the set. We had this delicious pianist, Saul Chaplin, and Saul and Gene would troop along, and everybody would come and test the stage. It was terrifying because it was so flat! You see, the stages that I'd danced on were all raked, and this one was flat, endless, and completely slippery. Also, there was no give to the floor at all, which is terrible on your ankles, calves, and knees. So I would fall once or twice and mutter, "Well, it's so slippery, Gene." Then I would put resin on my shoes and leave great, big white marks. So Gene said, "Well, it's terribly simple. All we have to do is repaint the floor." So, every time we had a new set we had to repaint the floor. Then the painters just got into the habit of putting sand in the paint when I had to dance somewhere. But that didn't solve the problem, either. You see, on wood you don't slip; you can turn. The satin of your shoe just doesn't stay on the ground; it rotates. But, when you have sandy paint, it rips the satin, and your shoe sort of stays as your foot turns. I mean it was frightening! Anyway, we went through it, and on some of the dancing for my little numbers, which we started with, I was a great pain in the neck for everybody.

Also, I was feeding myself then, and I didn't know much about nutrition, and in order to keep slim I would just eat nothing. Consequently, I was very weak and very much anemic, but Gene was my defender. He'd say to me, "If you're too ill, just tell me and stand by me, and I'll say you're too ill, and we will collect insurance and go off one day, and you can lie in bed all day and rest up." But we finally did get it done, and I must say I was pleased with it.

Preston Ames:

Gene choreographed it, but Vincente was the one who was the director. We never lost the fact that he was the skipper. Gene also realized that you have to have one director. It's one thing to choreograph it and another thing to have the thing pulled together. After all, it wasn't just one ballet, one dance number, it was six or eight numbers, six or eight big sets, and you had to have a preconceived notion.

Gene Kelly:

I had already shot the insert numbers, but I did not want to shoot the ballet without Vincente, for two reasons—number one, we were not only colleagues but pals, which would have been reason enough, emotionally; but, number two, his eye, his experience, is just invaluable. Nobody does a musical alone. Nobody! Minnelli's eye for color is the great thing. I don't think you can find a better costume designer in the world than Irene Sharaff, but, when you get all the choreography done and get everybody down on the stage floor, you can always find that Minnelli will have some way to adjust the color so that we'll have a better composition, a better look. In the ballet, for example, when he came out of doing *Father's Little Dividend*, which just took him six weeks in all, the whole ballet was planned and staged. It was all ready. All we had to do was say, "Roll 'em." But Vincente was able to polish it even more.

One setting in the ballet, the Toulouse-Lautrec café scene, with various characters here and there, is a good indication of what he could do.

We both came out of the school of John Murray Anderson on Broadway; he was sort of our mentor. He knew what to do with color and light. He was a great man of the theater, and Minnelli and I had worked under him. He was just great! Anderson could put a blue light on a scene and make the scene work where it wouldn't work with an amber or pink light. Like Minnelli, he was not a dance director. He just had this kind of an eye. Anyway, I remember, in the Toulouse-Lautrec scene Minnelli said, "Let's switch these two people around," and he switched them. He put the chap who's in blue down front, I remember very well, moved him down front and moved somebody else about 5 feet in back, and it was suddenly much better than Irene and I had visualized it.

Arthur Freed (Producer):

Then we just did it. We shot the ballet in a couple of weeks, without a flaw. You've got to prepare; then it's easy.

Preston Ames:

Arthur Freed was purring like a Cheshire cat because now this thing which he had always wanted to do had come to life. It had happened.

7

Postproduction

Gene Kelly (Actor and Choreographer):

People in the business thought we were crazy. They heard about the
ballet—you know, seventeen minutes' worth of dance. Everybody said,
"Oh, my God! What are they up to now?" I ran into one of the deans
of show business one night, and he said, "I hear you did a ballet with
no songs." He shook his head solemnly and said, "I hope you know what
you're doing, kid."

Preston Ames (Art Director):

At the point following the ballet, we were at a complete loss on how
to end the picture. How do you bring two people together when one
of them, Gene, is on the top of a platform, looking down on a street,
which was four levels below, where stood Leslie.

Knowing how Vincente loved stairs, anything that had levels, I
mustered my courage and said to him, "What would you think of the
idea of having Gene running down steps, Leslie running up steps, and
having them finally meet, overlooking all of Paris?" Well, you threw a
crumb to Vincente and he expected a banquet back. He said, "I don't
know how you're going to do it, but do it."

As a hubcap to this whole thing, we had built some cement stairs for our version of *Kismet*, the one that was done with Ronald Colman and Marlene Dietrich, back five or ten years previous to this, and here these stairs were, sitting on our back lot. They were great stairs; they were wide, and they afforded us enough room to do something. They probably went twenty feet in the air, but I needed three of them, and I only had one. I needed Kelly's platform and then three runs down to a street, which would then overlook all of Paris. So I went up on a boatswain's chair with a boom, and I had them drag me all over the place at the level which I thought this would work. I went back and sketched the operation as I saw it should be. To make a sketch of this was one thing; to face reality was something else. With Vincente, you never presented him just a pretty picture. You had to substantiate it with the fact that you could get this on camera. Vincente was always one for looking through his camera and setting up his people accordingly. It was almost a fetish with him. The camera operator, the cameraman—sure they knew their jobs, but he had to give the final little touches which were indispensable to his way of operating. Anything that you gave him he had to be able to actually do.

Going back now to our stairway, we showed him a sketch of these three stairs going down, with the platform foreground where Gene is and the street below and all of Paris in the background. Obviously, the first question is "Vincente, is this what you had in mind?" It isn't a question of "Do you like it or don't you?" It is, rather, "Is this the story you wanted to tell?" It was, and he was very happy with it. Then we went into step two, which was the realization of this thing.

At this time, we had at our studio a man by the name of Dupy, and Dupy, in the Matte Painting Department, had developed a device called the Dupy Duplicator. Everybody thinks that the duplicator was part of his name, but it wasn't. His duplicating machine allowed us to record a camera operation—tilting or painting—so that, if we were to go on our back lot where the stairs were and photograph a scene with this particular thing and then tilt our camera up, we would be able to take this same camera and the duplicator and put it back in the studio and, with our matte painting, do the same operation on a painted background. The details of this operation are quite complicated, but be satisfied in knowing that the Dupy Duplicator allowed us to finish the picture as we had planned, using our one staircase from *Kismet* and a six- by five-foot painting of Paris. On the screen, Kelly and Caron run up three flights of stairs and embrace in front of a landscape that is a 180-degree view of Paris at night. This whole operation—the running up the steps, bringing the film back into the studio, and rephotographing it in front of the painting of Paris—I imagine took three or four weeks. Incidentally, the Dupy Duplicator won an Academy Award this same year.

Ed Woehler (Unit Production Manager):

The last day they shot the ballet, I'm finished with it. Then it goes into the postproduction period—the dubbing and the editing. Our department still paid for the orders and ordered the actors. It still dribbled on. If they needed an actor for dubbing, or they needed more music, or they wanted to go back to do a retake, or if they needed anything, then it's still alive. Until the picture is finally released, it isn't finished in our department. There's always that little bit that has to still be done. Somebody's got to do it, and they always call. They'll call and say "we need" this or "we need" that, and then we have to execute that piece, providing it fits into the general plan and they want to spend the money.

Rick Ingersoll (Office Boy):

Gene Kelly threw me off the set once. After they had finished shooting, they were still there, doing poster art. I brought a tour in. He and Leslie were posing for the eight-by-ten camera in dance positions that they would use for advertising. He bawled me out because he didn't realize that I had permission to go on the set. Later, he found that out and came up to the office in the clipping room to apologize.

Preston Ames:

The person with whom I became very closely associated, once we finished shooting, was the film editor. She was a gal that I had never met, because I had never worked before with a film editor. This girl needed my help in very few places. It wasn't a question of whether I could contribute in the sense of telling her how to cut her film, because she knew more about cutting film than most people at the studio, but it was a question of timing. Did I have an idea for a particular little kind of tricky sequence that we had laid out for popping in pictures, or a transition from one to another? "How did this work?" and "How can we cut from one thing to another?" There was a togetherness which was terrific on that. The girl's name is Adrienne Fazan, an extraordinarily outspoken, strange, wonderful, creative female. She was quite something.

Adrienne Fazan (Editor):

I had Editing Room 21. As you came into MGM from the Washington Boulevard side, there were two narrow buildings, with an alley between them that leads to the commissary. There are stairs going up one of those buildings to a balcony and a bridge, and that bridge led right into my cutting room.

It was always agreeable, working on a picture with Freed. He was one of the producers (thank God) that would run with the director and the cutter. There are some producers who won't do that, and there are some directors who will not run, or work, with the producer. That makes it difficult, when the cutter is in the middle. I would run with a director, and when he wanted so-and-so I'd say, "But the producer said" this and that. "Aw, the hell with that; do it!" But Freed wasn't like that, and he trusted Minnelli. When he hired a director on a picture, he gave him the responsibility and trusted him. It was easy working on the Freed pictures. Besides, it's easier to cut musicals than dramatic films. With musical numbers, you go by the music; it's very easy. The dancers and the director take great pains to match action.

Gene Kelly:

In the cutting stage of the picture, I had a steady day-to-day work relationship with Adrienne. The dance numbers were all shot to be cut on a certain beat. When you get a good cutter like Adrienne you say, "Now, in the middle of that turn on the third beat of the bar, as I'm turning, cut to this other angle, and it won't look like a cut"; it won't look like a change. It's not that it won't look like a cut to the practiced eye; it will be a cut, but the audience will not be aware of it. If you want to make the audience aware of a cut, then make them aware of it. If you want the feel of flow, in soft numbers, in numbers with continuity of movement and, let's say, a certain slowness, it's good not to make quick cuts unless you're going for an effect of quick cutting within that framework. That's been done in commercials, but if you want the dance to have a very slow fluid feeling, let's say, "Our Love is Here to Stay," you don't make the audience aware of the change in camera angles.

In filming a dance, you compose each piece of film so it goes together with the next piece. It always matches, because dancers, you see, do the same thing every time. If they don't, they hit each other in the nose or they trip each other. You have to rehearse so that the turn you do this take is exactly the same turn next take, whether the camera's here or there. It's done exactly on the same beat on the sound track.

People have often asked me about the choreography on certain pictures, and I find that they do not understand that a really good film choreographer, as opposed to a stage choreographer, will compose for the camera. Each series of steps has to be shot from a certain angle to be seen best. There is always a "best" angle. You don't, or, I should say, you shouldn't, go down on the set with a dance number and then start trying out different angles on it. It should be composed for certain camera setups to *begin* with. The cutting of it, therefore, should be pretty much mechanical. I would say that there are times when accidental elements creep in, but very rarely. If you look at the ballet and, all of a sudden, in front of that fountain, the *pompiers* come by in their gleaming helmets, and they wipe across the frame and go into the next cut, you know, that can't be an accident, that has to be down pat.

I cut, my philosophy anyway, just simply, so that people can see the scene better. If we have a scene, and the camera is over your shoulder, and you say to me, "Now, what did you do?" and I say, "I shot him." Cut! I'd say "Oh, my God! I certainly can't be over your shoulder and see the expression in your eyes at the same time." That's a very simple way of doing it. Sometimes, in the dance number, no matter how well prepared you are when you're doing this kind of cut, you're going over here and I bring the camera over there. In that case, Adrienne will say, "Let's delay it for another beat before the turn." Sure that happens, but rarely. If it doesn't happen the way you've set it up on the stage, then I'd be very sad indeed.

Adrienne Fazan:

The dailies were very important. In fact, if some of the scenes were too dark or too light or too red or too yellow or too something or other, we would order new prints at the lab's expense. In those days, they had a different system than they have now. Nowadays, if we want a corrected reprint, the studio has to pay for it because nowadays they print everything on a one-color basis. But in 1950 we had corrected prints for the dailies. Everybody wanted the best, even for a work print. They couldn't wait to see how good it was or how beautiful the colors came through.

Minnelli would only look at the film in the projection room and almost never on the moviola. He'd say, "That's not long enough; stay longer. I want him to disappear." He always liked long dissolves, like ten-foot dissolves. In those days, because of colors, the norm was a four-foot dissolve.

Minnelli would never shoot a lot of film. He would only give me enough for the sequence he liked especially well. Mr. Minnelli was a little stingy. He never gave me enough close-ups. He wouldn't break up a sequence the normal way. Every director shoots a long shot, medium shot, close-up, over the shoulder, and so forth. Well, Minnelli wouldn't do that. He'd give me a close-up here and there, sometimes not where I wanted it so that we could cut out a whole page of dialogue that wasn't needed. Sometimes we would take a two-shot of two people and blow it up so it would become a close-up of one person—just for a look or something, in order to eliminate some unnecessary footage. Minnelli sometimes fell in love with certain sequences, and he didn't want them to be broken up or shortened. So he shot that way on purpose, so that it could not be changed in the editing room.

He also moved his camera from here to hell and back. That didn't present me with any problems, because I didn't have any cutting to do. All I did was a little cussing. The producer or Margaret Booth, MGM's Editorial Supervisor, would say, "Go to a close-up; cut in some close-ups." "I haven't got them!" That's why we sometimes would blow up.

Leslie Caron (Actress):

When the film was over I was put on layoff. Twelve weeks out of the year, we were not paid. It was called layoff, and so it was very hard. Of course, I was very economical. I had even put a little money aside, not trusting anyone to help me, ever. I was really like an orphan. I had no work. There was nothing for a long time. They waited to see the results of *An American in Paris*. There must have been three months where I didn't do anything, just nothing. I started giving classes and started acting with my teacher. I also moved to a new apartment, which I think cost $50 a month. It was one room.

Adrienne Fazan:

After I had sequences cut, I would show them to the director, and he would make comments. With Minnelli, he would mostly say, "Too tight," especially if it was somebody walking. He would count very slowly, "one, twooo, threeee, fourrrrrrr, cut!" When I got the film on the moviola, I would count a little faster, which, of course, was all right because I could lengthen the scenes later the way he wanted them. In the final editing, Freed would come in. Then it was up to the producer and the director to argue it out, and they would tighten the picture. Margaret Booth would yell and scream. "It's too slow!" She liked everything very tight, so I would trim it down some more.

Mr. Freed and Minnelli were the first ones to see the first cut. They ran the picture right through and did not make any remarks. The next day, after they had mulled it over in their minds, we would look at one reel at a time and then start to make changes. Changes would mostly be elimination. Once in a while, they would see a close-up and say, "Take it out; stay in the master shot," or "Put a close-up in," or "Stay on the shot longer," or "Trim it." Mostly, it depended on the time of the picture, how long it was. If it ran over two hours, which the first cut always did, they would look for places to eliminate a whole sequence.

Gene Kelly:

Two numbers were cut out because the picture was just too long. This was Freed's decision.

Every picture that I've ever done, we've had to cut one ballad, and sometimes two. Mainly, the reason is that ballads are love songs that come late in the picture—somebody singing, "I Love You"—and it's a *fait accompli*, it's been done. The audience already knows it. No matter how beautifully it's done, they're really wrapped up in the story by this time, and the ballad slows things down. So out goes the ballad. That happened in *On the Town* and in *Summer Stock*. Judy recorded a ballad called "Boys and Girls Like You and Me, We Go On and On," a Rodgers-and-Hammerstein song, one of the greatest ballads ever written. I think she did it in two pictures. Frank Sinatra did it also. It's never been in an MGM musical. "Boys and girls like you and me, we go on and on. Kings and everything, they have their day and are gone." It's applicable to anything. It always had to be done near the end of the picture and, therefore, was expendable.

Now, about "Crush on You" in *An American in Paris:* In my great wisdom, I said, "Well, since I have this whisky Irish tenor and nobody's interested, I'm going to sing a love song, which is a short love song, and it's going to be done with such humor and panache that it will just have to survive." It was cut! Guetary's number, around the same section of the picture, was also cut. He did his number thinking in the bistro, and I was sitting up in the window, again at my place, and the cuts were from where he was to where I am. That's one Vince and I worked out together. There was no dancing to it. It was just a musical number, and we liked it. We saw the rushes and were crazy about it. But that's one of those things.

What really hurt, though, was cutting "I've Got a Crush on You." I love that song; it's one of my favorites. It was all done in the little area of my room. It was charming, just dancing around in my little, silly room. Oh, I put in so much work! God! I rehearsed longer on that than I did on the whole "Singin' in the Rain" number! Then to lose it!

Nina Foch (Actress):

Now, after the picture was over, there was a scene that I had that's gone on the cutting-room floor. I always built a characterization so that, at one moment only, or possibly two, you really see the human being underneath. In life we do not speak what we mean, ever; we bullshit! I mean, we've been taught as children to say, "Kiss Aunt Louise," and you hate Aunt Louise. Normally, we talk about nothing in life, and so I build characterizations in that way so they're like a Persian carpet; there are thousands of little things that I build, so I don't give a shit if you see any particular one of them, because they will accumulate. So

I build this Persian carpet, and I decide the moment at which I'm going to let you have it to let you see who I really am. It'll suddenly come, and if you miss it you've missed it. If I want you to understand, if I am busy trying to make you understand the person I am, you won't understand the person I am, right? One of the cardinal rules of acting: You must not want to explain; it must just happen. All right, the explanation of Milo in *An American in Paris* is in this last scene. Earlier on, she is really Vivienne Segal in *Pay Joey*; she's a killer. But the thing that makes Milo so touching was in this last scene at the black-and-white ball, where I get drunk because I realize that I've lost Gene, and I'm sitting at the table with Oscar Levant, talking about men and why men don't love me. Minnelli says, "Let's do the scene; let's not rehearse; let's just do it." Beautiful. So we did it, and it was marvelous, absolutely *marvelous!* I think it's one of the best pieces of acting I've ever done. I'm just buzzing, about to be a weepy drunk, half-laughing, and suddenly up comes this truly lonely, lonely little girl whose daddy never loved her. That's not in the lines, but you can see she's that kind of woman. A piece of confetti gets in my champagne glass, and I see it, take it out, and look at it. I stop in the middle of the scene, and Oscar takes the time to really look at it. I look up; then I think about it, what it is that's in my glass. "Oh, it's a pill," and I take it like a pill. It's a beautiful moment. I saw the scene, and I knew I had that picture wrapped up. In this scene I reveal how really lost and desperate I am; I mean that's what's in it. It looked ridiculous for Gene to go off with Leslie when you see that scene, because the sympathy is all with Milo; it's got to be.

Acting is my business, and I'm not one to grab the prize, but when I saw this I said to myself, "Oh boy! Shit, man! You've got this. You've got it." I mean I can smell it when it's there; it has a smell after a while. I knew in *John Loves Mary*; I didn't have to wait for the critics. It's all over you; it stinks on you. It smells the other way, too. I've had that other smell, too—"flop sweat" we call it in the theater. Anyway, I got this letter from Arthur Freed, which I have in my files somewhere, saying that he was terribly sorry but that he had to cut this scene out of the picture because it made Leslie seem unsympathetic for Gene to go off with, considering how my scene had played, and that he was forced to take it out of the picture. He wanted me to know, however, that it was an incredibly fine piece of work. So I have a letter for my pains. But you can't eat letters, right?

Adrienne Fazan:

After the first cut, I would make my changes. Then we would run it again, and they might make a few more changes, mostly very little, unless the picture was in trouble. We would finally run it for the music people, reel by reel. After each reel, the producer and the director would talk scoring, and I would order my dissolves or whatever opticals had to be ordered and get it ready for scoring and sound effects.

Preston Ames:

My final budget figures worked out this way: I had a budget of $79,000 on the book, and I spent $81,000. That's 2½ per cent off, which is not bad. With the ballet, I had as a budget $37,000, and, as it turned out, I spent $49,000, which is 30 per cent over. Actually, when you consider what we had, that wasn't too bad either. There were constant changes of treatment and then constant corrections. Nobody was ever happy with it until it was finally finished. We were groping half the time for the right thing before we hit upon it. Well, that experiment might cost 10 or 20 per cent more than you anticipated, but we were out to do it properly or not at all, and that's why there's the difference in the overage between the book and the ballet.

George Gibson (Head of the Scenic Art Department):

After we had finished with the backings for the ballet (let's take the Renoir), I would assign a stock number to it; say, it was 5747, then the name of the picture, *An American in Paris*, then the set and the size of the backing. Then there would be a description—"Renoir: *Pont Neuf*, *American in Paris* Dream Sequence." Then it would say "day" (or "night"). I had a standard chart on which I added each thing as we did it.

After the backing was shot, it would be struck, and it would come back to the basement and be assigned a rack number and recorded in the stock book as number 5747 in Rack D #57. Now, naturally, how many times are you going to use a Renoir or a Dufy backing? Not many

FORM 72

METRO-GOLDWYN-MAYER PICTURES
CULVER CITY
CALIFORNIA

INTER-OFFICE COMMUNICATION

To ___ MR. GIBBONS _____

Subject ___ CLOSING COSTS OF PRODUCTION #1507 ___

From ___ ART DEPT ___ Date __ 1-17-51 __

Jan. 1951

PROD: 1507 - "AN AMERICAN IN PARIS"   A/C - 711   A/C - 711-1

Prod: Started: 8-1-50
Prod: Closed   1-3-51

		Estm. Cost	Actual Cost	Estm. Cost	Actual Cost
01.	Ext. Montmarte St & Square	6062	4803	----	9
02.	Ext. & Int. Cafe	11,433	11,039	825	471
03.	Int. Pension Stair & Hall	5339	6128	---	20
04.	Int. Pension 3rd Floor	4113	4471	107	343
05.	Ext. Beach & Quai	10,784	10,015	----	229
06.	Int. Maison Duclos	1200	1377	----	---
07.	Int. Henri's Apt.	1995	2135	----	12
08.	Ext. Cafe & Quai	1155	872	----	---
09.	Int. Milo's Hotel	1211	902	----	---
10.	Int. Cafe Florida	3501	3405	----	---
11.	Int. 2nd Fl. Bed Room	450	580	---	---
12.	Int. Milo's Hotel Suite	968	939	---	---
13.	Ext. Stage Door & Alley	817	901	----	---
14.	Int. Stage Stair	3863	9460	----	359
15.	Int. Artists' Ball	11,704	8617	----	506
16.	Int. Nicer Studio	841	850	----	8
17.	Int. School des Beaux Arts	---	98	----	---
18.	Ext. Perfume Shop	463	740	----	---
19.	Ext. Nicer Studio	310	343	----	---
20.	Ext. Terrace - Artists' Ball	3631	3042	---	433
21.	Ext. Artists' Ball & Stairs	4166	3080	----	301
22.	Int. Symphony Hall	4710	2936	234	250
23.	Int. Henri's Car	95	105	----	---
25.	Ext. Montmarte St. - Ballet	2798	3220	379	417
26.	Ext. Champs Elysees - Ballet	1467	1772	----	42
27.	Int. Moulin Rouge Ballet	3006	3435	135	155
28.	Ext. Place de la Concorde- Ballet	14,506	24,073	2618	1996
29.	Int. Baroque Set	488	1153	60	83
30.	Int. Victorian Set	395	671	----	---
31.	Int. Louis XVI Set	488	948	---	17
32.	Int. Modern Set	447	743	----	---
33.	Int. Jacobean Set	497	898	----	7
34.	Int. Biedermier Set	487	788	--	---
36.	Ext. Opera Ballet	7672	9052	250	393
37.	Ext. Carnival Square - Ballet	6735	7435	275	212
38.	Ext. Flower Mart - Ballet	3728	4364	----	53
39.	Ext. Guetary Poster	110	150	----	---
40.	Ext. Sketch	193	395	----	---
41.	Ext. Quai - Montage of Sketch	100	167	----	---
43.	Ext. Montmarte St.	200	43	---	---
44.	Ext. Fountain - Ballet	285	585	---	---
	Sub-totals	126,417.	136,089.	4883.	6946.

10 556   29 073

111,911   111,956

Closing Costs for Art Department

INTER-OFFICE COMMUNICATION				
To **MR. GIBBONS**				
Subject **CLOSING COSTS OF PRODUCTION #1507**				
From **ESTIMATING ART DEPT** Date **1-17-51**				

	PROD: #1507 -"AMERICAN IN PARIS"	A/C - 711		A/C - 712-1	
		Estm. Cost	Actual Cost	Estm. Cost	Actual Cost
70.	Int. Milo's Car	80	118	---	---
71.	Int. Jerry's Taxi	35	78	---	---
72.	Ext. Notre Dame - Montage	65	32	---	---
73.	Ext. Opera Montage	50	103	---	---
	Sub-totals	230	331	---	---
	TOTALS - - - - - - - -	126,647	136,360	4883	6946
	Cost - A/C 711 & 712-1		143,606.		

times. So I decided that this was something that could be written off completely as subject matter in our stock. Along comes a need for something else, so you take the Renoir backing out and you repaint it with another subject matter entirely. It will still carry the same stock number, but now it will have a new description, which has to be inserted, for example, "Arizona desert, day cloud sky, yellow foreground." We repainted all the *An American in Paris* ballet backings in this fashion.

Adrienne Fazan:

After we got a final cut from Freed, the negative was taken and cut at Technicolor. They take the master print and match it to the cutting print. Before they would make the first answer print, we would run the work print with them. The director, especially, would be there to tell them that certain scenes weren't dark enough or light enough or red enough or something. He would tell them, "This is to be a special effect." After the negative was cut, I would get the first answer print. After we got it back, we would all look at it and scream at the color.

It would go back to Technicolor for corrections until we got what we wanted in a release print.

The camera original film was destroyed because MGM didn't have the room to store it. They would keep the work print sometimes for five

American - Paris Ballet

Set	Budget	Estimat	Cost.
Ext. Champs Élysées b & w & color - Dufy :	3600	1467 -	1547
Ext. Place de la Concorde Dufy -	9500	14506 -	22,070
Ext. Flower market Renoir -	3400	3728 -	4168
Ext. montmartre Street Utrillo -	4400	2792 -	2755
Ext. Fountain (Blues Number)	3900		585
revamp Ext. Place de l'Opera. Van Gogh -	3900	7672 -	8047
Int. moulin Rouge. Toulouse Lautrec -	3900	3006 -	3045
Ext Carnival Square. Henri Rousseau	4400	6735 -	7066
Total	37.000 -		49,283 -
Over budget		12,283 - (30%)	

Fountain on place de la Concorde.	simple scheme 3580	perforated scheme 7000	cost 9500

Budget Memo

years and then destroy it. They would also keep all the trims of the picture for about five years, until all the foreign releases were out. After the picture was cut and the negative was cut, they would make trailers from the outtakes.

Alan Jay Lerner (Author and Screenwriter):

When I came back to California, I saw the rough cut of *Royal Wedding* the same day I saw a rough cut of *An American in Paris*. In those days, writers didn't hang around. I did what I had to do and went home. Well, when I saw *Royal Wedding* I was ready to commit suicide. I realized what an amateur I was as far as that film was concerned. But, when I saw *An American in Paris*, I turned to my friend Lilly Messinger and said, "It's going to win the Academy Award." I told her that it was the best musical that I had ever seen.

Rick Ingersoll:

Once the picture was completed and all the features and copy were written, more and more people got involved in it. It then became advertising; it became exploitation, tie-outs, tie-ins, openings, premieres, whatever it might be. As the picture went on, more and more and more people got involved, until finally, at the time of the preview and release, the entire publicity and advertising departments would be involved.

Howard Strickling (Head of the Publicity Department):

As soon as the picture is finished, you make the maximum effort in presenting the film to the press. You work on the theory that everything is as important as you make it. So, when you get a picture like *An American in Paris*, that looks very big, you take it and have a sneak in Santa Barbara or San Diego. That gets in the press: "MGM is so excited about *An American in Paris* that they are sneaking it in key cities." As a matter of fact, what we would do many times is not tell anyone we invited from the press for the preview where we were going. This builds up an aura of importance for it. We'd just say, "Be in front of the administration building at 5:30." Everyone would meet, and there would be six cars, and the cars would take off, and no one would know where they were going.

Then we'd try to get stories in the trade papers the next day about the audience in Santa Barbara going wild over the picture. We'd get the theater manager to send wires about what a sensational response there was to the picture. Then we'd have a second sneak, in Long Beach. Here we would tip off one of the columnists about the sneak preview. He'd be very happy because this is a big scoop for him, and he'd write a big thing for it. Pretty soon, you get the picture in the air. Finally, when you get down to having your official preview, you make it almost like a premiere. You have special programs printed up and special seats reserved. Special members of the press are invited with their wives and families. Members of my department would take certain people to dinner first and then escort them to the theater as their special guests. All this to give it that important build-up.

Arthur Freed (Producer):

The first preview we had of *An American in Paris* was in Pasadena. It was disastrous!

Vincente Minnelli (Director):

The first preview was a natural disaster. The sound went off. I'll never forget it, because you couldn't hear any dialogue. It was all kind of like under water. And hardly any music. But, for some reason, no one stopped the film. I guess everyone was too dazed. And it went on and on. We came back to Ira's house, and all of us were so bewildered that we were ready to cut our throats. Then, a few days later, we had another preview, in some other theater, where the sound was all right, and it was sensational. But that first one was awful—the most awful thing I've ever gone through in my life!

Arthur Freed:

The reviews were pretty good, but the critics didn't like the story line. They said it was weak. Myself, I think it was the right story line for the Gershwin music.

Newsweek (October 8, 1951):

On the debit side is a silly story by Alan Jay Lerner about an ex-patriate artist Gene Kelly who greatly appeals to a rich blond *patronne* while making poor headway with a *poule* who works for a perfumer. This situation is scarcely relieved when the dancer Kelly, the singer Georges Guetary and the pianist Oscar Levant, Gershwin's relentless Boswell, indulge in some of the heaviest handed plugging to which buoyant Gershwin tunes . . . were ever subjected.

Bosley Crowther (Film Reviewer, *New York Times*, October 14, 1951):

Mr. Kelly's the one who pulls the faint thread of Alan Jay Lerner's peach-fuzz script into some sort of pattern of coherence and keeps it from snapping in a hundred pieces and blowing away.

Étienne Chaumetier (Film Reviewer, French Magazine *Positif*):

One is left breathless by this giddy succession of images in which all is at once unexpected and impeccable. Is there a French director (Jean Renoir included) who could use Dufy, Renoir, Utrillo, Rousseau, Toulouse-Lautrec, surrealism, and pictures of history and genre (let us not forget *Les Charmes de l'Existence* by Kast and Gremillon) with as much verve and exactitude.

William Hogan (Film Reviewer, *San Francisco Chronicle*, November 27, 1951):

. . . to borrow a realistic expression from the film trade press, this is entertainment for "mass and class" alike. It is an unqualified success, the best entertainment of its kind.

Arthur Knight (Film Reviewer, *Saturday Review*):

Everything about this picture is calculated to the last detail, to the last effect, to the last dollar. And MGM with several million dollars tied up in this production gently but persistently keeps you actually aware of each dollar in every foot of film—and especially in the climactic title ballet, a number spread over an entire sound stage and involving all available ballet dancers west of the Mississippi. But even this proves less interesting, less imaginative, less inventive than the ballets of *Red Shoes* from which it clearly derives.

New Statesman and Nation (August 18, 1951):

By far the most original and successful ballet the cinema has devised will be found in the last twenty minutes of *An American in Paris*. Let me emphasize that this new screen ballet is not merely a bit of film ingenuity such as, portentously and rather horribly, we have experienced from *Red Shoes*. . . . it attains a genuine art of its own.

Variety (August 29, 1951):

Metro has another sock box-office winner in *An American in Paris*. Film is one of the most imaginative musical confections turned out in years. Miss Caron is a beauteous, lissome number with an attractively pert personality and plenty of s.a.

New Yorker (October 6, 1951):

Never too tightly confined by its slender story, *An American in Paris* skips from love in the moonlight to handsome ballets with the greatest of ease and Mr. Kelly is always ready, willing and able to execute a tap dance.

Los Angeles Examiner (November 19, 1951):

Sheerly enchanting is *An American in Paris*. The most imaginative, original, chic and dazzling musical of the year, or of last year and probably of next year and the next.

John K. Sherman (*Minneapolis Star*, November 11, 1951):

Everybody will soon be talking about the ballet that climaxes the new film at the World, *An American in Paris*, and naturally I want to get my word in before I'm drowned out. This swirling, kaleidoscopic dance number is one of the most imaginative sequences in recent Holly-wood musicals. It's a little overdone, of course, but not to the extent of losing its artistry or lessening its impact on the eye. It's a terrific climax to a terrif picture.

Richard L. Coe (*Washington Post*, November 7, 1951):

An American in Paris is the best musical I've ever seen.

Arthur Freed:

Critics are funny on musicals. You know, you can practically start with all of Cole Porter's shows. They murdered them! They murdered George's *Rhapsody in Blue*. Ira keeps a whole set of bad reviews at the house. The thing was not to do a biography of George. That had already been done by Warner Brothers in 1947. The thing was to do something with humor, which the Gershwin music has, and to really let the audience hear it done right. I thought our characters were good, and I thought they were real.

Alan Jay Lerner:

The criticism that I remember was about the sentimentality of it. There has always been the kind of critic that views the musical as being the intellectual brothel. They can go and see the girls and the pretty legs; they don't want to be bothered with the story. They don't want to be asked to feel anything. They just want to go and get their jollies. Every time you write a film or a play, you get two hundred reviews. After a while, you get to be immune to them. I know that the first review that I ever read of *An American in Paris* was in the *New*

York Times, and that was a bad one, but the picture won an Academy Award. Also, the first review that I ever read of *Gigi* was terrible, and that won an Academy Award also. But I would rather not have bad reviews, thank you very much.

Daily Variety:

San Francisco, Oct 3. [1951]—Rave reviews and upped prices are helping *An American in Paris* to go for a sock $40,000 on its initial week at the Warfield.

New York, Oct. 11—Broadway first-runs got a nice mid-week hypo with the close of the world series games and an all-day rain today. Standout is *An American in Paris*, plus stage show at the Music Hall. The Metro musical finished its first week with a smash $158,000 and is holding to a very big $20,000 today, the first day of the second round.

New York, Nov. 4—*An American in Paris* is still in the chips with around $86,000 in four days of fifth week at the Music Hall for the outstanding money in the city. Figure is sufficient to insure a sixth session.

Los Angeles, Nov. 13—Long holiday weekend and a half-dozen new films are helping Los Angeles first-run theaters to their best week since Labor Day. . . . A big factor in the $206,000 prospects is the tremendous pace of Metro's *An American in Paris*. Picture established a single day record at the Egyptian a giant $12,200 take. *Paris* did an incredible $6,400 in the 1,538-seat Egyptian Sunday. Aiding the record pace are prices that range from 80 cents to $1.50, against regular scale of 70 cents to $1.10.

Chicago, Dec. 3—*Streetcar Named Desire* seems due for fine $17,000 in fourth week at the Grand. Fair is *An American in Paris* third frame at the State-Lake.

Boxoffice (December 8, 1951):

In its first run engagements in key cities over the country *An American in Paris* has run up a box-office score of 184 percent of normal business. In Cleveland it did 355 percent of normal business at the Stillman and has been running for seven weeks. While this was the highest percentage tallied, Boston, Minneapolis, Pittsburgh and San Francisco did business of 200 percent or over and there is every reason to believe that when it goes to the neighborhoods and the small town houses, the reaction to it will be almost as good as in the first run houses.

Irene Sharaff (Costume Designer):

I was excited really at seeing the ballet, because I left just before the ballet was finished. I had to go back to New York, and I saw it at a screening in New York. I must say I was terribly excited by seeing it. I mean there it was. But, like all things you leave, you feel slightly removed from something you've done. After it's done, there it is.

Rick Ingersoll:

It has been said that the studio would pool their votes and everybody in the studio would vote for *An American in Paris*, or that orders came down from L. B. Mayer that *An American in Paris* will be *the* picture. Later on I was a member of the Academy of Motion Picture Arts and Sciences, and I never had contact with anybody in the studio saying this is how you should vote. In many cases, I didn't vote an Academy Award for the MGM picture or the MGM star if I felt that something else was better. But, on the other hand, if I was undecided or I didn't feel one way or the other, I would vote for the MGM project. I remember thinking, at the time when *An American in Paris* received its nomination, that it was no surprise. Those four other pictures nominated were very strong and marvelous. Everybody recognized their excellence, but they weren't really to everybody's emotional tastes. *An American in Paris* was the first of its kind. It was a joyous picture!

Arthur Freed:

I knew we would be up against my good friend George Stevens with *A Place in the Sun*. I was even surprised when we got nominated.

Howard Strickling:

Once it is nominated for an Academy Award, we publicize it like you would shoot a bird. You aim at something. So you figure out how many members there are in the Academy. Then you decide how you're going to reach those Academy members. There's no sense in publicizing the picture by taking an ad in the *Los Angeles Times,* because the voting is within the business. Arthur Freed has great contacts, and Johnny Green and Gene Kelly and Sydney Guilaroff and Helen Rose and Cedric Gibbons and Alan Jay Lerner all have great friends. Now, we don't pressure anyone, because more people have lost Academy Awards by trying to oversell people. Mr. Mayer used to have a policy of never high-pressuring or overselling people to gain votes, but we would be concerned that every Academy member see *An American in Paris,* so we would set up special screenings, and maybe Johnny Green or Arthur Freed or Alan Jay Lerner would bring all his friends to the studio for a screening.

Leslie Caron:

For the Awards ceremony, I was given an escort and asked to read the foreign-language entries and winner. They made a dress for me. They were very nice. They asked me if I liked the design, and I thought it was very nice.

Mary Ann Nyberg (Freed Unit Dress Designer):

When I first joined the Freed unit, there was nothing for me to do. Then Leslie Caron was to go to the Academy Awards, and it was so special. This was my first meeting with her. Freed said. "My God! Make a dress for her—you know, something marvelous." So I did an Empire style dress that I thought she would look marvelous in. It was all shades of this and layers of that. I took it down to the workroom, and there were a number of designers there that had been there for many years, and they were kind of tough ladies. The head of the Wardrobe Department for twenty years was a man by the name of Sam Kress. So he took my design and gave it to somebody. A couple of days later, I get a call to go down to wardrobe. They called me to ask if I wanted panels cut on the bias, on the edges, or in the middle. I said I wanted them straight and the bias in the middle. Well, I was constantly getting these idiot tests. Then I would get another call for some other niggling thing. Now, in the meantime, these are hours of work, and hours equals money. While they waited for me to come down there, they were still on their hour time chart.

Eventually, I went to Freed and said, "They have approximately five women on that one dress, and none of them can make up their minds about finishing, cutting, anything." Freed said, "I've got it. They are testing you. No matter what happens, stick it out." The phone rang about that time, and it was Kress. Freed said, "Sam? Yes, Sam. Oh. No kidding? You mean the cost of the dress is up to $700 on the hours alone. That doesn't cover the . . . I see . . . uhuh, uhuh. Well, I'll tell you what, Sam. I don't want that dress to cost under a thousand. Just keep going and put everything you have into it. We want Leslie's dress to be the most beautifully made dress that ever came out of Metro." Literally what was happening was with that first dress they were going to try and throw me out. If I hadn't known everything, that dress would never have been made. But that's a normal thing in a studio. It's very tough. You have to be good to survive. But the dress was made, and it was marvelous, and Leslie did wear it to the Academy Awards.

Preston Ames:

I'll never forget it as long as I live, the day of the Academy Awards. I said to Mr. Gibbons, "Are you going to be there?" And he said, "No. This is your evening." Never had he given me five cents of credit for just being alive. I'd just done my job, and I'd done my job well; otherwise I wouldn't have been there. But to tell me that this was my evening I'll never forget as long as I live.

Alan Jay Lerner:

I remember that the Academy Awards were presented on a Thursday night. The day before, however, I had to fly to New York because I learned my father had to be operated on on the day of the Awards. One way or the other, it didn't seem to matter whether I went, because I didn't think I was going to win. I was stunned that I had even been nominated.

My father was operated on on the day of the Academy Awards presentation. I left the hospital around nine o'clock and went to a friend's house and listened to it on the radio.

The RKO Pantages Theater, Hollywood, California, March 20, 1952

Charles Brackett (President of the Academy of Motion Picture Arts and Sciences):

It is my function to report on the state of the art, and in 1951, the year under consideration tonight, the state of the art of motion pictures was extraordinarily good. It was in 1951 that motion pictures really took the measure of the new medium, television. . . . It's possible that Mr. Cinema may have gotten a little thick around the middle and a little drowsy, but suddenly he was wide awake and all muscle. Suddenly he was calling on every resource at his command—great spectacle, superb beauty, subject matter exactly attuned to the current mood of the country, which is not a superficial or frivolous mood. So the World Series was spilling into a lot of living rooms for free; around the corner *The Great Caruso* and *David and Bathsheba* were playing, and they too were irresistible. Senator Kefauver came along with his glittering catch, and on the screen was *A Place in the Sun*, with its emotional truth deeper than the truth of mere fact. *An American in Paris* more than adequately answered Baron Leone, and the deeply perceived realities of *A Streetcar Named Desire* could stand up even against Sid Caesar and Imogene Coca. All through the months, the great pictures came crashing through in a way to sell the heart.

Zsa Zsa Gabor:

Those nominated for the best achievement in costume design for color are: *An American in Paris*, Metro-Goldwyn-Mayer, Orry-Kelly, Walter Plunkett, and Irene Sharaff; *David and Bathsheba*, 20th-Century Fox; . . . *The Great Caruso*, Metro-Goldwyn-Mayer; . . . *Tales of Hoff-*

man, a Michael Powell and Emeric Pressburger production, Lopert Film Corporation. The envelope please. The winner is Orry-Kelly, Walter Plunkett, and Irene Sharaff.

Walter Plunkett:

Truly, this is a most unexpected surprise. I thank you for Orry-Kelly, and I thank you for Irene Sharaff, and I also thank Irene Sharaff because I think some of her inspired and wonderful work is the only reason I have this. Thank you very, very much.

Gower and Marge Champion (alternately):

Those nominated for the best achievement in art direction of a color production are *An American in Paris,* Metro-Goldwyn-Mayer, Cedric Gibbons and Preston Ames, set decoration; Edwin B. Willis and Keogh Gleason. *David and Bathsheba,* 20th-Century Fox; . . . *On the Riviera,* 20th-Century Fox; . . . *Quo Vadis?* Metro-Goldwyn-Mayer; . . . *Tales of Hoffman,* a Michael Powell and Emeric Pressburger production, Lopert Film Distributing Corporation, British. The envelope please.

The winners are Cedric Gibbons and Preston Ames for *An American in Paris.*

Preston Ames:

I wish to thank Cedric Gibbons for having given me this opportunity to do anything that could be like *An American in Paris.* Thank you very much.

Keogh Gleason:

Thank you very much.

Darryl Zanuck:

It is always a great honor and privilege to either give or receive the Irving G. Thalberg Award as the best producer of the year. What exactly is a producer? I believe it was Socrates who said, "A movie producer is the man who spoiled a picture if the picture is a failure." Plato is alleged to have said, "If it was a hit, the producer had nothing whatever to do with it." I have no desire to argue with either Socrates or Plato. There are many kinds of producers. The Irving Thalberg Award goes to a creative producer, frequently a talented individual who also possesses the ability to organize and coordinate the talent of others. Generally, the inspiration for a film, good or bad, starts with the creative producer. Tonight we break a precedent. For the first time, a producer of musical films is being honored by the Academy. A producer of musical film works with many writers and directors on each individual film—the story writers, the music writers, the story director, the dance directors, et cetera. He is, by necessity, the creative center of this particular project. The man you have selected to honor has earned the right to be known as a "creative producer." His productions this year alone, *Showboat* and *An American in Paris*, are perfect examples of creative art. Mr. Arthur Freed.

Arthur Freed:

Thank you, Darryl. Thank you, Charlie. For this honor, I'm deeply grateful. All I can say is that the name of Irving Thalberg twice is the most important name in my professional life. First when I came to Metro, when I came to work with him, and tonight I hold the award that holds his name in my hand. Thank you.

Vera-Ellen:

Those nominated for best achievement in cinematography, color production are *An American in Paris*, Metro-Goldwyn-Mayer, photographed by Alfred Gilks, ballet photographed by John Alton. *David and Bath-*

sheba; . . . *Quo Vadis?;* . . . *Showboat;* . . . *When Worlds Collide.* . . . The envelope.

The winners are Alfred Gilks and John Alton for *An American in Paris.*

Alfred Gilks:

Ladies and gentlemen, I want to thank you very much, indeed. I'm humble, very proud, and I'm very proud of the great team that I worked with.

John Alton:

I wish to thank Mr. Vincente Minnelli for his confidence in our work. Thank you.

Charles Brackett:

An honorary Academy Award is given to Gene Kelly for his extreme versatility as an actor, singer, director, and dancer but specifically for his brilliant achievement in the art of choreography on film.

Donald O'Connor:

Now, ladies and gentlemen, I would like to present those nominated for the best scoring of a musical picture. And they are *Alice in Wonderland,* Walt Disney Production, RKO Radio; . . . *An American in Paris,* Metro-Goldwyn-Mayer, Johnny Green and Saul Chaplin; . . .*The Great Caruso,* Metro-Goldwyn-Mayer; . . . *On the Riviera,* 20th-Century Fox; . . . *Showboat,* Metro-Goldwyn-Mayer. The envelope please. Thank you.

The winners are Johnny Green and Saul Chaplin—*An American in Paris.*

Saul Chaplin:

Thank you very much.

John Green:

I'm not going to let him get away with it. We couldn't have done it without Solly.

Clare Boothe Luce:

The last category is "story and screenplay." The writers of the following took blank sheets of paper, their own experience or some historical event and transformed those blank pages into the text of a finished picture. The nominees are *An American in Paris*, Metro-Goldwyn-Mayer, story and screenplay by Alan J. Lerner; *The Big Carnival*, Paramount; . . . *David and Bathsheba*, 20th-Century Fox; . . . *Go for Broke*, Metro-Goldwyn-Mayer; . . . *The Well*, Harry M. Popkin, United Artists. The envelope please.

The winner is Alan Jay Lerner for *An American in Paris*.

Nancy Olson (Mrs. Lerner):

On behalf of my husband, I want to thank all of you, and congratulations, darling.

Jesse L. Lasky:

You know, as I looked over the list of nominated pictures this afternoon, I was struck by one thing—the uniform excellence of these motion pictures. Now, as for my private preference, well, I'd be just as happy to see this contest end in a five-way tie. But, obviously, fate must be more precise, and the envelope will contain no such happy resolution. The nominees for the best production of 1951 are *An American in Paris*, Metro-Goldwyn-Mayer; *Decision Before Dawn*, 20th-Century Fox; *A Place in the Sun*, Paramount; *Quo Vadis?* Metro-Goldwyn-Mayer; *A Streetcar Named Desire*, Charles K. Feldman Group Productions, Warner Brothers. The envelope please.

Oh dear! The winner is *An American in Paris*, Metro-Goldwyn-Mayer.

Arthur Freed:

Thank you, and thank you for my brilliant associates who made this possible, Vincente Minnelli and Gene Kelly, and a great studio with real courage and leadership, who supported me. Thank you.

Preston Ames:

Twenty years ago and I remember that night as clear as if it were yesterday. I was with my wife, and as they started to open the envelope I said to her, "I think I'm going to be quite sick." I had a premonition. My name was called and I was alone, so the first thing I did was to acknowledge Cedric Gibbons for what he'd done, for allowing me to have this wonderful job. I meant every word of it; that was all I said. It was a moment that was afterwards even more terrific because I suddenly realized that I had won over his associate Bill Horning, who had just finished *Quo Vadis?* and who had gone to Rome and built a studio and built a whole department and created really a magnificent picture. The next day, I went to Mr. Gibbons and I said, "Mr. Gibbons, I'm afraid I'm not worthy of this award, because I feel that Mr. Horning is the one that should have had it." And he said, "Mr. Ames, yours was the more popular picture."

Alan Jay Lerner:

I remember sitting on the floor, leaning up against the sofa, with a cup of coffee in my hand. When they announced that I had won, I can remember throwing the coffee up and hitting the ceiling with it. Later that night, I went back to the hospital to see my father as soon as he came out of the sedation.

Moss Hart used to say that, in the theater, you either get less or more than you deserve. In movies, you very often win an Academy Award for what you did last time but didn't win one for. I thought that Vincente certainly deserved his Oscar for *Gigi*, but I think he always won it as much for *An American In Paris* as he did for *Gigi*.

Ed Woehler:

I said to Minnelli after Gilks won the Academy Award for color cinematography, "You should hate every cameraman you work with."

Variety (March 24, 1952):

In a move as surprising as its winning of an Oscar, Metro is withdrawing *An American in Paris* from national circulation Wed. The award would have caused additional revenue, but emphasis is now on *Singin' in the Rain*. Release dates on *Rain* have been moved up.

Nina Foch:

We were still all believing in the theater then. We were all still believing that New York was the place. I lived in New York all through the 1950's because the action was there. I mean you could study there; you could work. You can't take *An American in Paris* seriously. It's a waste of serious work, not of course for a Vincente Minnelli or an Irene Sharaff but for a serious actress. *An American in Paris*—what can I say to you?

Leslie Caron:

What frightened me the most was not knowing what the whole profession was. I could dance on the stage, and that's frightening enough; you know, anything could happen. You can fall, you can break your foot, you can lose your shoe, you can lose your perfect balance, et cetera. But here I didn't know. For the eight months it took to complete the film, it was a nightmare.

And this whole atmosphere wasn't really friendly. I was used to people who were rough but profoundly friendly—the real thing. I mean tough; you know: "Aw, come on, you can do it." Here there was flattery but complete indifference. I was like a cat thrown into icy water and left to swim. I don't know; it may be absurd to have such a vision and to reveal it. I don't know how the others react. I know Rita Hayworth tells quite candidly the horrors of being under contract, and enough girls have committed suicide to prove the point, but you had to keep a deep secret about your state of golden slavery.

But I also must confess I was very interested in the acting. It was a new experience. It was terrifying, true, but I could see that there was something in it that would interest me. I decided immediately upon finishing the film that acting was something to examine more closely.

Daily Variety (March 21, 1952):

. . . pic is *Glory Alley* in which Ralph Meeker and Leslie Caron co-star. Although Meeker draws top billing in the credits, the trailer for the pic opens with a shot of Miss Caron and soundtrack exclaims, "Oo-lah-lah, that *American in Paris* gal." Windup is another shot of actress with narrator saying, "Don't miss that *An American in Paris* girl, Leslie Caron."

The Globe (Camp Lejeune, North Carolina, April 17, 1952):

"Miss Shaped Charge of 1952" was the title bestowed this week on MGM starlet, Miss Leslie Caron, by the boys of Ammunition Company, 2nd Ordnance Battalion. Chosen from personally autographed pictures of many young stars, including such lovelies as Liz Taylor, Monica Lewis and Esther Williams, Miss Caron won a near unanimous vote for her new designation. Results of the contest were sent to the MGM publicity department.

Record Jacket Blurb from the Original MGM Soundtrack
Album for *An American in Paris*:

That's music, by George! That's music by George Gershwin—direct from the soundtrack of MGM's lavish production, *An American in Paris*.

Gershwin's music has graced many a movie, but never so successfully as in this winner of the 1951 Academy Award.

Gene Kelly was the globe-trotting American; Leslie Caron, the *Parisienne* who taught him the meaning of ooh-la-la; Georges Guetary, the debonair Music Hall star; and Oscar Levant as the eternal emigré without whom Paris just wouldn't be complete.

The high point of the movie was the title ballet, originally written back in 1928. But in its selection of other Gershwin songs, the film became almost a retrospect of the composer's career. " 'S Wonderful," for instance, from Gershwin's 1927 *Funny Face*, "Paradise," from an early edition of the *George White Scandals*. "I Got Rhythm"—the song that launched Ethel Merman in *Girl Crazy*.

Here, then is a great parade of Gershwiniana—direct from one of the screen's most glittering films.

Alan A. Antik (Technical Advisor):

All of a sudden, after the picture was finished, Minnelli became extremely pleasant. Maybe in his mind he realized the extent to which I was responsible for helping him. Later on, I met him several times, and as he would drive by he would wave at me with great enthusiasm.

George Gibson:

It was a great picture for me—a great picture because it gave us a whole new scope of things to do and new ideas and attitudes about things. This, at that time, was a change. We had done musicals before in various stages, but all the talent that we had was in the process of development. With *An American in Paris*, we began to reach an acme, a top spot, a point where all of the talent was really working together. Then several pictures afterwards—*Band Wagon, Singin' in the Rain*—we maintained our peak, but, the more we improved, the less the business needed us. It's a tremendous denial of everything. You think the more you improve the more you're desired. It wasn't that. We were painting, when I retired, better things, more convincingly, more realistically, easier, and with greater facility; and there was less need for them. The business changed, and people began making pictures in real places. There was less need for any phase of the *making* of motion pictures as the years have gone on.

Irene Sharaff:

After seeing the picture, there were certain things I would have liked to change. I used two shades of color together that I didn't like. Every time I try to use them again (it was a strange shade of orange and a burnt sienna), every time I start putting those two colors down on paper, I say, "Unh unh, remember *An American in Paris*; they didn't work."

Preston Ames:

The Paris street we created lasted as long as the lot it was built on lasted. It's burned down now. So that's about twenty years. That was a thing that we created that was very pleasant. The rest of the things were put aside or destroyed. The telephone rang years after—people wanting to know "What did you do with those paintings that you did for the ballet in *An American in Paris?*" They couldn't appreciate the fact that the paintings were forty by four hundred feet. To them, they were just Utrillos or Toulouse-Lautrecs or something. That's why I say when we started out we really went *gung ho*—a crazy idea that we never let go of. It was something!

Gene Kelly:

The following summer, while Arthur Freed and I were on vacation in Paris, we arranged to show *An American in Paris* to Raoul Dufy. The arrangement was that we would show it to him in one of the screening rooms in the MGM Paris office. Dufy arrived on time and was wheeled into the room by his nurse, for he was very old. The four of us—Dufy, his nurse, Arthur, and I—watched the picture. Now, Arthur and I were literally sweating with fear. After all, here we were, showing one of the great painters of the world our treatment of his work. Well, he just chortled; he was so pleased. After the house lights went up, he asked if we would show him the ballet again, which we joyously did. He thought we had all done a wonderful job.

Dore Schary (Executive Vice-President in Charge of Production):

The books on *An American in Paris* are not closed yet, because we never sold our movie rights. The last thing Arthur Loew and myself did, before the big blowup at Metro, was to prevent the company from selling the films. They were offered $50 million for them, and we demonstrated to them that that was ridiculous. The last figure I heard was that they had already gotten about $130 million out of TV. I'm sure everytime they want to show *An American in Paris* they can probably get today a million bucks or close to it.

PART III

8

Twenty Years Later

Rick Ingersoll (Partner, Allan/Ingersoll Public Relations):

Think of this, that from 1950 until whenever, the only female stars developed by MGM—I mean *developed* by MGM—were Leslie Caron, Debbie Reynolds, and maybe Pier Angeli. There was just no development as there had been in the 1930's and the 1940's. 1950 was the time L. B. Mayer left the studio. Then they started dropping the June Allysons, the Greer Garsons, and the Van Johnsons, mainly because their contracts were running out. I surmised that they just didn't want to have that heavy financial weekly payroll to meet. Some of the stars were making $7,000 or $8,000 a week. Also, I think MGM began to realize that they could get these actors back by the picture rather than keep them under contract.

Ed Woehler (Retired):

Oh God, that's where the whole thing in pictures is today, in salaries. We used to get stars for $25,000 a picture. Now, you have to spend about $300,000 to $400,000 to get the same actor. So that's how it's jumped up, and, because of such demands, they're pricing musicals right out of the business.

Vincente Minnelli (Director):

There's been a great change in musicals. It started, actually, with Alan Lerner, when he did *My Fair Lady*. Now, when we did *Gigi*, the same thing was happening; also Rodgers and Hammerstein with *The King and I*, where the songs are almost like dialogue. They carry along the story. Now the trouble is with Europe, which is a great market for musicals. Getting translations that have style and verve to them and sing the same thing is very difficult. It didn't seem to hurt the foreign market on Jerry Robbins's *West Side Story*, because the situations were so strong that they practically carried you along. You could tell when the boys walked down the street that they were gangs. All the choreography was done that way. That did quite well in Europe. A lot of musicals then were like *An American in Paris*, where we had no worry, because the melodies were so well known. Everyone knew all the songs. But, when a drama like *Gigi* is done, or *My Fair Lady*, where the lyrics are definitely as important as dialogue, then you have trouble.

Gene Kelly (Director):

Now, if you sign fellows to do musicals the various guilds and unions require, and correctly so, that the rehearsal time be paid, so there's a certain kind of thinking in making this particular kind of picture today that's so completely tied up with economics. That's number one. Number two: When they are made, they're brought from Broadway, and then they're sacred cows; you can't touch them. The thing, you know, is that you mustn't tamper with them, you must re-create them on film. I can't blame the business executive who says, "Well, this show made money for five years." And you say, "Well, look I'd like to try this." "Don't try anything; it's a money-maker, and I just payed $20 million for it," you know, "don't mess with it."

Walter Strohm (Retired):

The thing that made the studio possible was the amount of pictures that they were able to turn out. That the good ones would pay for the bad ones. Now, when they only turn out eight or nine pictures and they cost so much money, you can't keep a big studio running. It's just economically unsound to keep a big studio unless you can make a big product, and, if you don't have a big product, get rid of the studio quick. As quick as you can. I think there are other elements also that have so changed the whole business of picturemaking, and that is why the big studio is gone. Gone—I don't have to *think* that—it *is* gone. I don't think it's ever coming back in the same form as it was. The big screen, the ease of going on location, equipment being modernized to the point where they can carry out a little recording system in a bus and take a scene—so it's eliminated a lot of the technical things that we had at the studio that made it possible to make our kind of picture. I don't know whether they're going to be able to make high technical pictures when they've sold all this equipment. Maybe they don't use it. Maybe they don't know how to use it. Maybe that was a period of picturemaking that's passed, where we used a great number of miniatures, painted backings, and process work. Look what went into the making of *2001*. Now, where did they get the equipment to make that kind of a picture? I was over there when they were making it, and it was a very, very complex job. I don't know where you do those things if you don't have a studio or the organization that will take the time to develop it. Maybe that kind of picture's gone; maybe it's forgotten.

George Gibson (Retired):

Bill Horning was Cedric Gibbons's assistant, and one time we were down on the stage and we had some problem that had to be solved, and I had said something to Horning about "Well, gosh, Bill, what are you supposed to do? You can't read people's minds." And he said, "You've done a pretty good job of it for twenty-odd years." This kind of thing exists, and it exists with creative people. It has to, because a creation is not a cut and dried "It's going to rain tomorrow" or "It's raining now." It's an intangible sort of description of something, and you're very lucky if you can get this something out of the air. We were kind of lucky about things like that.

It takes talent, but I think it takes more experience. You know, you learn pretty much through association with people. This is the value of an association that is a continuing fact. You can't say, "We need a scenic artist; hire him," "We need a painter; we'll hire him," or "We need a carpenter; we'll hire him, and we'll get this picture made." This is all against the whole concept of any kind of a creative endeavor. *Creativity demands a continuing relationship with people,* the people who work for you and you, who, in turn, work for somebody else. It's the only way that I think any kind of creative effort can be accomplished. We weren't aping anybody. We were doing a job that was a very demanding and highly disciplined type of job. We couldn't do it any other way. Everything had to go into it that we knew how best to put into it.

I have no idea what will become of my Scenic Art Building. I have no idea. It's still there, of course, but it will be closed down as of the end of next week. All I know is that that building represented the best that there was in the field of scenic art, both as a place to work and to the personnel who were working in it. It was the best there was, best there's ever been.

Preston Ames (Art Director):

The studios supplied us a lot of things. They gave us, for example, Arthur Freed, Alan Jay Lerner; they gave us Gene Kelly; they gave us the greatest musicians. There was a stable of talent there. There it was. Use it; make something out of it. Today, you would have to go all over the world to get these things and put it together. We had the stages, we had the tools, we had the savvy, we had the manpower, and we were geared to do this kind of thing. No studio is geared to do it anymore. They can't get the talent; it doesn't exist. They've destroyed it only because there's no need for it. As soon as there's no need for this talent, it disappears. It dissipates just like anything else. It's gone. I'm only saddened to see talent dissipated because the present director, the present producer, the present writer, is reluctant to use any of these things. He abhors it. To him it's the antithesis of what he wants.

The present group of people that are coming up deny it only because they're afraid of it. I don't know. I think it's competitive. I met a director the other day who wanted no part of me, because I was telling him what I could do and he didn't want to be told what I could do. He didn't want to be told anything. He wanted to tell me what to do. Well, that's fine, but he dismissed me, and that was the end of that.

The film-makers of today don't want sets; they don't want stages; they don't want experienced people. They want to experiment themselves, and, in their experimentation, I think they're eventually going to come back, not as strongly, but I think they're going to come back to what we were doing a good twenty years ago.

Ed Woehler:

I worked at MGM for twenty-eight years, and that's a long time, but I don't go back now. I'll tell you why. They let all my friends go out there. They closed their Construction Department; they closed the Art Department; they closed everything. They sold off all their props, and, to me, I think they've lost all their chance of becoming a big studio again, because people rent space to get whatever is available there, like the sets and props, et cetera. They don't have anything to give them anymore. They just rent out a cold stage now. You can go anyplace to get a stage, but at Warner Brothers you can get their back lot, their props, and their wardrobe.

There was a time when there was just no stage available to rent at Metro—thirty-one stages just going all the time. Right now, there is one stage operating over there. One stage! You know, Lot 3 was one of the greatest lots in the picture business because we had a big backing out there; we had the big lake; we had the big waterfront street; we had the Saint Louis street; we had three western streets. But they sold it all. They're tearing it down. So all they have now is Lot 2, which is where the streets were—the Hardy street, railroad stations, the city street, the Verona square. I understand they're getting rid of that, too. We had wardrobe out there, too. We could dress any period that you thought about, but they sold all the wardrobe at the auction.

They don't have the talent. There's nobody out there securing it, you see. Mayer always had men out looking all the time. He had scouts; he had people in New York looking all the time. In the old days, you knew pretty well what your cast was, because they wrote the stories for the people in the film. Mayer would take care of all the talent. He kept some great talent there. You had a feeling on that lot that they made the best pictures in the world, which they did. A great feeling!

Saul Chaplin (Producer):

I went to the MGM auction. As I walked in, I heard the album from *An American in Paris* playing on the PA, and I walked around and saw all those costumes from the ballet that were going to be on sale. I couldn't stand it. It was so sad.

APPENDIXES

An American in Paris

MUSICAL NUMBERS

PROD. 1507

Sc. 1–11	*EXT.*	PARIS AND PENSION (1)
		a—Walking Theme
		Paris shots
Sc. 1		b—Blues Themes—PIANO
3X1		Jerry's walking pantomime
3X2		
3X4		
3X5		

Sc. 12	*INT.*	JERRY'S ROOM (2)
15		
16	*EXT.*	CAFE
	INT.	ADAM'S ROOM
		OSCAR LEVANT
		a—Narration and piano ending with
		"*NICE WORK IF YOU CAN GET IT*"
		b—Henri sings last 8 bars.

Sc. 18	*INT.*	CAFE (3)
		HENRI'S RETROSPECT
		a—Mirror frame—LISE'S SOLO
		"*EMBRACEABLE YOU*"

Sc. 30   *EXT.*   *CAFE* (4)
Jerry dances with old woman.
Kelly
Guetary
Old lady (dances)
Middle-aged lady
   "   "   man
"BY STRAUSS"

Sc. 30A   *EXT.*   *STREETS* (5)—*Jerry walks to Montmartre.*
a—Walking Theme
"AMERICAN IN PARIS"

Sc. 39   *INT.*   *ADAM'S ROOM* (6)
a—#1 GERSHWIN PRELUDE
(LEVANT'S PIANO SOLO)

Sc. 43   *INT.*   *FLODAIR CAFE* (7)
a—MEDLEY OF 4 GERSHWIN SONGS
    (by colored orchestra—BENNY CARTER)
    4th number in medley is:
    "OUR LOVE IS HERE TO STAY" (Lise
    hums)

Sc. 44   *INT.* *MILO'S CAR* (8)
    "OUR LOVE IS HERE TO STAY"
    (Jerry hums)

Sc. 46–47   *INT.* *JERRY'S ROOM* and *INT. CAFE* (9)
a—Adam plays . . .
    Henri sings to Lise in cafe.
b—Jerry makes Steinberg figure in his room.
    "LOVE WALKED IN"

Sc. 50   *INT.*   *JERRY'S ROOM* (10)
a—Jerry sings and dances in bed.
    "THAT CERTAIN FEELING"

Sc. 62   EXT. STREET (11)
              a—Jerry dances down street with French
              children.
              "I GOT RHYTHM"

Sc. 63   INT. ADAM'S and JERRY'S ROOMS (12)
              a—Jerry sings and dances.
              b—Adams plays piano and sings in his room.
              "TRA-LA-LA"

Sc. 64   INT. HENRI'S ROOM (13)
              a—Henri hums.
              "STAIRWAY"

Sc. 68–69   EXT. QUAI (14)
              a—Jerry and Lise on *Quai.*
              (Jerry sings—they both dance.)
              "OUR LOVE IS HERE TO STAY"

Sc. 71   INT. THEATRE (15)
              a—Henri sings on Music Hall stage.
              (Show girls)
              "STAIRWAY TO PARADISE"

Sc. 85   INT. ADAM'S ROOM (16)
              a—Adam plays piano solo.
              (MUSIC TO BE SELECTED)_____

Sc. 100–103   PARIS—MONTAGE (17)
              a—shots of Jerry working.
              b—shots of Jerry with Lise.

Sec. 105   EXT. RIVER BANK BY BRIDGE—
                    JERRY'S RETROSPECT (18)
              a—Jerry and Lise in Paris.
              b—*"SOMEBODY LOVES ME"* (no vocal)

Sc. 106   *INT.   and EXT. CAFE—EXT. BOIS*   (19)
108   a—Henri and Jerry
                            "S'WONDERFUL"
                         b—Jerry sings to Lise.
                            "S'WONDERFUL" (reprise)

Sc. 122X2   *INT.   BALLROOM*   (20)
148   a—Dance number to be selected (Sc. 122X2)
                         b—Dance number to be selected (Sc. 148)

Sc. 122X5   *INT.   BALLROOM*   (21)
                         a—Art students' ball arrangement:
                            "LIZA" (Levant's Solo)

Sc. 122X6   *INT.   BALLROOM*   (22)
                         a—Henri sings at Ball. (Group sings with him)
                            "BUT NOT FOR ME"

Sc. 153   *BALLET*   (23)
                         a—Jerry and Lise.
                            "AN AMERICAN IN PARIS"

AN AMERICAN IN PARIS

PROD. 1507
STAFF LIST

TITLE	NAME	STUDIO PHONE
PRODUCER	Arthur Freed	1112
SECRETARY	Helen Wendt	1112
SECRETARY	Mary Milligan	1112
DIRECTOR	Vincente Minnelli	1154
SECRETARY	Janet Kay	1154
UNIT MANAGER	Ed Woehler	1143
ASST. DIRECTOR	Al Raboch	1246
2nd ASST. DIRECTOR	Fletcher Clark	1246
SCRIPT SUPERVISOR	Grace Dubray	1269
CAMERAMAN	Al Gilks	414
OPERATOR	Al Lane	414
ASST.	Matt Kluzic	414
TECHNICIAN	Henry O. Imus	414
STILL MAN	Frank Shugrue	414
ART DIRECTOR	Preston Ames	1587
SET DRESSER	Keogh Gleason	273
PROPERTY MAN	Harry Edwards	273
2nd PROPERTY MAN	Stanley Hutchinson	273
SOUND MIXER	Stan Lambert	321

TITLE	NAME	STUDIO PHONE
STAGE MAN	Cliff Wright	321
GAFFER	Wesley Shanks	214
BEST BOY	Camden Rogers	214
MAKEUP	John Truwe	247
HAIRDRESSER	Helene Parrish	389
MEN'S WARDROBE	Charles M. Zacha	531
WOMEN'S WARDROBE	Vicky Nichols	675
CUTTER	Adrienne Fazan	521
ASST. CUTTER	Ed Hartzke	521
PUBLICITY	Emily Torchia	654
MUSIC	Saul Chaplin	1134
ASST. DANCE DIR.	Carol Haney	1278
WRITER	Alan J. Lerner	1375
TECHNICAL	Alan A. Antik	1187
ASST. TO DIRECTOR	Jane Loring	475
ARTIST	Gene Grant	1492

AN AMERICAN IN PARIS

CAST

Jerry Mulligan	Gene Kelly
Lise Bourvier	Leslie Caron
Adam Cook	Oscar Levant
Henri Baurel	Georges Guetary
Milo Roberts	Nina Foch
Georges Mattieu	Eugene Borden
Mathilde Mattieu	Martha Bamattre
Old Woman Dancer	Mary Young
Therese	Ann Codee
Francola	George Davis
Tommy Baldwin	Hayden Rorke
John McDowd	Paul Maxey
Ben Macrow	Dick Wessel

MINOR PARTS AND BITS

Honeymoon Couple:	Don Quinn
	Adele Coray
3 Boys (Bubble Gum)	Lucian Planzoles
	Christian Pasques
	Anthony Mazola
Smiling Young Man	Charles Bastin
Man	Carli Blinor
Nuns	Jeanne Lafayette
	Louise Laureau
Man at Shutters	Captain Garcia
Man with Books	Charles Millsfield
Woman with Cats	Louise Colombet
Postman	Alfred Paix
Young Man at Mirror	Leonard Mazola
American Girl	Noel Neill
Maid	Nan Boardman
Jack Jansen	John Eldridge
Kay Jansen	Anna Q. Nilssen
Woman at Table	Louise Lareau
Man at Table	Albert Pollet
Woman on Phone	Wanda Lucienne
Woman Customer	Madge Blake
Waiter	George Dee
Driver	Art Dupuis
Man	Charles Mauu
Man	Albert Pollet
Waiter	Albert D'Arno
Bit Artist	Peter Camlin
Bit Artist	Jeanne Lafayette
Bit News Vendor	Marie Antoinette Andrews
First G.I.	Sam Strangis
Second G.I.	Herb Winters
French Girl	Jeanne Lafayette
Bit Painter	Dudley Field Malone
Bit Bearded Painter	Louis Laurent
Bit Rugged G.I.	Greg McClure
Bits in Audience	Leo Mostovoy